British Colonial Rule

British Colonial Rule and the Resistance of the Malay Peasantry, 1900–1957

Donald M. Nonini

Monograph Series 38/Yale University Southeast Asia Studies
Yale Center for International and Area Studies

Yale University Southeast Asia Studies
James C. Scott, Chairman
Marvel Kay Mansfield, Editor

Consulting Editors
Hans-Dieter Evers, Universität Bielefeld
Huỳnh Sanh Thông, Yale University
Sartono Kartodirdjo, Gadjah Mada University
Lim Teck Ghee, Institute for Advanced Studies, Kuala Lumpur
Alfred W. McCoy, University of Wisconsin
Anthony Reid, Research School of Pacific Studies, Canberra
Benjamin White, Institute for Social Studies, The Hague
Alexander Woodside, University of British Columbia

Library of Congress Catalog Card Number: 92-53707
International Standard Book Number: 0-938692-47-X paper
0-938692-48-8 cloth

Distributor:
Yale University Southeast Asia Studies
Box 13A Yale Station
New Haven, Connectitut 06520

Printed in the U.S.A.

The Law doth punish the Man or Woman
Who steals the Goose from off the Common,
But lets the greater Felon loose
That steals the Common from the Goose.

Anonymous Eighteenth-Century
English Proverb

Contents

List of Tables

Map

Preface

Fifteen years ago, the late Malcolm Caldwell wrote that "peasant discontent and actual resistance were virtually *always* rumbling somewhere in Malaya throughout the British period—something that requires research and documentation."[1] Although much work on peasant resistance has appeared since then, a large part of it the superlative studies of Malaysian scholars, Caldwell's point is still a timely one. This book represents an attempt to synthesize a large body of materials on peasant resistance to the colonial state and colonial capitalism over more than a century of British imperial rule and influence on the Malayan peninsula. In it, I attempt to delineate the forms resistance took, to set out the dialectic between the formation and growth of the institutions of British rule on one side and the emergence and internal differentiation of a "Malay" peasantry on the other, and to evaluate the various explanations given, both by mainstream theorists and radicals, for the "underdevelopment" of this peasantry. Indeed, in what follows, I hope to show that these three tasks are inextricably connected at the levels of both theory and historical process.

I claim no great originality for what I have written, which has depended on the labors of a large number of conscientious historians and social scientists, many of whom would not agree with the controversial views expressed here. Indeed, the effort undertaken in this book might better have been carried out by a Malaysian, and I am sensitive and receptive to just this criticism. If there is a justification for my having written it—other than the "pure pursuit of knowledge" to which positivist scientists are so devoted—it lies in two areas. First, much of the history of the North, for which those of us in the North remain accountable, lies in the past "colonial encounter" with the South and in its contemporary consequences. The enduring leitmotif of this encounter was and still remains the underlying and pervasive racism of the colonizers and managers of empire. This racism, grounded in the political economy of modern imperialism, is still very much with us. This book represents an attempt to reflect on the historical contours and limits of the racism of the North, while considering as well its obverse—the resistance of the dominated—in one very specific, changing situation, that of "British" Malaya. Second, there seemed to me to be a need for such a synthesis as the one attempted here in order to affirm the historical time depth and the intensity of such popular resistance to British colonial rule in Malaya. Such a synthesis, in effect, represents a fundamental critique of the triumphalist narratives of a regnant transnational capitalism (still, if residually, centered in the North), told by its scholars of fortune, which have focused in a onesided way on one of Southeast Asia's development "success stories."

Finally, should it happen by way of good fortune that this study in any way serves as a source of empowerment for those who are its subjects—the rural *Bumiputras* of the twentieth century—then this alone would more than justify its writing. It is to them, with their enduring and courageous spirit of resistance, that this book is respectfully dedicated.

A Note on Measures, Geographic Units, and Miscellany

One Malaysian *relong* represents .71 acres. One Straits Dollar has, since 1906, been set at 2s. 4d. as the official currency during the colonial period.

I have resisted the conventional practice of delineating at this point the political-administrative units of British Malaya, i.e. Straits Settlements, Federated Malay States, Unfederated Malay States, Malayan Union, and Federation of Malaya. Their political definitions are given in the text in the order of their chronological formation. This also serves the purpose of demonstrating the limitations of their political definitions for an economy and history of resistance of the Malaysian peasantry.

I have used the terms "plantation" and "estate" interchangeably to refer to commercial agricultural units of more than 100 acres. Wherever possible, I have confined that term "Malaya" to the British colonial period, and the term "Malaysia" to the period since independence in 1957, but invariably (e.g. in the phrase "Malayan peninsula" for what is now officially called "Peninsular Malaysia") there has been some historical crossover.

——————————————————

Over the past two years since the completed manuscript was submitted to the publisher, much new scholarship on rural Malay society and British colonial rule in Malaya has appeared. Other recent studies have either belatedly come to my attention, or have only become available to me in the interim. Although the pressures of time make it impossible to incorporate the findings of this scholarship into the present book, several studies are so pertinent to its themes that I can only mention them here in lieu of the extended discussion they deserve.

Among the former, it is necessary to refer to *The Underside of Malaysian History*, edited by Peter J. Rimmer and Lisa M. Allen.[2] I am deeply sympathetic to the avowed goal of the editors of that collection—"contributing to a people's history of Malaysia."[3] The articles by Barlow, Drabble, and Loh in Part I of the volume ("...In the Countryside") are directly pertinent to the argument of the present book. In addition, there is the ongoing critical analysis of the postcolonial and contemporary political economy by Jomo K. S. in two works, *Growth and Structural Change in the Malaysian Economy*, and *Beyond 1990: Considerations for a New National Development Strategy*.[4] Among the latter is a major and important study in local-level historical anthropology, *From British to Bumiputera Rule*, by Shamsul A. B.[5] This is an outstanding monograph that consistently and carefully traces the interaction for more than a century between national- and regional-level processes of political economy (e.g., the formation of colonial state policies against Malay rubber cultivation) on the one hand, and class and social relations occurring in one Malay *kampung* (village) in the state of Selangor on the other. This work adds substantially to out comparative historical and ethnographic understandings of this interaction in the case of rural Malay villages in rubber-growing areas of the Malay peninsula. I believe that Shamsul's fine study complements the findings of the present book. Patrick Sullivan's *Social Relations of Dependence in a Malay State*[6] provides a new and thoughtful interpretation of the phenomena of slavery and debt-bondage in precolonial Perak. Although sympathetic to his historical materialist approach, I have found that my conclusions in chapter 2 differ fundamentally from his own; the issues clearly need discussion in depth elsewhere.

D. M. N.
March 1992
Pulau Pinang, Malaysia

Acknowledgements

This book began many incarnations ago as a First-Year Essay in the Department of Anthropology at Stanford University in 1975. I have therefore first to thank its readers who encouraged me to carry the analysis further, Bridget O'Laughlin, Frank Cancian, and the late Michelle Rosaldo. It underwent further refinement under the influence of G. William Skinner, whose rigorous scholarly concern with spatial and temporal structures has much inspired the approach to political economy taken here.

The book has undergone many changes, as I have undertaken various professional ambulations. In Malaysia I received assistance from many friends and scholars, but I would particularly like to mention Paul Kratoska and Lim Mah Hui. At the New School for Social Research, both Melissa Ennen and the late Stanley Diamond were of great help, in different ways, in developing and clarifying the argument. At Chapel Hill, I have greatly benefited intellectually from the company of my colleagues in the Department of Anthropology, and financially from a Junior Faculty Development Grant provided by the administration of the University of North Carolina. Both made further work on this book not only feasible but pleasurable as well. Finally, I would like to express my great appreciation to my own "invisible college" of friends and colleagues. Many made tangible and intangible contributions to the argument. Among them I would particularly like to thank Jim Scott, Craig Lockard, and Tom Patterson for their careful and critical readings of the entire manuscript.

Any errors of fact or interpretation remaining in this book, despite the interventions of those mentioned above, are mine alone.

CHAPTER ONE

Introduction

Prologue

Marxist approaches to the underdevelopment of the Malaysian peasantry[1] have, until recently, belonged largely to what has been called the "world systems" approach.[2] Advocates of this approach have presented an argument with the following logic. They have first described and analyzed Malaysia's relationship with the more inclusive world capitalist economy, from the beginning of the British colonial period to the present; they have then set out a set of functional preconditions for the successful operation of capitalism within Malaysia as part of this more inclusive world system; finally, they have proposed that these preconditions have constituted the major structural determinants of the proletarianization, impoverishment, and immiseration of the Malaysian peasantry. For instance, Michael Stenson writes,

> The key to the evolution of Malaysian society according to these perceptions is to be found not so much in the cultural dynamics of the Malay, Chinese or Indian communities as in the evolution of the world capitalist economy and the class structure of Malaysian society. Contrary to those who would still emphasize the "autonomy" and uniqueness of South-east Asian history, I would emphasize its transformation in the late-nineteenth and the twentieth centuries by the common force of capitalist imperialism. No part of South-east Asia has been more fully enmeshed in this process than West Malaysia.[3]

From this it follows that as a requisite,

> the Malay peasantry was discouraged from entering the rubber export economy as smallholders and instead were encouraged to produce rice in order to complement rather than compete with the interests of British capital. Their function was to provide both a stable political base and cheap food for Chinese and Indian labour. . . . An important consequence was the ossification of Malay economic and social structure.[4]

Similarly, Bach has stated that "the continued success of rubber and tin fully integrated Malaysia into the world economy whereupon it was essential for all that Malaysia remain successful, at least until her resources were no longer needed. These are the circumstances of 'dependency' at the international level."[5] As a consequence, "subsistence farmers have been integrated into the market economy through their need to borrow money."[6] This need therefore makes them susceptible to exploitative moneylenders-cum-shopkeepers, and they are forced to sell their lands to exploitative landlords and become tenants. Participating in the "unequal linkages" between the rural agricultural sector and the industrial and plantation sectors, "padi farmers provide much of the rice crop which goes to feed the other labourers."[7] The Malaysian peasantry thus plays its part in the maintenance of Malaysian capitalism. Other examples of the "world systems" approach to the Malaysian peasantry could be given.[8]

This approach has represented an important critique of earlier so-called "cultural" and demographic explanations of the poverty and immiseration of the Malaysian peasantry, the vast majority of whom are ethnically Malay.[9] These explanations pointed to endogenous factors within the Malay peasantry as exclusive determinants. Malay predisposition to "leisure" rather than to work, an egalitarianism militating against capital accumulation, peasant conservatism inhibiting technological innovations, spendthrift habits of consumerism rather than saving, and Islamic laws of inheritance requiring the partition of an estate have all been cited.[10] Moreover, unfavorable and invidious comparisons are made with the culture of "the wealthy Chinese," comparisons referred to by Stenson in the quote above. Similarly, others have pointed to demographic factors, holding that rural population growth drives up rents, leads to land fragmentation and landlessness, inhibits technological progress, and causes per capita consumption to fall.[11] In general, there are serious theoretical and empirical shortcomings in such neomalthusian "population pressure" models.[12] Both kinds of endogenous explanations have played an ideological role by providing "blame the victim" stories available for use by the apologists for capitalist development in Malaysia.

The "world systems" approach has provided a long-needed corrective to them. Thus, claims such as "to set the Malay peasant on the road to economic progress requires changes in his habits of thought and attitudes"[13] and "ultimately the explanation [for rural land concentration] must be sought in the increase in the Malay rural population which has outstripped any increase in rice production"[14] have been refuted by "world systems" theorists who have pointed to the economically subordinate role to which the Malay peasantry was consigned by colonial and neocolonial development. Insofar as rural "population pressure" and such cultural factors as Islamic laws of inheritance have contributed to the immiserization and proletarianization of rural Malays, their effects have been both relatively minor and historically specific. They occurred only from the 1960s onward, after the major transformations of rural Malay life that took place during the colonial period, and are discussed in subsequent chapters.

Similarly, what has been called a "structural" approach to peasant poverty has been complemented and extended by the "world systems" argument. The "structural" approach holds that poor rural Malays have been subject to exploitation by non-Malay moneylenders and middlemen, and by rich Malay landlords-cum-agrarian capitalists.[15] While accepting the structural account in most cases, "world systems" theorists have pointed to the exogenous structural conditions tied to the needs of capitalist accumulation, at both national and international levels. The specific determinants cited by "structural" accounts are thus seen as a subset of more inclusive factors inherent in the operation of the world capitalist system.

However, in recent years a number of objections among Marxists have arisen with respect to the "world systems" approach. They have derived largely from an alternative perspective within Marxism. Stanley Diamond has argued that the "world system" is no more than an analytical construct of those who overemphasize the integrative effects of capitalist markets, wherever these arise, as autonomous determinants, and who neglect the role of military force (and attending ethnocide) in such "integration." According to Diamond, the deference paid to the capitalist market leads to the reification of a "world system," and the concept has little theoretical value as currently defined.[16]

Other critics have argued in a related way that the "world systems" model presupposes the emergence of a world-wide functional system that operates mechanically in terms of functional prerequisites and linear cause and effect determinants. Specific colonial and postcolonial societies have not only been viewed as subordinate or "dependent" on the activities of international capitalists—something with which no Marxist in general would disagree.[17] Rather, critics state, "world systems" proponents have often allowed this nonexceptional claim to become another quite different one: that *all* features of the underdevelopment of the Third World, including transformations in peasant societies dominated by the capitalist mode of production, have occurred *because* of the functional requirements of the world capitalist system, which contribute to the objective of advanced capitalist accumulation. Local, regional, and national events and processes in the Third World, including those in which peasantries are bound up, have thus been seen as caused, in a determinist way, by the functional needs of the "world system." The views of Stenson and Bach, among others who have written about the Malaysian peasantry from the "world systems" perspective, appear to be typical of this functionalist perspective.

Critics have argued that there are serious logical and empirical problems with this world functionalism—many of them generic to functionalist explanations,[18] others specific to "world systems" theory itself. First, the emergence of the world capitalist system was by no means continuous or linear, but was rather a dialectical process in which dynamic instabilities —due to shifting national balances of power, alliances between European and indigenous Third World classes, contradictions both between and within European colonial capitalism and colonial states—and in which *resistance* from peasants, proletarians, and tribal peoples have meant that the outcome of this process was by no means predestined or determined. Moreover, the expansion of capitalist enterprise and of state power and the resistance of subaltern groups to such expansion has varied over space by region and locale. Thus, Worsley has argued against Wallerstein's *The Modern World System I* that

> of course, primary resistance did not prevent the onward sweep of capitalism and its final consolidation. In the dialectic of opposition between rulers and ruled, the rulers of the core countries had their way. But the triumph was long in the making, and the hegemony of capitalism has been a very uneven process along the way, in different zones, at different times, and with differing degrees of penetration and success.[19]

Thus the point should be made that class societies are always dialectically rather than mechanically constituted: they emerge out of struggle between classes and class-based groups, their evolution is open-ended, subject to chance and contingency, and those who are dominated in the process can never be reduced to mere objects of manipulation by ruling classes.

Second, the need for capitalist accumulation, in either metropolitan or peripheral countries, can never be said to determine uniquely or completely the existence of its supposed functional prerequisites: here, the particular forms of proletarianization, landlessness, low productivity, and immiserization of a Third World peasantry such as Malaysia. To believe that it does is to engage in teleological thinking rather than scientific inquiry: there are simply no logical or empirical justifications for assuming that these functional prerequisites will come into existence merely because they meet the needs of the functional system of world capitalism, or for that matter, the functional subsystem of Malayan capitalism.[20] There have always been domains of "free play" and indeterminacy in Third World societies; the histories of their class formations cannot be reduced to the overarching logic of the "world system."[21] Joel Kahn has made the point specifically for the Malay peasantry:

> this list in no way exhausts functions performed by the village economy in aiding national accumulation and supporting the existing power structures. The point to be made is that a variety of such linkages exist and have existed in the past. What needs emphasis is that the forms of village economy cannot be deduced simply from the functionality of the linkage (for example cheap labour could be guaranteed by any number of mechanisms); [and] that outside interests must make use of situations given to them by history.[22]

A third criticism is that "world systems" theorists have proven particularly unable to incorporate cultural, political, and ideological phenomena into their explanations of the play of forces of production and exchange in the emergence of the internally differentiated "world system." They have failed most crucially in two areas—in their interpretation of the state as monolithic in peripheral capitalist societies and in their neglect of the totalizing character of colonialist and neocolonialist orders. I turn to the first of these below in my discussion of recent work on the British colonial state in Malaya.

As to the second area, "world systems" theorists have tended to focus—at times exclusively—on economic processes (e.g. emergence of cash crop production) and the coercive power exerted by colonial regimes to buttress these; they have failed to consider that colonial and neocolonial societies display a totality of dialectically constituted cultural and ideological mechanisms, themselves modes of power, exerted on one hand by those who colonize, on the other—and usually in opposition —by those who are colonized. Not only force, but "acculturation" in government or missionary schools, the financial cooptation of indigenous elites, the manipulation of religious prohibitions, the use of courts of district chiefs, the creation of a colonial civility and etiquette based on an ideology of "natural" status differences between colonialists and various "tribal" or "racial" groups among the colonized—these and much more represent *cultural* mechanisms aimed at regulating the behavior of those who are colonized, and even worse, converting them to consent to their own exploitation. Conversely, there are cultural forms of resistance that emerge among those colonized—revitalization movements, work slowdowns by "lazy natives," rebellions and banditry, counterhegemonic ideologies opposing capitalist values and worldviews, and much more—that are part of colonial social systems. Here again, Worsley's critique of Wallerstein is appropriate:

> The establishment of colonies, therefore, was a process of political economy, not a 'purely economic' process governed by the play of the market. It entailed the construction, not just of systems of production, but of government and taxation; a total racist social order; and a strong machinery of ideological control in order to suppress existing cultural values and institutions where these could not be accomodated to the new order and where necessary or feasible, replacing them by imported ideologies, especially Christianity, and the institutions—the Church and the religious orders—with which to enforce them.[23]

Indeed, a leading advocate of the "world systems" approach has conceded that "here [the dissolution of societies based on status] is a definite place where processes of consciousness and ideology enter as integral to the theory of capital accumulation on a world scale. But it is also here that we come to an almost abrupt halt theoretically."[24] But cultural and ideological mechanisms within a totalizing social order, such as those mentioned, must be accorded some autonomous role in the history of the creation of the modern Third World and not appended as an epiphenomenal afterthought to "real" economic and political processes conceived in the most narrow sense, as is done by "world systems" theorists.

In contrast to the "world system" perspective, in recent years an alternative humanist and historicist Marxist approach to the underdevelopment of the Malaysian peasantry has appeared. This new approach has several related aspects. First, it places a strong emphasis upon the resistance of the Malay peasantry to class and state domination under colonial and postcolonial capitalism in Malaysia—a resistance engendered by rural Malay culture grounded in noncapitalist relations of production.[25] Recent work by historians on the widespread resistance, at times violent, but customarily covert and unspoken, by rural Malays to British colonial rule and to indigenous aristocratic despotism has led to the rejection of the platitude—which appears to be shared by "world systems" theorists as well—that popular Malay response to colonialist policies was a passive and placid one. This study draws directly and for inspiration on their work.[26] Several scholars have pointed to the role of Islam in the rural Malay challenge to Malaysian capitalism and the state, such that it represents an alternative moral charter for those who have opposed domination by foreign and state capitalists, by landlords and merchants, and by those elites—both Malay and non-Malay—who support them.[27]

Others have pointed to resistance by contemporary Malay peasants to the strategems of foreign and Malaysian capitalists and to state bureaucrats. For instance, James Scott has shown that Malay agricultural laborers respond to landlord depression of their wages not by strikes or other overt action, but by what he calls "everyday forms of resistance" such as covert work stoppages and slowdowns, theft, and sabotage.[28] Rural Malays working as wage laborers on state plantations have adopted strikes and covert actions, similar to those described by Scott, in the face of wage cuts and employer pressures to intensify production.[29] Overt forms of peasant protest, such as the 1974 Baling demonstrations, the 1980 "riots" by padi farmers in the Muda scheme, and conflicts between Malay settlers and FELDA (Federal Land Development Authority—the government land settlement authority) have also been reported.[30]

A second aspect of the alternative approach is the attempt to recapture Malay peasant subjectivity (i.e., intentional praxis) and consciousness as these have developed during the confrontation between European capitalist and peasant noncapitalist modes of production—an attempt to recreate a history of popular Malay experience "from the bottom up." Work in this area has just begun, but it is important to note that, as might be expected, the most comprehensive work to date has been done by Malaysian scholars. Shaharil has reconstructed the "voices" of Kelantanese peasants as they sought to confront colonial capitalist and official attempts to dispossess them from their land, from the early 1900s onward.[31] Cheah has studied the relationship between "social banditry" and popular Malay culture in northern Kedah in the early twentieth century; it is clear from his work that there exists among contemporary peasants a strong oral tradition that honors violent resistance to landlord oppression and British rule.[32] Shaharil has recently traced both the sources of popular discontent and the eschatological Islamic dimension of peasant consciousness present during the Trengganu uprising of 1928.[33] And Zawawi has interpreted the emergence of a proletarian consciousness among Malay peasants on a Trengganu oil-palm plantation, and developed a critique of the "world systems" approach, such as it is, to class consciousness.[34]

A third feature of an alternative Marxist approach to the underdevelopment of the Malaysian peasantry is one that sees the colonial state not as a monolithic entity, but rather as a highly differentiated structure within a more inclusive imperial system and mediating between this system and local-level communities. There are three distinct aspects of the history of the colonial state that require consideration here. First, colonial Malaya was a complex, evolving system connected to higher (i.e., more geographically inclusive) levels of the British empire, and responded to the perturbations and oscillations inherent in the development of industrial capitalism. Far from being autonomous, the British colonial state responded to these changes by instituting reforms and adjustments; these responses, in turn, led to the emergence of further contradictions and interaction effects, which posed new problems for the state and to which it had to react. Responses, however, were by no means monolithically coordinated, nor were they aimed solely toward successful capital accumulation for colonial capitalists, for the British administration was itself internally differentiated. It reflected class differences between different British and other European groups within and outside the state, conflicts between factions within the administration allied to differing groups at higher levels, competition between rival departments within the bureaucracy, and contrasting ties and allegiances to the various classes and ethnic groups among the colonized. In this alternative perspective, then, where state policies and maneuvers vis-à-vis the Malay peasantry appeared to be coordinated and uniform and to further the interests of colonial capitalists, this must be explained and cannot simply be assumed away as "world systems" theorists are inclined to do.

Second, the congruity of the organization, aims, and policies of the colonial state with the cultural and ideological mechanisms of attempted "hegemony" (in Gramsci's sense) mentioned above cannot be taken for granted. Rather it itself becomes problematic, for the colonial state is only one source, although a major one, for these mechanisms. Finally, as recent theoretical work in the study of state formation suggests, particular attention must be paid to the history of expansion of colonial state power and the various forms it assumed over space, as this expansion was directed against both precolonial elites and the local kin-ordered communities from which the latter drew tribute in the precolonial period.[35] Thus a crucial focus of inquiry must be on the three-cornered struggle between the colonial state, these elites, and local communities over control of peasants' means of production—particularly their own labor and land—as this struggle changed over time.

The implications of this new perspective on the Malayan colonial state for understanding the transformation of the Malaysian peasantry lie in the regions of contingency and "free play" that the internal contradictions of the colonial state opened for peasant praxis and resistance. The British colonial state was at no time completely unconstrained in its initiatives against the Malay peasantry, as the reconstruction that follows makes clear.

In this study, I adopt the alternative humanist and historicist Marxist approach whose main features I have sketched out—an emphasis on Malay peasant resistance; an attempt—albeit indirectly—to recover Malay lower-class subjectivity, and a focus on the mediating character of, and internal contradictions within, the British colonial state—and situate these within the historically contingent process of "primitive accumulation." First employed by Marx in his observations on the growth of nineteenth-century English industrial capitalism and its effects on the English and Irish countrysides,[36] the concept of "primitive accumulation" has been most perceptively applied to colonial societies by Giovanni Arrighi. In his landmark study of capitalist development and indigenous labor in Rhodesia, he proposes:

> primary [i.e. primitive] accumulation can be defined as a process in which the nonmarket mechanisms predominate and through which the gap between productivity in the capitalist sector and productivity in the noncapitalist sector is widened. The process is completed when the gap is so wide that producers in the latter are prepared to sell their labor-time "spontaneously" at whatever wage-rate is consistent with steady accumulation in the capitalist sector.[37]

The histories of the "underdeveloped" societies of the Third World, in Southeast Asia as elsewhere, suggest that in retrospect the process of "primitive accumulation" has been a major historical regularity of modern colonialism, even if it has been contingent and open-ended. At first the instabilities brought on by the linkage of the colonial economy to international capitalism provide indigenous producers with a competitive advantage over European capitalists, and they thus threaten the prospects for capital accumulation within the colonial capitalist sector. However, these instabilities are dampened by the colonial state which deploys various "nonmarket mechanisms" against indigenous tribal peoples and peasants—wars and punitive expeditions; coercion of head tax and labor corvée; dispossession from the land through its outright seizure as "Crown land" or through its privatization; prohibitions on the raising of certain crops or cultivation regimes (e.g., shifting cultivation); monopoly sale and pricing of commodities such as opium, liquor, textiles and salt; monopsonistic controls through "marketing boards," and the establishment of native "reservations" in geographically peripheral and infertile areas, among others.

During the period in which these state-initiated "nonmarket mechanisms" distort and transform noncapitalist relations of production among the peasantry, colonial capitalists invest profits, increase productivity, receive state subsidies, and eventually accumulate capital. At some point in the trajectory of this process, the colonial capitalist class overcomes its initial competitive disadvantage vis-à-vis indigenous producers. As the colonial system matures, we find among the indigenous peasantry diminished agricultural productivity, landlessness, lowered consumption, and physical immiseration. At an even later time, a rural proletariat emerges which sells its labor power to agrarian capitalists or migrates to towns and cities to swell the ranks of unemployed and underemployed people—a subproletariat forming an "industrial reserve army." What then is the relationship between these "non-market mechanisms" of the state, capitalist development, and peasant resistance on one side, and the usual outcomes of the primitive accumulation process—peasant proletarianization and immiseration—on the other?

I am not implying that the process of primitive accumulation represents the *only* form of appropriation occurring within colonial societies, but only that it tends to dominate their evolution. Where there are other classes that appropriate the social product—such as non-European merchant and usury capitalists, rural landowners, and petty industrialists—their interests more often than not are subordinated to those of colonial capitalists. In colonial societies, conflicts between appropriating classes have proven common, but have most frequently been resolved in the favor of colonial capitalists through the deployment of power by the colonial state. For instance, colonial authorities enacted laws against excessive profit-taking by non-European merchants, landowners, and moneylenders. These measures were conventionally phrased in the idiom of "benefitting the natives" and served as the charter for "enlightened colonialism," while, in fact, they reaffirmed the prior claims of colonial capitalists over other appropriating classes to the social product of the peasantry. Indeed, an official ideology of protecting the "birthright and inheritance" of the "Malay yeoman-peasantry," and the contradiction between its precepts and the actual processes of appropriation were recurrent *leitmotifs* throughout the colonial history of Malaya.

This book, then, sets out to deconstruct the following paradox. How is it that the process of primitive accumulation, which is neither historically inevitable nor predetermined, has yet occurred with such tragic regularity in the emergence of the Third World? And in the instance of the Malaysian peasantry, what part have peasant resistance, popular culture, and internal contradictions within the British colonial state played in this process?

In what follows, the historical analysis of chapters 2-7 is largely confined to Malay society on the western coast of the Malayan peninsula, since the emergence of a proletarianized rural Malay population on the east coast had its own distinctive features that would require separate treatment. It should be noted, therefore, that the regional division in terms of political economy between west and east coasts crosscuts and, for present purposes, overrides the administrative division between Federated Malay States and Unfederated Malay States that marks the conventional histories of British colonial Malaya. Thus changes occurring among the Malay peasantries of Kedah and Johore fall within the history of rural Malays on the west coast, although full recognition must be given to the distinctive character of these states as members of the Unfederated Malay States. In addition, the historical reconstruction that follows does not presume to be a comprehensive synthesis of rural Malaysian history during the colonial period—an enterprise far beyond the scope of what is attempted here. Instead, the effort is both different and more modest: to provide an interpretation of the major causes and sources of transformation of the Malay peasantry during the colonial period. Drawing on the work of historians, anthropologists, and other scholars, I attempt to explore the paradox of primitive accumulation set out above. I begin with a description of the condition of rural Malay society as of approximately 1960, three years after Malaysia's formal independence from the British.

The Malaysian Peasantry Transformed, Circa 1946–1960

For Malaysia, the period from the end of World War II and the Japanese occupation to the granting of Independence in 1957 has been most memorialized as "the Emergency"—the insurrection by the Malayan Communist Party against the British and the counterinsurgency measures successfully used to defeat the guerrillas.[38] A focus on the important political events of this period, however, has led, until recently, to a comparative neglect in the study of the changed economic conditions of the Malaysian countryside and of the Malaysian peasantry. On one hand, these conditions cannot be understood independently from the experience of the seventy years of colonial rule that preceded them. On the other, they are conditions that the peasantry of an independent Malaysia had to and still has to confront: growing proletarianization, landlessness, marginalization, and, relatively, a falling standard of living.

From the end of the war through the 1960s, observers throughout rural
Malaysia noted extensive land fragmentation, the existence of a large population
of landless tenants in Malay villages and engaged in part-time and seasonal wage
labor, and the emergence of a class of Malay full-time wage laborers. In many
villages, there were, as well, clear signs of incipient land concentration by small
groups of landowners.

For West Malaysia as a whole, the 1960 Census of Agriculture showed that
seventy percent of all rural farms were less than five acres in area, and 50 percent
were less than three acres.[39] The two major crops of the Malay peasantry during
this period were rubber and "wet" padi, or irrigated rice. In the rubber-producing
areas in the south and on the west coast, extensive tenancy and land
concentration were both reported. For the village of Kampong Bagan in Johore,
Husin Ali summed up the land tenure situation as, "the landlords, comprising
16.1% of the 124 residents studied, control over two-thirds of the land, wh'le
19.3% of the people . . . own 72.4% of the land. On the other hand, the ter .nts
and/or laborers who make up 29.1% of the people own only 3.8% of the land."[40]
Here and in other rubber-growing areas, tenancy took a sharecropping form in
which, under the *bagi dua* arrangement, landowner and tenant split the yield of
rubber tapped each day according to a fixed proportion.[41] In Jendram Hilir, a
village in Selangor, villagers were almost completely dependent on rubber
tapping for income, unlike in Kampong Bagan, where coconut growing was also
important. In this village, twenty households out of 108 owned no land at all, and
those who had land owned an average 4.5 acres; 52 individuals from 22 village
households worked regularly for others under the *bagi dua* system.[42] In Jelebu
district, in Negri Sembilan, where a mixed economy of both rubber tapping and
padi growing predominated, almost 46 percent of all households owned no
rubber plots, despite the fact that rubber tapping was the principal source of cash
income. Swift also noted the appearance of land concentration in Jelebu: there
was "an increasingly large class of low status share-tappers, and a small group of
wealthy men controlling an increasingly large share of the society's productive
assets."[43]

As for rice cultivation, for West Malaysia as a whole 78 percent of padi
farms were below five acres in area, and only 3 percent were ten acres or
above.[44] Of all major rice-growing areas, the Kedah Plain, long noted as the
largest area of Malaysia's "rice bowl," has been most systematically studied for
this period in terms of land fragmentation and concentration and rates of tenancy
and rural wage-labor. The *Census of Padi Planters in Kedah, 1955* found that the
average padi farm size in this area was only 5.1 acres, and that land was highly
unequally owned, with farms under 2.8 acres constituting 32.5 percent of all
farms but only 10.1 percent of the total area, while at the high end of the farm-
size distribution, farms greater than 7.0 acres made up only 17.9 percent of all

farms, but composed 43.0 percent of the total area.[45] Moreover, 42.1 percent of all padi farmers were pure tenants, owning no land.[46] Several village-level studies support this latter conclusion for the area as a whole in this period: for four villages studied, the percentage of padi-farming households that owned no land and operated as tenants varied from 44.1 to 56.1 percent.[47]

By the mid-1950s, conditions for tenants in this area had deteriorated with steady rent increases, cash rents increasingly substituted for rents-in-kind, and the appearance of cash deposits required by landowners from tenants to reserve land for the next season.[48] During the decade from 1955 to 1965, tenants in the area declined marginally from 42.1 percent to 41.4 percent, the beginning of a long-term trend through the 1970s toward a decline in tenancy.[49] However, this denoted no improvement, for increasing numbers of peasants were unable to obtain land at all, even by renting in, and had either to become full-time agricultural laborers, to out-migrate to work at wage labor elsewhere, or to settle and cultivate land beyond the Kedah Plain. According to the definitive study on land tenure in the Muda Scheme on the Kedah Plain, during the decade from 1955 to 1965 among padi cultivators, "either a substantial degree of out-migration occurred as many peasants were forced to become agricultural laborers, thereby not appearing in the farm statistics, or a combination of the two processes took place. In the Muda area out-migration was probably the main factor."[50] By the late 1960s, a substantial number of rural Malays on the Kedah Plain had become agricultural laborers; a study by the Food and Agricultural Organization and the International Bank of Reconstruction and Development (FAO-IBRD) in 1972-1973 concluded, on the basis of its sample, that 5.4 percent of the rural Malay population in the area were full-time farm workers.[51] Two village studies suggest that in some farming villages —particularly those close to Alor Star or another urban center in the area—the percentage of peasants working as wage laborers was even higher, from about 15 to 25 percent.[52] This represented the beginning of a trend toward proletarianization that was to accelerate in the 1970s and 1980s. In one comparative study, Husin Ali reported substantial concentration of land in two villages, one called Kangkong, located on the Kedah coast, whose main economic activity was rice cultivation; the other called Kerdau, in western Pahang, with a mixed economy based on both rice growing and rubber production:

> for those [land holdings] under three acres, 67.7 per cent of the people in Kangkong are in this category and they own only 19.2 per cent of the land; in Kerdau 26.6 per cent of the people own only 6.0 per cent of the land. . . . In contrast, those within the categories [of holdings] above eighteen acres present the reverse picture: in Kangkong 5.5 per cent of the people own 33.0 per cent of the land [and] in Kerdau 6.3 per cent of the people own 24.9 per cent of the land.[53]

Similar conditions of small farm size, high tenancy and land concentration, and increasing rural wage-labor rates prevailed in other areas where padi growing predominated. Nearby in Province Wellesley (Seberang Perai), in one irrigated rice scheme 41 percent of all padi farmers were landless tenants.[54] Several miles to the south in Krian district, another important "rice bowl" area, a comparative study observed in two adjacent rice-growing villages that 34 and 35 percent, respectively, of cultivating households were those of landless tenants; that cultivating households grew padi on an average farm size of 3.5 acres in the first village, and of 2.8 acres in the second; and that 2 percent (one of 48) and 16 percent (21 of 131) of all households were, respectively, either supported by full-time wage labor (both agricultural and nonagricultural) or had heads of household who were unemployed.[55] This same study pointed to another common feature among padi cultivators: that they frequently resorted to seasonal or part-time employment in addition to cultivating their own fields. In the two villages studied, 60 percent and 57 percent, respectively, of all padi cultivating households had heads who worked either seasonally or part-time in work as diverse as agricultural wage labor (e.g., during padi harvest), fishing (as boat crew members), rice mill wage labor, teaching, carpentry, barbering, and tailoring.[56]

The findings of at least one study suggest that these conditions were not limited to the west coast states, but could be generalized to padi-growing areas in the east coast as well. In the state of Kelantan, 29 percent of all agrarian households were landless, and according to Nash, "of the more than 15,500 farm families in Kelantan, less than ten percent own the necessary rice and other land to meet their minimum standards of adequacy."[57] In the village he studied no less than 26.3 percent of the adult labor force were agricultural laborers, rubber sharetappers (under *bagi dua*), or unemployed.[58] It is a plausible thesis that the same fundamental causes of rural Malay immiserization and proletarianization in the west coast analyzed in the present study affected peasant communities in the east coast as well, with important differences arising from the location of these communities in West Malaysia's national periphery (see chapter 5, endnote 22). However, this thesis cannot be pursued further here.

Through this period, the one rural nonagricultural occupation in which Malays participated in great numbers was coastal fishing. Here a combination of very small-scale fishing operations, concentrations of capital in the form of individually owned motorized boats and purse seines, and the widespread presence of Malay share-laborers as members of boat crews existed by the 1960s on both west and east coasts of the peninsula. On the west coast, boats, purse seines, and other productive property were owned by Chinese *taukeh ikan* (fish traders who also provided fishermen with credit and loans), whereas *taukeh ikan* on the east coast were ethnic Malays.[59]

Firth observed that by the 1960s, in the eastern states of Kelantan and Trengganu, there was a marked increase in the proportion of Malay fishermen who were without capital and had to work for shares of a boat's catch, compared to the time before the Japanese occupation.[60] A similar change from the period before the occupation appears also to have taken place among Malay fishermen on the west coast. In one study, Husin Ali observed that the village of Kangkong on the Kedah coast showed a "process of accumulation and dispossession" leading to the concentration of boats and nets in the hands of nine persons, while twenty-two persons were share-laborers dependent on the former.[61]

Changes in ownership during this period were accompanied by falling productivity in all major areas of the rural Malay economy except padi growing, and even here the increase was one of productivity only, not income. A comparison of the year 1950 with 1958 shows that for the four major sectors of Malay peasant production, smallholder rubber production declined by 14 percent, smallholder copra by 34 percent, and fish landings by 9 percent, with only padi showing an increase of 14 percent.[62] In the case of padi growing, in 1960 the average real income of a padi cultivator remained almost exactly the same as in 1947, while the number of padi cultivators declined by 15.4 percent.[63] In 1962, Fisk concluded that

> despite the general prosperity of the Malayan economy and the general rise in the level of the GNP, the trend of productivity in the backward peasant sector has been downwards rather than upwards . . . it means that probably nearly 20 per cent more people are living off the same, or possibly slightly less total production than they were 10 years ago.[64]

From the available evidence, it is probable that for most Malay peasants, real incomes were static or declined during this period.[65]

It is also in this postwar period that rural Malays were first observed in substantial numbers either working as full-time, permanent wage laborers or seeking such work. In addition to the ethnographic evidence already given, statistical findings based on comparisons between the 1947 and 1957 population censuses demonstrate both the absolute number and the increasing proportion of rural Malays having to resort to wage labor. Table 1 shows that on a state-by-state basis, there was a consistent increase of from 3.1 to 33.9 percent in the proportion of wage laborers among the economically active Malay population in agricultural occupations, with a median increase of 10.3 percent.[66] Important sources of rural wage labor in the postwar period were plantation work and government employment.

In the years after the Japanese occupation, surprised government labor officials noted how rural Malays were flocking to rubber plantations to work as tappers and manual laborers for the first time in Malayan history. For instance,

TABLE 1

Numbers and Percentages of "Malaysians"* Who Were Wage Earners Within the Economically Active Population in Agricultural Occupations in 1957, and Changes in Percentage of "Malaysians"* Who Were Wage Earners Within the Economically Active Population in Agricultural Occupations, 1947-1957, by State.

STATE	NUMBER WAGE EARNERS 1957	PERCENTAGE WAGE EARNERS 1957	CHANGE, PCT. WAGE EARNERS 1947-1957
Malacca	12,332	57.2	+33.9
Johore	41,691	45.2	+25.3
Penang	8,431	32.6	+23.2
Selangor	12,883	28.0	+16.6
Perak	25,366	23.8	+13.0
Negri Sembilan	7,408	21.8	+ 9.0
Kedah	30,509	21.4	+ 9.0
Trengganu	9,631	15.6	+10.3
Pahang	6,302	12.6	+ 6.8
Kelantan	17,378	12.4	+ 6.5
Perlis	1,213	5.2	+ 3.1

Sources: Del Tufo 1949 Tables 103-104; Department of Statistics, Federation of Malaya, 1958: Vols 2-13, Table 16.

*Note: "Malaysians" consisted of "Malays," "Indonesians" and "Aborigines." See Footnotes 66, 68.

the *Annual Report of the Labour Department of the Malayan Union* for 1947 noted that

> Malays are now going through an interesting transition in that they are moving slowly and gradually away from the traditional village economy to a wage economy. This process is very slow and needs encouragement as the Malay with his long history of independence will only accept a wage economy when he is fully confident that he understands it and that he is not going to lose any real degree of independence.[67]

For instance in 1947, no less than 59,000, or 20.3 percent of the plantation labor force, were "Malays," and their number continued to grow, absolutely and relatively, through 1960.[68]

Rural Malays in great numbers also sought employment with the government as police, truck drivers, postmen, and laborers in this period. For example, in 1948, 32,000 Malays were recruited as "Special Constables" as part of the administration's counterinsurgency efforts.[69] A Keynesian ironist might argue that if there had not been an "Emergency" to ameliorate the unemployment crisis then developing among rural Malays by providing government work, one surely would have had to have been invented. This, however, was no long-term solution. For, as one leading economist delicately put it in 1967, "Indeed an important problem today is to stop the long queues of Malays at many of the Labour Exchanges from getting longer!"[70]

To summarize the available ethnographic and statistical evidence, through the postwar period to the 1960s, Malay peasants experienced extensive land fragmentation and falling productivity and incomes; many owned no land and worked either as tenants, sharecroppers, or wage-laborers for landowners. A large proportion had become permanent wage-laborers for plantation enterprises or for the colonial government. These were qualitatively new developments, as the following pages show. To understand the causes of their appearance, it is necessary to start with a reconstruction of the late precolonial period in which noncapitalist, tributary relations of production prevailed.

CHAPTER TWO

The Precolonial Period

Introduction: Issues in Precolonial Malayan State Formation

Data on precolonial Malay society drawn from nineteenth-century sources are sparse, fragmentary, and often unreliable. This makes definitive statements impossible. All the same, sufficient data are available to indicate that the regional and local political and social systems found in the Malay peninsula in the mid-nineteenth century were diverse and extremely differentiated in terms of political organization, stratification, and settlement ecology. But then difficulties become even more obvious, for, although variation can be intuited, its full extent and underlying causes are not clear, given the nature of the data. The reconstruction of precolonial Malay society presented in this chapter is therefore at best provisional, and the conclusions drawn from it extremely tentative.

An historiographic note is needed here. Although the precolonial period per se, if defined as prior to active British intervention in the Federated Malay States in 1874, can be formally distinguished from the years that followed, in fact European and Chinese inland penetration of the peninsula proceeded outside the authority of formal colonial rule during the years from the late eighteenth century up through the 1870s in the future Federated Malay States, and through the early 1900s in two other western Malay states—Kedah (1909) and Johore (1919)—covered in this study. From the British and Chinese sides, this longer period that spanned the Treaty of Pangkor in 1874 was one of continued and then accelerated energetic (and even frenetic) extension of British political influence over these states, and of further commercial penetration by Chinese of their economies, a process begun in the late eighteenth century. From the Malay side, it was one of continued but increasingly weakened political resistance to British encroachments combined with active engagement over the same period with the new trading systems initiated by British and Chinese commerce in the Straits Settlements and the Federated Malay States. For purposes of exposition, this chapter is confined to the years before 1874, but it must be kept always in mind that, given the existence of these long-term developments over this longer period, the year chosen to mark the periodization is, to some extent, arbitrary.

In what can be only a very schematic reconstruction given the limitations of data, I wish to advance the following propositions. First, precolonial Malay society in the nineteenth century was not in the strict sense a "society" but rather an assemblage of regional social systems in various phases of state formation and class differentiation. In all instances, these social systems were class-based rather than unstratified like those of certain tribal peoples in the same region. By the mid-nineteenth century, the state formation process within these social systems was characterized in most instances by relations between three major classes—Malay commoners or *ra'ayat*, and Chinese tin miners and agriculturalists on one side, and the ruling class led by Malay "rulers" or *raja* on the other. However, class differentiation in no way characterized the social organization of most villages (*kampong*) in which Malay *ra'ayat* lived, because the large degree of residential segregation entailed the separation of Malay commoners from both members of the Malay ruling class and Chinese laborers.

Second, a basic unit of social organization of precolonial Malay society consisted of what I call here the Malay *ra'ayat* kin-ordered village community. Previous accounts of precolonial social organization have emphasized the importance of the Malay nuclear family and dyadic patron-client ties. I propose to complement these accounts by arguing for the existence of a kin-ordered village community which would go far to explain the dialectics of precolonial state formation and the character of peasant resistance within this process. It is probable that day-to-day class relations between members of the ruling class and the *ra'ayat* most commonly took the form of interactions between kin-ordered communities and state elites.

Third, the dialectical relations of state formation were structured primarily in terms of struggle by the ruling class over the control of the labor and products of the Malay *ra'ayat* and Chinese laborers, and *not* over land and its resources (except tin). This was in distinct contrast to the struggle between the *ra'ayat* and the new rulers of the colonial period, in which access to land—and its commodification—were central features. In the precolonial period, relations of exploitation instead took the form of taxes on tin production and exports; of import duties on opium, spirits, rice, and other trade goods consumed by the *ra'ayat* and Chinese miners; of corvée labor; of debt-bondage and slavery; of export taxes on goods produced by the *ra'ayat*; and of tithes on *ra'ayat* produce exacted in situ.

Fourth, precolonial Malay states appear to be one variety of what Michael Adas[1] has referred to as the weak "contest state" common to many preindustrial settings in Southeast Asia, Africa, and elsewhere. The characteristics of such states deserve attention for they constrained options available to the peasant *ra'ayat* both prior to and after the establishment of British rule in 1874. Fifth, as was true elsewhere, in Malaya there appears to have been associated with these states what Adas calls "avoidance protest" by the peasant *ra'ayat* against ruling-class exactions, which sought, often successfully, to limit ruling-class exploitation to within tolerable bounds. Such avoidance resistance included flight, transfer of allegiance to another lord, and several other strategies discussed below. As a result of the effectiveness of avoidance protest by the peasant *ra'ayat*, the continued existence of ruling-class power in most states depended on a *modus vivendi* in which major forms of exploitation were directed by the ruling class not against the *ra'ayat*, whose loyalty was thereby assured, but against Chinese laborers. It is therefore crucial to distinguish those forms of exploitation and sources of revenue which made major contributions to ruling-class wealth but had little direct effect on the lives of the *ra'ayat* (such as tin export taxes and opium farms) on one hand, from those sources which provided relatively little in the way of ruling-class income but had a major impact on the *ra'ayat* (such as corvée labor, debt-bondage and slavery, and import duties on staples such as rice) on the other. Avoidance protest by the *ra'ayat* constrained the ruling class of each state to maximize the former, but minimize the latter, whenever possible. From this vantage point, instances of peasant resistance to state policies and actions observed in the colonial and postcolonial periods in a sense represented no less than the continuation of a long tradition of avoidance protest or resistance, albeit transformed in terms of specific strategies, from the precolonial period.

In what follows, these five propositions are developed, and evidence—such as it exists—is brought to bear on them.

Deconstructing the Notion of "Malay Society"

Malay "society" prior to British accession with the Treaty of Pangkor in 1874 is, properly speaking, a misnomer, for the Malay populations of the peninsula during the two preceding centuries could best be described as residing in distinct concentrations within the boundaries of several maritime- and riverine- based states or *negeri*. In most cases, inland concentrations of Malay populations in settlements in each of these states —Kedah, Perak, Selangor, Negri Sembilan, and Johore—were separated from those of other states by overland topographic barriers—mountain ranges and coastal swampland dividing the major river basins—as well as by the obstacles to transit posed by tropical rain forests. Within a state, given these geographic constraints, the principal lines of communication and trade were the rivers that extended inland from the coast. The primary form of transport of both people and goods was river boat; travel by foot on jungle paths and elephant tracks was a secondary form. In places, jungle paths were important however, as where they connected inland settlements to riverine villages or allowed travellers carrying trade goods to bypass downriver settlements of chiefs, and thereby escape the exaction of tolls and taxes.[2]

Such interaction as there was between states was generally by means of maritime commerce. Settlements in coastal locations, especially those situated at river mouths, could take best advantage of such commerce, although in some areas overland trade did take place, often with the objective of evading tolls associated with river trade.[3] Therefore, what existed during this period prior to active British intervention were several more or less autonomous state polities in various phases of formation or dissolution, poorly integrated within, and connected without by premodern transport and communication technology and facilities.

Moreover, not only does precolonial Malay "society" as such disappear on closer inspection, but so also does the label "Malay" itself. By this time the various "Malay" populations of these states consisted not only of the "Malay" descendants of wet-rice cultivators of several centuries' settlement in the peninsula (in many locales, themselves the cultural and genetic products of encounters with aboriginal Negritos, Chinese, Siamese, and Europeans), but also of recent immigrants. Achenese from northern Sumatra, Menangkebau from eastern Sumatra, Javanese from Java, and Buginese from Suluwesi were the greatest in number.[4]

What made this congeries of culturally distinctive groups specifically part of a "Malay world" were the use of a common language and its dialects (even if only as *lingua franca* in places); the existence of a constellation of cultural self-descriptions centered on being the followers of Islam; and the adoption of—or being made subject to—a common form of political domination called *kerajaan* or the "condition of having a *raja* [ruler]" within a state territory on the peninsula. Defined in these terms, the "Malay world" extended far beyond the peninsula to islands to the west (Sumatra), the east (Borneo) and the south (the Indonesian archipelago). "Malays" belonged to this world in that they were different from groups not so identified—i.e. aborigines, Chinese, Europeans, or Siamese.

Such a characterization is, however, most valuable when taken as a classifying device for historical inquiry and not as a label reflecting a unitary cultural, much less social, reality. The extent to which those nineteenth-century peoples across this vast geographic area who were identified by others as "Malay" considered themselves on a day-to-day basis to be so—or acted in solidary groups vis-à-vis other groups—is problematic. That is, we cannot assume the existence at that time of a self-ascribed "Malay" ethnic identity. Indeed, if one of the central theses of this study is correct, this identity was forged in the course of the colonial experience. To the contrary, the precolonial period was marked by strong antipathies between different "Malay" cultural groups—particularly between those who saw themselves as autochthonous *(anak negeri)* and those who were recent immigrants *(anak dagang)*—since villages tended to be homogeneous in terms of the regional origins of their residents, and to be aligned by origin with chiefs opposed to one another in the feuds and succession struggles of the period.[5]

Class Divisions: Rajas, Chiefs, Ra'ayat, Chinese

Malays lived in precolonial "Malay society" (in the sense just qualified) within state systems, *negeri,* whose ruling classes controlled—or attempted to control—the lives of their subjects within specifically bounded territories. A *negeri* was territorially defined by the area within the basin(s) or catchment zone(s) of one or more of the rivers debouching on the waters of (what are now called) the Straits of Malacca, the Straits of Johore, or, in the east, the South China Sea. A major division within this society, therefore, was that between the ruling class—led by the *raja* or ruler of the state, called *Yang Di-Pertuan* or "Sultan"—and its subjects, the "commoners," or *ra'ayat.*

In addition to the ruler and his immediate family, members of the ruling class included his male patrilineal kinsmen (including potential heirs to the sultanate, the *waris negeri*); affines of the royal family (usually already cognatically related to it); and non-royal (or in Kedah, royal) "chiefs," their families, and their kinsmen-cum-retainers. A "chief," generally with the title of *Dato'*, was a member of the ruling class who held rights over the people residing within a district *(daerah)* defined by the basin of a river tributary or subtributary, and over trade passing down or up the section of river within the district. Gullick describes the spatial scope of a district as "either an area lying on one or both sides of a reach of the main river of the State or . . . a side valley down to the point of junction with the main stream."[6] In theory, rights over the people and river trade within a district were conceded to the chief by the sultan in return for loyalty to him. In fact, however, more often than not, such a concession was no more than the formal recognition of a *fait accompli*—the control over a district's territory by a powerful chief.

The ruling class in each state was endogamous, with the exception of a relatively small number of marriage alliances between royal families of different states. The ruling class of a state consisted of the bilateral descendants (or in Negri Sembilan, the matrilineal descendants) of the sultan and district chiefs. The relatives of a chief, along with his debt-bondsmen and slaves, formed an entourage of followers upon whom he could call for military and administrative service, as well as the extraction of wealth from Chinese miners and the *ra'ayat* of his domain by means of "farming out" rights to specific taxes, corvées, and produce. Most members of this entourage resided in the village of the chief—usually the largest village in the district—who in turn, imitating the sultan, withdrew both physically and ritually from contact with the *ra'ayat.* As a result, except for the chief's (or sultan's) village, other *kampong* of a district were composed exclusively of *ra'ayat.*

All other Malays were members of the *ra'ayat.* The great majority of these were "free" peasants. In contrast, a small but significant minority were debt-bondsmen (*orang berhutang*). These latter had contracted loans with their chiefs and, since they were unable to redeem them, entered into a form of indentured service to their chiefs. Debt-bondsmen possessed the right to purchase their way out of service formally, but in actuality were rarely able to do so.

In addition there resided in chiefs' *kampong* non-Malay slaves, *hamba abdi*—non-Muslims such as aborigines and Africans (imported by Arab traders or by Malays returning from the *haj*). Their status was permanent and inherited, but their de facto position appears to have been much the same as debt-bondsmen, who, as Muslims, could not be enslaved.

Although the proportion of the non-ruling population who were either debt-bondsmen or slaves is not definitively known, estimates from certain states suggest that they were very few in number. In Perak in 1879 they appear to have composed about six percent of the Malay population; in Pahang for 1889, between three and six percent; for Negri Sembilan at about the same time, Gullick notes that "except at the royal palace . . . there were few" in the state; and for Kedah as of 1909, they constituted about one percent of the Malay agricultural population.[7] This small number, however, may well have belied their social importance, as I suggest below.

Although, properly speaking, they were not subjects of the sultan or his chiefs and thus not part of "Malay society," Chinese tin miners and other coolies must nevertheless be mentioned because, by the mid-nineteenth century, their activities generated large revenues for the ruling class. In the central western states of Perak, Selangor, and Negri Sembilan, tin had been mined for several centuries by Malays using crude sluicing techniques. By the 1820s Malay district chiefs in these states had contracted with Chinese secret society leaders to organize immigrant Chinese laborers (from Kwangtung and Fukien provinces in southeastern China) in *kongsis* to work in the mines.[8] In the 1870s tin mining concessions were given to Chinese in Kulim and Krian districts in southern Kedah.[9] By the 1840s, Chinese formed the vast majority of the mining population in these states. In Johore from the 1840s onward, Chinese coolies working on gambier plantations provided large revenues through the *kangchu* system to the Temenggong (later Sultan) of Johore and his government, in the form of opium and spirit farms.[10]

What, then, were conditions of life in Malay *ra'ayat* peasant communities of the period?

The Kin-ordered Malay Village Community and State Formation

In the mid-nineteenth century most of the settled Malay population in the western states were wet-rice cultivators depending on rainfall trapped by crude irrigation and drainage works to water their fields. *Ra'ayat* population tended to concentrate near the mouths of major rivers in nucleated settlements on alluvial plains or cleared swamplands; inland, settlements were dispersed in linear fashion along the major river and its tributaries. Settlement population sizes and densities tended to fall as one went upriver and suitable land for wet-rice cultivation became more scarce.[11] Peasants planted as side crops both annuals and tree crops, such as coffee, tobacco, sago, bananas, corn, sugar cane, tapioca, and coconut, areca, betel, durian, and other fruits.[12] They also engaged in coastal and riverine fishing. In foothills and highland areas, or where tin was being mined, e.g., in Selangor and lower Perak, peasants engaged in dry-rice swidden cultivation.[13] Some worked seasonally in tin mining.

It has been argued that wet-rice "productivity" under these conditions was generally low compared to that found in present wet-rice areas using modern cultivation techniques, indicating a precolonial status of economic "backwardness." This is generally ascribed to two causes. One is that the accumulation of a surplus of rice or some other crop invited confiscation by a district's chief or members of his entourage, thus discouraging excess planting and high yields.[14] The other is that the extensive labor inputs needed for constructing adequate irrigation and drainage works for higher yields were not forthcoming, except perhaps under elite compulsion.[15]

Nonetheless, some clarification is needed here, for there are two meanings for "productivity"—productivity *per acre* and productivity *per labor hour*. Generally, the former sense is assumed and the latter ignored, as when modern wet-rice production in Malaysia and elsewhere under "double cropping" and other Green Revolution innovations is being discussed and often promoted. However, double-cropping is relatively *un*-productive, that is inefficient, in terms of labor inputs: large per acre yields are associated with enormous investments of labor or its machine energy equivalent and of other inputs as well. Generally, the major increases in effort and drudgery involved have only been achieved through direct and indirect pressures from the modern state to increase production, and this is surely true in the case of Malaysian peasants, as later chapters demonstrate.[16]

In contrast, wet-rice cultivation in the precolonial period was no doubt highly labor-efficient—like other forms of premodern agriculture (such as swidden) in land-plentiful areas, and not associated with state compulsion. Under the prevailing conditions, field sites that were relatively advantageous in terms of effort required for drainage and irrigation would have been chosen. It is probable, if we judge from recent single-cropping, wet-rice cultivation practices in Malaya, that wet-rice cultivation was but one element in an intricate man-made mini-ecosystem based on the highly efficient extraction of environmental resources with, for example, buffalo foraging on off-season field stubble, and with fish and shrimp being caught in ponds and drainage channels.[17]

Given later pieties by British colonial officials to the effect that rural Malays showed "inherent laziness" because of the ease with which they met their food needs, and that their extensive land use practices such as swidden, or *ladang*, were "wasteful," this distinction is an important one. Equally critical, however, are that in this precapitalist era the kin-ordered *ra'ayat* Malay community would have discouraged capital accumulation, and that production yields were limited in any case by the number of producers in one's family, and by the lack of either storage facilities or, except for Kedah, markets for surplus padi grown by local cultivators.

Although most wet-rice cultivation was for the subsistence of the peasant family, the Malay *kampong* was by no means self-sufficient.[18] Peasants purchased goods such as textiles, salt, and tobacco, which they could not produce themselves; they sold goods such as rattan, gutta percha (a kind of gum or resin) and other forest products and—in the unique case of Kedah—padi and rice, all of which were exported beyond the district or even the state.

Most accounts of rural Malay social organization in the precolonial and early colonial periods have provided a somewhat atomistic portrait of rural Malay life in the *kampong*. It has been argued that the basic unit of production and consumption was the Malay nuclear family.[19] Members of the nuclear family cultivated padi lands together, resided together, and ate meals together. For many theorists, associated with the central economic role of the Malay nuclear family unit was the absence of any corporate descent groups that might hold land and organize village political, economic, and ritual life. A notable exception was Negri Sembilan, where there existed an (ethnologically) unusual matrilineage organization of Menangkebau immigrants from Sumatra and a form of landholding vested in women and grounded in local "custom," called *adat perpatih*. For some authors, it was even the *ra'ayat* individual who was the real unit of Malay village society. For instance, according to Wong, "the economic activities of the Malays had become individualized in the sense that land was cultivated by a single individual or a family for his or their own livelihood."[20] It has been claimed that beyond the individual per se and "his" nuclear family, the major social ties made by peasants were vertical—patron-client links between individual *ra'ayat* and chiefs and other influential members of the ruling class. Banks writes, "the Malay social system lacked clans and lineages of the African type. Instead, the Malay system accentuated individual ties to patrons and sultans as opposed to community-based groupings. This may have encouraged extracommunity alliances and their proliferation across the archipelago."[21]

However, while not denying the existence and importance of such vertical ties, I would like to argue here that a fundamental unit of *ra'ayat* social organization, the kin-ordered Malay village community, has gone largely unnoticed in the literature. Moreover, there is at least good circumstantial evidence both for its existence and for its centrality in the dialectical relationship between the precolonial *ra'ayat* and its ruling class and state apparatus.

The kin-ordered *ra'ayat* village consisted of a moral community of families and individuals linked closely together by a variety of kinship and residential ties. The absence of formal descent groups among the *ra'ayat,* in all *negeri* except Negri Sembilan, *does not* imply that no local social organization existed beyond an aggregate of nuclear families. For the general case, as Keesing has warned us,

> that societies without corporate descent groupings are so common in the tribal world . . . should throw into question the great emphasis on corporate groups and on formal or "structural" systems of social organization . . . . Informal groups and networks, friendship as well as kinship, the texture as well as the structure of social life have increasingly commanded anthropological attention in recent years.[22]

Instead, we must look to solidarities between persons in the same village formed by kin ties beyond that of the nuclear family, by personal kindreds, and by affinal relations, and by interdependent relationships between neighbors and fellow residents of the *kampong*, as overlapping modes of structuring the kin-ordered *ra'ayat* village community.

Gullick, whose treatment of precolonial Malay kinship is by far the most comprehensive, has, in effect, suggested the basis for such informal structuring of the village community. He observes that during the period, "there was a definite preference for matrilocal marriage," and that "the sons left the homestead of their parents when they married and settled with their wives' families or elsewhere. In time, therefore, the homestead came to consist of sisters (or women more remotely related in the female line) together with their husbands and children."[23] That the existence, not to speak of importance, of such an informal female-centered unit *spanning* nuclear families in organizing everyday life might well have escaped the notice of androcentric colonial officials goes without saying. Given the long recognized participation of women within agricultural production (e.g., groups of women transplanting rice) and the general sharing of decision-making between men and women in contemporary Malay peasant families noted by many anthropologists, it is justifiable to suggest that this informal female-centered domestic unit, each linked to other similar units in the *kampong* through agnatic, cognatic, affinal, and neighborly ties, was the fundamental structure of Malay village life in the precolonial period. However, it was one that was largely unnoticed by European observers of the period, and one that has subsequently been ignored. Moreover, closely related kinfolk resided near one another in the village: "a hamlet of half a dozen houses might consist only of a single group of kinsmen led by one of their senior members. A larger village would consist of the 'founder family' and several other separate groups of kinsfolk."[24]

All the same, villages were not exogamous, and perhaps a majority of marriages occurred between families in the same village; for a man, because of matrilocal post-marital residence, "[t]here was a considerable inducement to him to marry within his own village."[25] Unfortunately, *pressures* on a man from his female kin (mothers, aunts, sisters, brothers' wives, etc.) to do so have been given little weight or scholarly attention.

What we can infer, then, is the existence not of a congeries of unrelated nuclear families coincidentally residing within the *ra'ayat kampong,* but of a village community made up of female-centered domestic units complexly (and often redundantly) interlinked as kindred and affines, neighbors and fellow residents, within the same locale.

Late precolonial portraits by European officials and observers of Malay village life imply social relations verging on self-destructive anarchy within the realm of production —atomization prevented only by the strong hand of ruling class authority—the chiefs and the local village headmen, the *penghulu.* For instance, Gullick argues from these descriptions about wet padi production that

> the existence of larger contiguous blocks of padi land than the holdings of individual families imposed a measure of concerted action. There are advantages in working land in such blocks . . . . But the advantages of a larger contiguous cultivated area are lost if there is no common timetable for planting operations. If each plants as he pleases, one will want the fields to be drained off for reaping while the padi of another is still green. Pests lurk in the plots of mature padi and sally forth to devastate the growing plants nearby. Despite these compelling reasons for concerting padi planting operations, *there was great difficulty in imposing a common programme.*[26]

By "common programme" Gullick makes it clear, in a quote from Hugh Clifford in Pahang that follows, that this was to be "imposed" by chiefs. However, there is need to be skeptical of this invocation of the function of formal authority for, although chiefs in the precolonial period might feasibly attempt to coordinate padi production in their own *kampong,* surely they could not have done so to any great extent elsewhere in their districts. Moreover, although one might expect to find the kind of atomized "beggar thy neighbor" situation depicted in the absence of authority in a few exceptional villages, it could hardly have been a widespread practice. The assumption that it *was* a widespread practice—that Malay villagers were incapable on their own of informally coordinating their padi-planting activities—is unjustified by ethnographic or historical studies of Malay village life, although it may accord well with Orientalist and Social Darwinist stereotypes about Malay fatalism, lethargy, and lack of long-term rationality. Indeed, this assumption is belied by Gullick elsewhere when he discusses padi cultivation in Negri Sembilan and implies the existence of a village community with informal sanctions toward cooperation: "in order to minimize loss through pests the whole village must synchronize its cultivation programme. Thus each stage from the first operation of mending the dams up to the junkettings of the harvest season becomes a village occasion. The family which cuts itself off from this become strangers in the village."[27] It is difficult, moreover, to understand how it would have been possible for Malay *kampong* to exist as social systems for any length of time under these conditions, and yet stable communities without ruling-class leaders present to coordinate padi production clearly existed over long periods of time during the precolonial era.

I propose, instead, that kin-ordered village communities, organized through networks of interlinked female-centered households, engaged in informal and consensual decision-making, and led by *penghulu* and other prominent individuals were quite capable of synchronizing their own padi-production activities. They were also able to coordinate village labor in common irrigation and drainage tasks, etc., and, in fact, did precisely this during the precolonial period, with little or no assistance from members of the ruling class.

Although inequality certainly existed within the kin-ordered *ra'ayat* village community, this did not extend to the existence of classes within most *kampong*. Because members of the ruling class lived separate from *ra'ayat* communities, this major class schism was absent from the *kampong*. One possible line of inequality was that between the *penghulu* of the *mukim* (subdistrict) and other villagers, since the *penghulu* was appointed by the district chief and would have been his follower. There is indeed some evidence that the *penghulu* in some areas could command the labor of his co-villagers via corvèe, tax their produce, and fine them.[28] Nonetheless, his membership within the local kin-ordered village community, sharing kinship ties and common residence with other villagers, would have militated against the emergence of a full-blown class schism within the village. Another source of inequality, however, was the difference in time of original settlement. Members of female-centered domestic units whose ancestors had been the earliest settlers and had cleared or drained what had been forest or swamp land would have tended to be wealthier than other villagers. They usually had disproportionate power and authority within the village as *penghulu* or *ketua kampong* and their kinfolk. More recent arrivals were relatively less well-to-do and less influential. At the same time, however, the original settlers were not "landlords," for, in most areas, land was either not a commodity or—in the few areas where it was becoming a commodity, such as the Kedah Plain—the "landlords" were members of the ruling class who had overseen forest or swamp clearance and then sold or rented out land to *ra'ayat* clients. (Precolonial land tenure and its connection to surplus appropriation is discussed below.) Nor is there any evidence that individual *ra'ayat* villagers or their households, other than the *penghulu,* had control over the labor of other villagers, the produce they grew, or the imported goods they needed for livelihood, such as salt or, in times of deficiency, rice.

In short, there appears to have been little differentiation within the village community if by this is meant privileged access to or rights over labor or the means of production; in this sense, there were no class divisions within the village, except an incipient one between the household of the *penghulu* and those of other villagers in a *mukim.* Within the village community, there was little potential for capital accumulation; and it appears that redistributive mechanisms such as *kenduri* were fully operative in this period.[29] Rather, we can speak of a *relatively* egalitarian kin-based community, consisting of the members of one class. As Jomo has written,

> village ties, often overlapping with kinship relationships, were thus strengthened by communal organization and shared responsibility for various productive and other activities. Social differentiation . . . did not usually amount to class relations. Rather, village unity was perceived as the norm and supported by shared interests and a common lot.[30]

The conflict between the ruling class of each *negeri* and the kin-based *ra'ayat* village community—a leitmotif of precolonial Malay state formation—was both reinforced and constrained by the egalitarian character of this community. It is precisely this conflict, which focused in particular on surplus appropriation, that demonstrates the primacy of the kin-ordered village community over either families per se or individuals, for the most consequential forms of exploitation by the ruling class of the *ra'ayat,* such as corvée labor and import levies, were directed against or affected the village as a whole. It also appears probable that in most instances it was the kin-centered village community that was the locus of resistance to ruling-class exploitation. It is to these forms of exploitation and the resistance they engendered that the discussion now turns.

Modes of Exploitation

The division between ruling class and subordinate classes was reproduced over time by various forms of exploitation of the *ra'ayat,* of slaves, and of Chinese laborers, and by the use of the proceeds from this exploitation by the ruling class in each *negeri* to maintain its domination. The relationship between the ruling class and subordinate classes was a tributary one, in which the latter were required by coercion to provide social labor and a proportion of what they produced to members of the ruling class which the latter then employed to maintain themselves. Against certain colonial officials such as Maxwell, it must be argued moreover that, with a few exceptions, this tribute was not rendered to rulers or chiefs as a form of "feudal rent" for the land that the latter "owned." This becomes clear through the explication of precolonial land tenure given below.

The chief of a district, as a leading member of the ruling class, possessed rights to appropriate the produce of his *ra'ayat*, to require their corvée labor (*kerah*), to exercise *droits de seigneur* over *ra'ayat* women in his district, to levy taxes and tolls on the waterborne trade coming downriver from inland (e.g., on tin ore or ingots) or upriver from the coast, and to impose taxes on any tin mine production in his district. It must be noted however that, although "in theory" chiefs possessed a variety of rights over the Malay *ra'ayat*, in fact taxes and tolls often bore most heavily on Chinese miners and agriculturalists in the duties on opium and chandu, spirits, and gambling concessions. It was precisely this that comprised the *modus vivendi* between *ra'ayat* and ruling class in several precolonial Malay states.

According to Gullick, the major source of state revenues for the support of the ruling class were taxes from tin mining, assessed by chiefs either on tin carried by boats downstream or in situ at the mines. Between a fifth and a third of all output by value was diverted in this way.[31] After tin duties per se, taxes assessed on the opium and spirit trade and on the gambling concessions patronized by Chinese miners were large additional forms of revenue. In fact, it is not hyperbole to assert that in several *negeri*, state formation by the mid-nineteenth century onward was a process borne on the backs of Chinese coolies. The proceeds from their production and addictions subsidized the position of the ruling class and made possible its "sustained yield" relationship with the Malay *ra'ayat*.

Reliance on revenues from Chinese miners was confined to those states where tin-mining had become important economically by the mid-nineteenth century—Selangor, Perak, and, to a lesser extent, Negri Sembilan. In the west coast states of Johore and Kedah, the ruling class employed other mechanisms to generate the most important sources of revenues.

For Johore, the *kangchu* system has been closely studied.[32] Under this system, the Temenggong (later Sultan) of Johore farmed out the rights to establish gambier plantations on specific rivers in southern and western Johore and to gather taxes on opium, spirits, and gambling to wealthy Singapore secret-society leaders and merchants (*taukeh*) from the 1840s onward, in return for annual revenues. Through this period, the area that now conforms to the modern state of Johore consisted, at least in terms of population, almost exclusively of Chinese settlements. Trocki estimates that by 1874, Johore had almost 100,000 Chinese residents.[33]

In Johore, as in Perak, Selangor, and, to a lesser extent, Negri Sembilan, it was the Chinese coolie whose labor and addictions provided the wealth that filled state coffers. As Trocki has put it, "Singapore's economy was supported by the production and consumption of several hundred-thousand Chinese coolies who were locked in a perpetual cycle of indebtedness and opium addiction. Many of these resided in Singapore, but the vast majority lived and worked in Johor, Riau, Sumatra, and other nearby settlements."[34] Trocki describes what he calls the "gambier/opium economy" of Johore, which financed the government of the Temenggong by mid-century, as "a vast system of plantation agriculture held together by a combination of debt slavery, secret society terror, and opium addiction."[35]

For Kedah, according to Sharom, revenue farms on imports and exports had been established by the ruling class by the early 1800s, and were more or less all tendered out to a group of Chinese Hokkien merchants in Penang.[36] The revenue farms included those for opium, spirits, gambling, padi, and rice. As to the relative importance of the different farms, evidence for the period prior to 1874 is too sparse to draw firm conclusions, but for a later period for which data are available (1897-1901) Sharom found that the largest revenues derived in descending order from tax farms on opium and chandu, exported rice and padi, gambling, "customs" and spirits.[37] A plausible inference would be that prior to the opening of southern Kedah to extensive tin mining, tapioca, and rubber estate enterprises by Chinese in the 1870s, revenues from opium and chandu, gambling, and spirits would have been proportionately less, and those from exported padi and rice more, than for the later period. Kedah had been a source of rice exports to the island of Penang and to Province Wellesley from the late eighteenth century.[38] There is no doubt that these were taxed.

The situation in Kedah was representative of other *negeri* as well. The lack of agricultural self-sufficiency by Malay villages indicated the existence of regional trading systems, with each system based on coastal and riverine commerce and oriented to a major river and its tributaries. Control over such trading systems by district chiefs ensured their capacity to exact tax revenues from such traffic. Additional sources of revenues to chiefs thus derived from their taxation of goods imported upriver from the British Straits Settlements or from other states in the peninsula. According to Gullick,

> Malay chiefs also obtained revenue by taxing their Malay subjects. . . . Taxes were imposed on almost all varieties of trade goods. The Malay peasant

economy was by no means self-sufficient. Rice was imported in some
deficiency areas; salt, dried fish, opium, oil, coconuts, and textiles were all
staple trade commodities which could be taxed (usually at a 10 per cent *ad
valorum* rate paid in kind) as they passed the chief's riverside stockade.[39]

Unlike the revenues harvested from Chinese coolies, wealth extraction through
taxes on trade did have direct effects on the welfare of Malay *ra'ayat*.

All members of the *ra'ayat* of a district had to perform corvée labor, *kerah,*
for their chief or his entourage. Such forced labor might take a variety of forms.
According to Maxwell in 1884, "the cultivator may be required to give his labour
in making roads, bridges, drains, and other works of public utility, to tend
elephants, to pole boats, to carry letters and messages, to attend his Chief while
travelling, to cultivate his Chief's fields as well as his own, and to serve as a
soldier when required."[40] The precise nature of *kerah* obligations varied from
district to district, as each chief and his retainers had specific rights, often
sumptuary, vis-à-vis *ra'ayat* villagers. What is most important here, despite the
phrasing by Maxwell of *kerah* obligations as individual ones, is that—as he
himself makes clear—*kerah* was in fact organized on a *village-wide* basis by the
penghulu: "The *kerah*, or forced levy of men for labour, is effected through the
headmen of villages or districts."[41]

What I suggest is that the impositions of *kerah* on *ra'ayat* were mediated
by the *penghulu* of the village affected, who in turn was accountable to the kin-
ordered village community as a whole. Although his position was approved and
supported by the district chief, the *penghulu* would have had to derive his power
and influence within the village not so much from force or direct state power, as
from his nodal leadership position within this community. According to Gullick,
the *penghulu* was usually the member of a large kin group within the village,
related by kinship ties to many other villagers, relatively wealthy, and possessed
prestige due to his personal leadership qualities[42] —among others, presumably,
his ability to create village consensus around such potentially divisive issues as
kerah. The reaching of negotiated agreement within the kin-ordered community
over *kerah* (who could and ought to perform it) would have reinforced the
corporate identity of this community vis-à-vis the district chief and his retainers.

A similar argument might be made with respect to tithe exactions on
ra'ayat produce which apparently did occur in some areas. However, there is
little evidence to determine whether, when these were imposed, they involved
specific families, or were directed against the village community as a whole.

The data do suggest that, overall, tithes were relatively uncommon. The
question of the prevalence of tithes as a mode of surplus extraction has been a
disputed one. Although while Commissioner of Lands, Straits Settlements,
Maxwell argued that the *raja* had "the right of levying tenths and taxes" against
padi cultivators,[43] he was hard put to find specific instances of this "right" being

exercised. The one instance where he found a tithe on padi was in the Krian area, and this one instance has been characterized as extremely exceptional.[44] Further, Swettenham, British Resident of Perak in 1890, wrote of the precolonial period that "there was not . . . any system of payment by tenths." However, Swettenham went on to state that "the authorities, Sultan, State Officer, local headman, or anak Raja . . . dispossessed the occupants at pleasure, or helped themselves to any produce that they thought worth having whenever they felt able and inclined."[45]

These somewhat inconsistent data leave the impression that the tithe on produce was by no means systematically demanded, but that occasional impositions by individual chiefs or their retainers did occur. As I suggest below, there were constraints on such arbitrary exactions that arose from the resistance of the ra'ayat kin-ordered community.

Debt-bondage and slavery were also practiced and, as I indicated above, directly affected a small percentage of the ra'ayat and other subordinate groups (e.g., aborigines). Members of the ra'ayat became debt-bondsmen by borrowing money from chiefs or their retainers. Subsequently, when they were unable to repay the loan, they had to enter the service of the chief, formally only until the loan was repaid, but, in fact, far more often than not, for the duration of the life of the debt-bondsmen. The wife and children of a debt-bondsman also shared his status. Slaves and their families, who were non-Muslims, were the chattels of their chiefs.

Debt-bondsmen and slaves worked the padi fields of their chief, served as soldiers and petty retainers in his entourage, and performed domestic labor in his household. Some women in debt-bondage and slavery were forced to become the concubines of their chief or to enter into prostitution with the young men of his entourage. In this way and others, debt-bondsmen and -bondswomen were required to earn income for their creditors. Both debt-bondsmen and slaves could be transferred to the service of another master for a sum of money.[46]

Although, as I pointed out above, the proportion of the population in each negeri who were either debt-bondsmen or slaves was very small, nonetheless their example would have had the important demonstration effect of intimidating the ra'ayat on behalf of chiefs and other members of the ruling class. There are instances of chiefs forcing ra'ayat into debt-bondage. According to Sharom,

> in areas where debt-bondsmen were useful both economically and politically, chiefs tended to increase the number of such followers through a variety of means. Sometimes, a chief could invent a debt where one did not exist or he could impose a fine on an offense never committed. In this way the victim became a debt-bondsmen [sic], the pesaka or property of the chief.[47]

In this way, the oppressive lives of debt-bondsmen would have displayed to others the manifestation of the powers of the *raja* and district chiefs against troublesome *ra'ayat*. The effects of such terrorization resulted precisely because debt-bondage was an *individualized* status which left indebted individuals and their family members without the support of the kin-ordered village community against ruling class exactions. The mere possibility of this extremity might well have compelled peasants to comply with the demands of chiefs and their retinues when they would not have done so otherwise. At the same time, however, this possibility would have reinforced to the *ra'ayat* the advantages of collective, anonymous, covert, unorganized, "spontaneous" resistance to ruling-class demands—the avoidance protest of peasants in a contest state. Before turning to this subject, it is necessary to discuss briefly the issue of precolonial land tenure, given its later juridical importance to the British colonial state.

Land and an Indigenous Labor Theory of Value

Tributary relations between the Malay ruling class and the *ra'ayat* took the form of control, or attempted control, by the *raja,* chiefs, and their elite retainers over peasant labor and products and not primarily over land. Prior to 1874 with the extension of active British rule, land in most areas in Malaya was not a commodity, that is, a thing or object to be bought or sold as such, or to be "owned" in an absolute sense. For land to be treated as a commodity in this, the Western sense, there would have had to exist a set of jural state institutions buttressing the status of land as private property—mechanisms of land sale, registration, survey, eviction, etc.—which did not then exist. Nonetheless, there was a general trend toward the commoditization of land prior to 1874. These formal mechanisms began to appear in an inchoate form in the years after 1874 in, of course, the four states directly subject to British rule and also in other *negeri* (Kedah, Johore, Kelantan, and Trengganu) as a result of the cultural and economic influence of nearby British power within the region.[48] Nor was land, except in a few instances, a means of production controlled by the ruling class from which rent revenues from the *ra'ayat* could be drawn.

A major conclusion regarding precolonial land tenure is that the approaches toward land and views about it held by the ruling class, on one hand, and by the *ra'ayat*, on the other, must have been radically divergent. But since ruling-class domination was not predicated upon direct regulation of access by the *ra'ayat* to land, this divergence was of little practical consequence during the precolonial period. Later, during the colonial period, as the British came to control access to land, matters in this regard were fundamentally transformed.

Turning first to the *ra'ayat*, evidence suggests that peasants regarded land as a part of a permanent and inclusive commons of nature with which they established a relationship through their labor and production of use values, the necessities for survival. The prevailing abundance of land made such a stance possible. For instance, David Wong, one of the foremost scholars of Malayan land tenure, has observed of the precolonial period that "at the time when land was abundant, anyone could, as a simple matter of fact, clear forest land for cultivation and occupation. His more permanent continuous use of the land seemed just an essential facet of life in a sedentary peasant community."[49] And Wong writes that when it came to a cultivator wanting to clear forest land, the underlying philosophy was that the forest belonged to no man; abandoned land could be used by anyone since it had "gone back to God."[50]

What can be inferred is the existence of a peasant labor theory of value of land: that the value of a plot of land, or more properly of rights over it, lay in the amount of labor applied to transform it for human use. Kratoska, for instance, states that

> indigenous Malay law, then, provided that a person retained proprietary rights over land so long as the land continued to be affected by his labour, and when land no longer bore signs of the previous possessor's labour his claim to the land lapsed. The governing principle was that a person was entitled to the product of his labour.[51]

Thus, the value of a plot of land at any one time depended on the labor entailed in its specific prior use. According to this principle, land fell into one of three categories: wet-rice land or *sawah;* land cleared and cultivated by swidden methods or *ladang;* and land on which the cultivators resided and on which they had planted fruit trees, called *tanah kampong*. Wong illustrates the peasants' labor theory of value with reference to practices for taking up abandoned land:

> the basic principle was that if a person abandoned his land leaving it to become *tanah mati* ("dead land"), any other person could then take up such "dead land" by making use of it . . . Malay customs regarded *huma* or *ladang* land as "dead" upon its abandonment and hence open to any other person to appropriate it. [Footnote 13: "A *ladang*, abandoned after a few year's running, would be no longer, by the primitive method of agriculture, worth cultivating."] In the case of *sawah*, their customs permitted a three-year period of grace after the land had ceased to be cultivated before treating it as no longer *hidup* ("alive") in favor of the former cultivator. The length of the period seems attributable to the reason that after the lapse of such time, the uncultivated field would have become covered with brushwood and rank vegetation.[52]

Rights over *tanah kampong* lasted as long as the land was occupied and beyond that time as long as there was evidence of fruit trees.[53] Rights over land determined in this way were transmitted through time through descent ties between kin within the village community: thus, for example, the children gained rights over land first worked by their parents or mother's brother and later, as they became adults, by themselves.

According to Wong, where land had become scarce, dealings over land arose. In most instances, it would be more proper to say that it was not land itself that was exchanged, but rather *rights* over land derived from labor invested in it. Wong describes three kinds of transactions over land among *ra'ayat*:

(a) *pulang belanya*—"return of expenses": "the dealing was not quite a sale of the land but one of a take-over by way of recouping the original cultivator for his labour in clearing the land as well as for any crops he had cultivated or house erected thereon."

(b) *sewah*—"letting": "an arrangement whereby a cultivator allowed another person to cultivate his land for the return of a share in the produce crops or for a rent in kind or in money."

(c) *gadai*—"security transaction": one form in which a debtor becomes in effect a tenant to his creditor, and there is an apportioning of the produce he grows between the two. Another form, *jual janji*—"conditional sale": an arrangement in which a creditor takes over occupation of the land and all proceeds from the land go to him; the debtor can redeem the land by repaying his debt within a fixed period of time; if the debtor fails to repay, there is an "absolute sale," *jual putus*.[54]

Given the prevailing abundance of land, the first two kinds of transaction represented an arrangement by which each party could be compensated for his proportion of the total labor invested in successfully occupying, clearing, and planting crops on a plot of land. The third kind of transaction, *gadai*, appears to have represented an initial step toward the commoditization of land; Wong comments that "presumably 'security' dealings were relatively a late development in a peasant community."[55]

In contrast to the fairly straightforward, if scattered, empirical evidence available for the *ra'ayat*, the question of what rights the precolonial ruling class had over land and its resources has long entered the realm of general and etherealized issues about "feudal" rents, "eminent domain," "allodial" and "usufructuary" rights, and similar notions within British Victorian political discourse on an envisioned Asian feudal past. This is so because British officials of the early colonial period, the most frequent commentators on the subject, saw themselves as the inheritors of the precolonial ruling class, entitled to maintain its "feudal" rights over land, as they inferred these, in the name of preserving Malay "custom." The potential for their reaching self-serving conclusions on this subject should be quite obvious.

On one side, colonial officials (of whom Maxwell was the most articulate theorist) claimed that the Malay *raja* held "absolute property in the soil," while peasant *ra'ayat* possessed merely a "proprietary right" to land that they cultivated, which was nonetheless a "usufructuary right" subordinate to that of the *raja*. The "absolute" right of the *raja* or his deputies over land was on this view validated by the payment of the tithe on produce and corvée labor by the *ra'ayat*—in effect, kinds of "feudal rent" to the ruling class.

Against this view, more critical scholars have for the most part argued that no such concept of "absolute" or "total ownership of land" by the *raja* was widely recognized in the precolonial period. I am inclined to agree with this position, for the following reasons. First, there is little evidence, as I mentioned above, for the payment by the *ra'ayat* of the tithe as a kind of "feudal rent." Second, it is equally difficult to interpret corvée labor as a form of rent. Third, and most tellingly, the labor theory of value of land held by the peasantry was at complete odds with any purported overarching claim of "total ownership" by the ruling class. Supposing for the sake of argument that this claim existed, it appears to have made no practical difference in determining the appropriation of forest land or of previously cultivated holdings or in structuring of dealings over land. Nor in this period did state institutions for land registration, survey, or payment of rents exist. Even Maxwell himself was forced to concede that "the Raja's absolute property in the soil, is but a barren right. . . . Tenant right is the cardinal doctrine of the Malay cultivator, and, as long as that is fully recognized, it does not matter to him who or what functionary or power may, in theory, be clothed with the original and supreme right to the soil."[56]

In contrast to the *ra'ayat* labor theory of value of land, the rights to land on the part of the *raja*, chiefs, and their retainers in most instances appear to have been but an extension, validated by *force majeure,* of their powers of appropriation vis-à-vis their subject *ra'ayat* populations. As Wong put it,

> no one would seriously doubt that a ruler of such a kingdom was mindful, and aggressively so, of territorial possession. His territorial possession should, however, be understood in the context of political rule or power over the agricultural communities of people. There is no evidence to suggest that the imposition of monarchical rule on the Malay peasants . . . had resulted in the introduction of a tenurial system of relationship between the ruler and his subject.[57]

Although there is little documentary evidence, one can hazard the guess that there were two kinds of exceptions to this generalization for the period before 1874. First, in tin-mining areas, chiefs must have attempted to control day-to-day access to the specific lands on which tin ore was located, since the revenues from tin mining were crucial to maintaining the position of the ruling class in Selangor, Perak, and, to a lesser extent, Negri Sembilan; rights of Chinese mining *kongsis* to work these lands depended on rendering shares of income from the smelted tin or tin ore to district chiefs. Second, in the state of

Kedah during the late eighteenth and early nineteenth centuries, members of the ruling class supervised the construction of irrigation and drainage canals north of the Kedah river, leading to swamp clearance and settlement by Malay wet-rice agriculturalists. It is possible that the lands on each side of the canals constructed were then sold or rented out to *ra'ayat*; so at least was the practice when the Wan Mat Saman canal was later constructed, in the 1880s.[58]

The "Contest State" and Peasant Protest

Evidence from the precolonial period on the peninsula supports the notion that common and systematic peasant protest against and resistance to ruling-class exactions did not commence with the British colonial period, much less the period after Independence, but had existed prior to colonial rule.

Michael Adas[59] has argued that a common form of polity in the preindustrial era in Southeast Asia, Africa, and elsewhere in the non-Western world was what he has referred to as the "contest state"; his examples of this kind of political organization are precolonial Java and Burma. Moreover, he has also proposed that forms of peasant resistance that he calls "avoidance protest" are most commonly associated with such a state.

I suggest that precolonial *negeri* on the Malayan peninsula should be seen as variants of such a weak "contest state," and that, like precolonial Java and Burma, several forms of "avoidance protest" by the peasant *ra'ayat* against the ruling class existed and were more or less effective in constraining ruling-class exactions. Moreover, it was precisely the effectiveness of such peasant protest which led to a fairly unique solution to the problem of the weakness of the "contest state": the emergence by the early to mid nineteenth century of a *modus vivendi* between the Malay ruling class and *ra'ayat* by which major sources of state revenue were derived not from the *ra'ayat* but, directly or indirectly, from Chinese laborers by way of taxes on tin and tin ore mined by Chinese miners, and revenue from levies on opium, spirits, and gambling consumed or used by Chinese.

Adas characterizes the "contest state" as follows:

> central to this form of political organization is rule by a king or emperor who claims a monopoly of power and authority in a given society but whose effective control is in reality severely restricted by rival power centers among the elite, by weaknesses in administrative organization and institutional commitment on the part of state officials, by poor communications, and by a low population-to-land ratio that places a premium on manpower retention and regulation.[60]

As a consequence of these characteristics, conflicts appeared within the ruling class (the "elite") at several levels over control of revenues derived from control over peasants' labor and the goods they produced. Succession struggles and conflicts over territorial domains internally divided the ruling class; administrative performance by lower levels of the bureaucracy —especially the passing upward of revenues collected—was poorly monitored by the ruler; premodern means of communication set a ceiling on administrative capacity in general; ruling-class military organization and technology were relatively backward, leading to difficulties in the coercive control of subject populations; and peasant labor was scarce, relative to land available.

According to Adas, within the contest state, the means of protection of first resort by peasants against ruling-class exploitation were "village defense mechanisms" against excessive demands on peasant labor and production. These "defense mechanisms" took advantage of the characteristics of the contest state just mentioned, i.e. its administrative and military weaknesses, internal dissensions within the ruling class, low population-to-land ratio, etc. Thus, struggles between ruling-class factions and conflicts between the ruler and lower levels of bureaucracy over the proportion of revenues to be "skimmed off" before being passed upward led to grossly inaccurate record keeping on peasant production and its revenue potential.[61] Since revenue collection was commonly organized on a village basis, "collusion between village notables and the state's revenue collectors and the employment of a wide range of time-tested evasion techniques were the most effective ways in which cultivators were able to defend themselves against excessive elite demands on a sustained basis."[62]

Yet also present within the contest state, made possible by it, and often indistinguishable from village defense mechanisms were forms of "avoidance protest." This was defined by Adas as protest "by which dissatisfied groups seek to attenuate their hardship and express their discontent through flight, sectarian withdrawal, or other activities that minimize challenges to or clashes with those whom they view as their oppressors."[63] In precolonial Java and Burma, in addition to flight and withdrawal into religious cults or monastic movements, avoidance protest by peasants included the transfer of allegiance to new lords, petitions for redress to the ruler, banditry, arson, and sabotage.[64] All of these were alternatives to protest by peasants that directly confronted the military forces of the ruling class through rebellion or jacqueries. Adas observes that peasants engaged in confrontation protest only as a last resort, if ever, and that instead, the graduated repertoire of forms of avoidance protest preceded by village defense mechanisms were far more common. According to Adas, avoidance protest has largely been ignored by historians who have focused instead on the relatively rare instances of violent protest by peasants in the premodern era.

Avoidance protest was, by its nature, either collective but relatively unorganized with its practitioners largely anonymous or difficult to detect, or sufficiently ambiguous in its aims as not to challenge directly the authority of the ruling class.

Precolonial Malay *negeri* appear to share many of the characteristics that Adas has observed of the "contest state" in precolonial Java, Burma, and elsewhere. Succession struggles between various factions of royal families and ruling class lineages and struggles over territorial control between *raja* and chiefs and among chiefs were both rife to the point that they dominate the conventional narratives of histories of the eighteenth and nineteenth centuries for these states. (Kedah and Johore are partial exceptions to this generalization.) In most states, the bureaucracies were weakly developed—small in size, underfunded, and manned by the kinsmen and personal retainers of *raja* and chief, rather than by administrative specialists.[65] There were conflicts between *raja* and chiefs and between chiefs and their retainers over the amounts of revenues collected and retained.[66] Such conflicts were both by-product and cause of the generalized incapacity by *raja* and chiefs to exert their coercive and economic power over extended space. Premodern communication technology impeded the integration and efficiency of state bureaucracies, while premodern military organization and technology inhibited the efficient deployment of coercive power against the *ra'ayat* of each district and state. The comparative recency of settlement by Malay agriculturalists on the peninsula meant that population-to-land ratios were low, which in turn implied the need for the ruling class to adopt strategies of rule suited to the direct control of *ra'ayat* labor, rather than through its regulation of access by the peasantry to land or other means of production. In all these ways, precolonial Malay *negeri* were variants of the contest state.

Village defense mechanisms and forms of avoidance protest can be inferred and, in some cases, demonstrated to exist among the *ra'ayat* of precolonial *negeri* on the Malayan peninsula. The first line of defense against ruling-class oppression must have been the organization of the kin-ordered village community led by *penghulu* or *ketua kampong*. Here, because of the predictable absence of historical documentation, it can be only speculated that both the social organization of the kin-ordered *ra'ayat* village community (as described above) and the weakness of the precolonial contest state contributed to collusion between *penghulu* or *ketua kampong*, on one side, and the revenue collectors of chief or *raja*, on the other, to evade the payment of tax revenues, and that this would have benefitted all or most members of the kin-ordered village community.

About forms of peasant avoidance protest, we are on surer ground. There is some evidence of petitions by *ra'ayat* to *raja* protesting abuses of appointed officials, and to the effect that these were at least partially effective. Sharom writes:

At various intervals, the Kedah *ra'ayat* from different *mukims* sent petitions directly to the Sultan or Raja Muda. The most common of these were petitions against the irregular conduct of the *penghulu* in the administration of the *mukim*. And it is significant to note that such complaints were taken seriously and were attended to.[67]

In one case that Sharom cites, the offending *penghulu* was removed from office and banished from the district.

Peasant flight, the transfer of allegiance, and the threat of flight, as well as its effects in curbing abuses by chiefs and their retainers, appear to have been the most common form of protest mentioned in sources. Gullick writes that if a chief "oppressed them [the *ra'ayat*] unduly or failed to protect them from marauders, the people would flee away and settle elsewhere," presumably under another chief,[68] thus leading to loss of population in his district, fewer supporters, and lowered tax revenues. He continues, "in a Malay State a peasant had a moderate expectation of justice at the hands of his own chief because the chief could not afford to disintegrate the population of his district by a *general* course of oppression or injustice beyond what the conventions of the relationship between ruler and subject permitted."[69] Flight in a more limited manner also occurred; for instance, Maxwell wrote that in Kedah, "I have seen the Malay peasant running from his fields into the jungle at the sight of the Raja's elephants, lest he should be called upon to form one of the train."[70] The vision of an unpopular chief or Sultan's procession passing through deserted *kampong* bereft of willing and loyal *ra'ayat* must not, at times, have been uncommon.

Both *raja* and chiefs, for the most part, quite clearly recognized the potential for peasant flight as protest if a "sustained yield" strategy of moderate demands on *ra'ayat* labor and produce was not followed. Above all, these exactions were not to threaten peasant survival. It is noteworthy, for instance, that there are no recorded instances of the seizure of *ra'ayat* padi or rice stores by the ruling class, an action that would have certainly provoked extreme resistance. And corvée labor, *kerah*, was timed so that it did not interfere with the vital subsistence activities of rice cultivation. According to Raffles, writing in 1811 of Kedah, "certain months are allowed the many to plant and reap their paddy: and this when stored is sacred, and cannot be taken from their possession; with this exception all the rest of their time, exertions or acquirements may be taken by the King or his officers if so inclined."[71] Nonetheless, this does not mean that outmigration and flight to settle in another district or state, with a transfer of allegiance to another chief, usually under pioneering conditions, did not occur. The high frequency of flight during the mid-nineteenth century was, in fact, a testimony to the conditions of civil strife present from the mid 1800s onward in Selangor, Perak, and Negri Sembilan, where struggles over tin fields

between different Malay chiefs became associated with violent conflicts between
contending Chinese secret society factions during those years.[72]

For most years from the late eighteenth century to 1874, however,
conditions were far more stable in most states. What made such stability
possible, I propose, is that the ruling class in these states during this period came
to depend increasingly for its revenues on Chinese labor in one way or
another—from tin export duties in Selangor, Perak, and Negri Sembilan, and
from the opium, spirit, and gambling farms of Johore and Kedah and other states.
Malay *ra'ayat* avoidance protest was no doubt effective in making a "sustained
yield" relationship of political allegiance to the ruling class necessary for the
latter. What made this relationship possible, however, was the fact that the ruling
class in each of these states came increasingly to depend for its expanded social
reproduction on surplus appropriated from Chinese tin miners and
agriculturalists who were neither Moslems nor subjects of *raja* or chiefs. In light
of the claims of contemporary indigenist ideologies in Malaysia, this must be one
of the more ironic developments of early modern Malayan history.

The modes of peasant struggle against the state described here—the
deployment of village "defense mechanisms" against state officials and forms of
peasant avoidance protest such as petitioning the ruler for redress against official
abuse, flight, and the transfer of allegiance—continued, I suggest, up through the
British colonial period, albeit in a modified way. In the four chapters that follow,
specific manifestations of peasant resistance during the colonial period which
have left their residue in the written record will be discussed. It is, of course, far
more often than not impossible to document resistance in a systematic way,
given that British officials who kept the records generally had a vested interest in
denying its existence.

I conclude with a more daring proposition, namely that these forms of
peasant resistance have persisted up through the contemporary period of an
independent Malaysia. For instance, Adas describes one common means of
protest available to peasants in precolonial Java:

> disgruntled villagers—at times led by their headmen or, in other instances, in
> opposition to them—organized processions to the residence of the most
> powerful lord in the region, which in the vicinity of the capital meant the royal
> palace. The participants often concluded their march with a sit-in on the *alun-
> alun,* or great square, in view of the royal audience hall. They remained there
> until the ruler or one of his advisers heard their complaints and assured them
> that measures would be taken to reduce their burdens and punish the offending
> officials.[73]

This description can be compared fruitfully to that of two much more
recent incidents. In the first, Malay peasants, many of them starving, protested a
drastic fall in the price of rubber and the government's role in contributing to it.

There were "hunger marches by smallholders in the towns of Baling, Sik, Selama and Changloon in northern Kedah during the past month. Smallholders, finding it difficult to earn a living from their modest rubber plots, marched on a district officer's headquarters in Baling and were given a *gentang* (about 8 lbs.) of rice."[74]

The second incident was a protest by padi farmers of the Kedah Plain against a forced savings scheme involving coupons paid them by the government in return for buying their padi:

> a crowd of roughly ten thousand gathered in front of the state office building on January 23 to protest the *cupon* system and to demand a $M10 increase in the paddy price. When the chief minister finally appeared, he was shouted down, and the police and riot control troops . . . moved in to disperse and arrest demonstrators, some of whom fled in vain to the state mosque across the street.[75]

Observers of the contemporary Malaysian situation will recognize both of these incidents readily: the first was the Baling march and assembly of 1974; the second, the Alor Star demonstrations of 1980.

These incidents and what they imply for popular resistance are examined more closely in chapter 8.

CHAPTER THREE

The Emergence of Capitalism, 1874–1920

Part I: Colonial State Expansion and the Peasant Community

Introduction

In this chapter and the next, I discuss major developments in British Malaya during the years 1874 to 1920 as these bear on the dialectic of conflict and accommodation between the Malay *ra'ayat* and the new British colonial state. These years are chosen not as a matter of convenience, but because they logically represent an integral period of expansion for both European colonial capitalism and the colonial state—processes in which rural Malays were actively implicated, if not always in ways of their own choosing. By the end of this period, both processes had reached a plateau phase: by 1920, the fundamental institutions of British Malayan society were in place, initiating future paths of change which were to prove irreversible. In the colonial economy, production of tin, a wasting resource, had reached stable levels by 1905, and by 1920, growth in Malayan rubber production had saturated the international market.[1] By World War I, the revenues of the Federated Malay States had risen to an equilibrium level, around which they fluctuated in the years up to the Japanese occupation;[2] by 1919, all of the states of the peninsula were under some degree of formal subordination to the British rulers.[3] In this chapter I describe the major features of these processes as they bear on the Malay peasantry and the role of Malay peasant resistance within them.

This period was marked by five developments. First, the British expanded and consolidated their formal political rule over the peninsula. Second, (both a cause and effect of the first development) British officials established a rationalized bureaucratic state structure. Third, the colonial administration transformed land into a commodity and a form of private property. Fourth, with the determined encouragement of British officials, large-scale plantation and mining capitalist enterprise became the dominant forms of economic organization. Fifth, and a necessary condition for the fourth development, a large Chinese and Indian proletarian labor force under capitalist management appeared.

Based upon transformations in the colonial political economy, this period can be further divided into two subperiods: its first two-thirds (roughly between 1874 and 1905) and its last one-third (between 1905 and 1920). This chapter considers this first subperiod, although changes in the Malay kin-ordered village community are examined for the entire period. During this first subperiod the praxis of rural Malays throughout the western states was largely peripheral to major trends in the new colonial society. These trends centered on two processes—the growth of European and Chinese tin mining and plantation enterprise, particularly Chinese mining capitalism, and the emergence of a colonial state firmly under British control. The creation of a secure and stable state bureaucracy and its necessary financial precondition—the emergence and prosperity of European and Chinese tin mining capitalism—were central preoccupations of British officials in these years. The Malay *ra'ayat* played only a small role in these efforts, although indigenous Malay and Indonesian immigrant frontier settlers provided labor to clear and cultivate much forest land.

This is not to say that the economic, juro-political, and cultural transformations of these years had no effects upon the livelihoods or social organization of Malay peasants. During this first subperiod, for specific reasons discussed below, the Malay *ra'ayat* could be considered a relatively "underexploited" subordinate class vis-à-vis the state. It must be emphasized that these years were unique in that respect. Nonetheless, profound changes did occur in the social relations of production linking the Malay peasantry and exploiting classes, with critical consequences for rural Malays in later years. These changes were brought about by the persistent, albeit indirect, interference of the colonial administration in peasant production through its growing control over land, land alienation, tenure, and use, and through its implementation of new mechanisms for bureaucratic regulation of the day-to-day lives of the *ra'ayat* and extraction of revenues from them. Most crucially, these changes affected the kin-ordered *ra'ayat* village community by promoting class division within it, thus reducing its capacity to resist the expropriating programs and policies of the new British ruling class. They also represented the cynosure around which Malay avoidance protest against British rule centered in these years.

It is necessary to emphasize the gradual and uneven spread of British political power throughout the Malayan peninsula during this entire period. It would be a Eurocentric illusion and an affront to historical fact to suppose that triumphant British officials, soldiers, merchants, tin entrepreneurs, estate managers, and schoolmasters in the years immediately after the Pangkor Engagement in 1874 singlehandedly created the institutions of "civilization," colonial rule, and the *pax Britannica* throughout the peninsula. In fact, British imperialism in these early years of indirect rule was far from strong or secure in its grasp. The spread of British political and administrative influence was gradual, resisted both by members of the precolonial ruling class and also, although not often acknowledged, by the Malay *ra'ayat*. On the whole, the expansion of British power in the peninsula was not one of sudden and spectacular victories of imperial troops over recalcitrant natives in "punitive expeditions," although a few of these occurred to demonstrate conspicuously the might of British military power (e.g. in Perak against Malay chiefs involved in the assassination of Birch).[4] Instead, the British ascent to political dominance was a grinding day-to-day process of parasitism upon and then supplanting of non-European power structures combined with tactics tried successfully elsewhere in the empire. Officials employed a large repertoire of strategems against recalcitrant subject populations including, but not limited to, the Malay peasantry. British officials proceeded to attempt to regulate these varied populations more by wheedling, threats of force, drug peddling (i.e., of opium, liquor, and tobacco), flattery, financial cooptation, the imposition of new taxes, efforts to divide and rule, and coerced indebtedness, than by their actual exercise of overwhelming *force majeure*. Moreover, in the early years of this period, it was not British or other European large-scale enterprise that brought into existence the economic foundations of British rule, but rather the ventures of Chinese mercantile and mining capitalists and the labor of the immigrant Chinese proletariat.

At the beginning of this period, British military, economic, and ideological power was heavily concentrated in the Straits Settlements of Singapore, Penang, and Malacca. Beyond these urban coastal settlements, their power declined significantly. Beginning with the Pangkor Engagement in 1874 and British pressure immediately thereafter which forced the Malay ruling class of three western states—Selangor, Perak, and Sungei Ujong—to accept and act upon the "advice" of British "Residents," this power, exercised through the strategems mentioned above, gradually increased within these states over the first two decades of this period. This led in 1896 to their unification with Pahang and the remaining small states of Negri Sembilan under the centralized administration of the Federated Malay States.[5]

British imperial political power was least in the states under Siamese suzereignty—in Kedah, Perlis, Kelantan, and Trengganu —and in the state of Johore, where, in the years after 1874, Malay *raja* and their upper-class followers ruled formally independent of European influence. Because of the relative weakness of British power and influence in the three western states considered here (Kedah, Perlis, and Johore), many of the administrative innovations imposed by the British and the effects of these changes on both the structure of Malay village community and the capacity for Malay peasant resistance occurred later than elsewhere, beginning only with the years from about 1910 to 1930 when the British finally gained effective control over local administration. The process of uneven development means that the changes during this first subperiod in rural areas in what was to become the Federated Malay States, described in this chapter, occurred about thirty years later in these other states.

During this entire period, British colonial officials in Malaya were guided by two overriding, long-term goals. The first was to extend and consolidate British power and influence throughout the peninsula in the form of rule by Residents in the Federated Malay States and by Advisers by 1919 in all of the Unfederated Malay States. The second was to "open up" Malaya to both settlement and capitalist enterprise through the building of an infrastructure and provision of access to cheap land, labor, and capital. But this is not to say that there was some overarching, articulated master plan devised by British imperialists for the development of the Malayan peninsula in 1874. The weakness of British power made such a plan impossible. On the contrary, British Malayan officials during this period made necessary changes in specific policies directed to the means by which these goals were to be attained. Such changes were made possible by the high degree of administrative autonomy accorded colonial governors and their bureaucratic subordinates by the Colonial Office in London.[6] But they were made inevitable by the growth in British power vis-à-vis subject groups and classes on the peninsula.

From the Pangkor Engagement onward during this period, one can infer a process of the growth in colonial state power by which British officials at first grafted their functions parasitically onto the power structures of non-Europeans and then, over time, through the strategems already mentioned, came to supplant these structures with their own. This process of encroachment was evident repeatedly during this period, and is relevant to the problem posed below that one could call the "underexploited" character of the Malay peasantry.

Bearing Lightly the Burden of Subordination: An Underexploited Peasantry

One of the ironies borne out by the history of the Malay peasantry is that there are times when a class or group, although subordinate in major ways, may benefit temporarily from the incidental effects of exploitation of other subordinate classes and, for this reason, for a while at least, may bear lightly the burden of subordination. This was clearly true for the Malay peasantry during the first subperiod from approximately 1874 to 1905 and into the second. However, by the end of the period as a whole, the situation of rural Malays in this respect had begun to change radically for the worse.

In what sense were Malay peasants an "underexploited" class during these years? Sadka has written:

the material improvements which came to them as a result of British rule and alien immigration were genuine enough. In the first place they undoubtedly benefited from some of the more obvious consequences of an orderly administration. The wars which had depopulated whole districts came to an end. Slavery was abolished . . . it was a fertile source of injustice and cruelty, and its abolition was a blessing. Malays, like others, benefited from the improvement in communications; not perhaps from the railways . . . but certainly from the construction of roads and bridle tracks.[7]

Sadka states that, moreover, the benefits of "orderly administration" and improved communications cost Malays little, for "there was little pressure on them to provide labour for economic development," that is, for tin mining, plantation agriculture, and the construction of railways and roads.[8] Further, the "incidence of taxation fell lightly on the Malays," being limited to land rents and duties on forest produce among all sources of revenue for the colonial state.[9]

There is no reason to doubt the factual accuracy of Sadka's reconstruction here, but her interpretations of facts are open to question. Her assessment of the great benefits and small costs to rural Malays of the *pax Britannica* is reasonable only when measured contrastively against the brutal exploitation of the immigrant Chinese and Indian proletariats of this period by British and Chinese capitalists. When I state that the Malay peasantry in this period was "underexploited," this is not to say it was not exploited at all, but rather to call for the explanation of an apparent anomaly: why it was exploited less than other subordinate groups at this time, for there was exploitation indeed. After all, during this period, the British did gain control over access to peasant land and did impose bitterly contested land taxes and fees on peasants.[10] Moreover, to state as Sadka does, that "the incidence of taxation" fell lightly on Malays in terms of their contribution to total revenues is not the same as stating that taxes were light relative to the total cash budgets of most rural Malay households. As was true elsewhere in the British empire where the imposition of taxes on indigenous peoples decreased their self-sufficiency and increased their need for cash, Malays were forced to earn cash by casual wage labor and the sale of their produce in order to pay the land rents imposed by the colonial administration.[11] Nevertheless, Sadka is correct to state that rural Malays benefitted from relief from the depredations of civil war and the threat of debt-bondage, from the elimination of the occasional arbitrary exactions of the precolonial ruling class, and from access to the new railways, roads, and bridle paths that were constructed with the coming of colonial rule. Most important, rural Malays were not coerced into becoming wage laborers, nor were they prevented during the second subperiod from cultivating rubber.

Why then were the Malay *ra'ayat* so lightly exploited during most of this period? No recourse to the notions of "enlightened" colonialism offered by apologists for British imperialism need be made. Instead, the temporarily light mantle of oppression worn by peasants can be explained by two factors. One was the slow pace of the process by which British officials displaced non-European power structures and supplanted them with their own; this inhibited the growth of state power directed against the peasantry. The other was the fact that, throughout this period, the revenues of the expanding colonial state depended primarily on the exploitation of the Chinese mining and plantation proletariat through the state's monopoly of the sale of opium and other drugs this proletariat consumed and the exaction of duties on the tin it produced. The Malay peasantry, in short, was a class whose exploitation was neither necessary nor sufficient for the reproduction and expansion of the colonial state, and therefore a policy of benign neglect toward it was appropriate.

One example of the general process of encroachment on and supplantation of non-European power structures was, of course, in the area of administration. When British Residents first assumed their roles in each of the western states in the 1870s and 1880s, they supported more compliant members of the precolonial ruling class by permitting them to collect revenues from both precolonial and colonial sources such as taxes on import trade, tin duties, and land rents; to appoint *penghulu;* exercise *kerah* rights, etc. Over the next two decades in Selangor, Perak, and Negri Sembilan, and after 1909 in Kedah and 1910 in Johore, the British implemented and consolidated a new bureaucratic structure of control. This included Residents or Advisers at the highest level (governing in Council in the presence of the sultan or *raja*), District Officers in charge of districts at the next lower level, and *penghulus* (thereafter employees of the administration) at the lowest level, the *mukim*. Specialist departments (Surveys, Lands and Mines, Customs, Treasury, etc.) were also established. Even with the imposition of this new structure, it was only after several years of growing influence in the state administrations that Residents were able to displace completely or coopt the Malay elite and either eliminate their precolonial rights (such as *kerah*) or arrogate these to themselves and their subordinates, the (mostly British) District Officers. British officials were thus able only gradually to destroy the bases of power held by the Malay *raja,* chiefs, and *penghulu,* and to replace these with their own.

Two related developments in this process had direct effects on the day-to-day lives of the Malay *ra'ayat*. One was the centralization of revenue collection in the hands of British District Officers and the displacement of Malay intermediaries. This seems to have occurred in the western Federated Malay States only by the turn of the century; Sadka writes that

> from 1893 . . . rents were collected by district officers [in Perak], the functions of penghulus, as in Selangor, being to round up the rent-payers on collection day. In 1897 the Secretary to Government reported, "It is a rule in Perak (&

sh[oul]d be everywhere in Malaya) that no rents are collected by a Penghulu or Eurasian or native clerk."[12]

In Johore and Kedah, in contrast, similar changes occurred much later, due to the political independence of these states during most of the period. In Kedah, peasants were required for the first time in 1909 to pay land tax or land rent as a replacement for the older *kerah* obligation.[13] Land rents were to be paid not to the *penghulu* of a *mukim,* but rather to a newly created Land Office, presumably to the person of the District Officer or his subordinates.[14] Although most Kedah District Officers were Malay rather than British, collusion between *penghulu* and local village communities in the determination and setting of revenues vis-a-vis the state administration would no longer have been possible. In Johore, where most of the population was Chinese and state revenues derived from revenues collected from Chinese *kangchu,*[15] neither Malay *penghulu* nor British officials played a major role in revenue collection from peasants during most of this period. In 1910, Johore received a British Commissioner of Lands, Mines, and Surveys, and, under British pressure, new land enactments similar to those in force in the Federated Malay States and requiring land rents from cultivators were passed.[16] Presumably, after 1910 these land rents were collected by officers in district Land Offices as elsewhere on the peninsula, and the *penghulu* were bypassed.

The other development was the rationalization of the position of the *penghulu.* Kratoska has carefully reconstructed this change in the Federated Malay States.[17] It is evident that the objective of this drawn-out process, from the 1870s through the early 1900s, was gradually to transform the office of *penghulu* into one in which loyalty to the state administration's personnel and policies would override any preexisting allegiances of *penghulu* to local kin-ordered village communities and their welfare. British officials substituted regular salaries for *cabut* (percentages of duties collected from *mukim*) for *penghulus* and, as mentioned above, eventually eliminated them from revenue collection altogether. They set explicit criteria for their recruitment and promotion. They began to post *penghulu* out of their native districts and to transfer them to new postings frequently. Officials divided *mukim* into different classes based on their importance and set the rank of a *penghulu* depending on the class of the *mukim* he administered. They stipulated the duties of *penghulu* in empowering documents, the *surat kuasa.* All these measures provided sanctions and awards to constrain the performance of *penghulu* toward compliance with the policies and directives of the higher colonial bureaucracy, and to prevent them from allying with specific local kin-ordered *ra'ayat* village communities against the state. In Johore, the Malay *penghulu* appears to have been subordinated to the District Officer after effective British control was established in 1910. Over time his role diminished progressively to the point that, by the 1950s, he was "little more than a Land Office clerk."[18] In Kedah, in contrast, *penghulu*, although salaried after 1909, remained in their native *mukim* and, if Bailey's study of Sik district is representative, continued to play an important role as brokers between the villagers of their *mukim* and state authorities, a role enhanced by their position as relatively wealthy landlords.[19] The situation in Perlis seems to have been similar.[20]

The centralization of revenue collection and the rationalization of the office of the *penghulu* were processes whose gradual realization over more than two decades was indicative of the weakness of power of the colonial state vis-à-vis the Malay peasantry during most of this period. Even if British officials had directed their attention toward the peasantry instead of the immigrant proletariat, and sought to exploit rural Malays by forcing them into permanent wage labor, requiring that they cultivate certain crops, or demanding heavy taxes from them, *penghulu* and *ketua kampong* whose administrative reliability and loyalty to the state were assured and who could implement, monitor, and carry out such programs, simply did not exist "on the ground" in sufficient numbers to ensure their success. If there is any truth to the vaunted "pragmatism" of British colonial officials, it would surely have lain in recognizing just such weakness.

Thus it was for solid material reasons that "little pressure" was exerted by the administration on the Malay *ra'ayat* to participate in wage labor. The usual explanation given in the historical literature is that there were simply too few peasants to provide the massive inputs of labor required by the mining and plantation economy and the colonial state. Although this is obviously true, it should also be pointed out that the healthy aversion to wage labor and passive resistance (e.g., evasion) by peasants to British efforts to recruit them into the colonial labor force simply imposed on the colonial state prohibitively high costs for securing the compliance of the relatively small number who were present, given the weakness of its power at this time.[21] As Sadka herself points out:

> Malays would not offer themselves as a permanent labour force. . . . Since the standard of living offered to their labour by planters and miners was inferior in every social value to that already enjoyed by Malays, and so low in material values that Malay standards could hardly have been worse, it followed that Malays could not be recruited for continuous field or mine labour except by force, and such an idea was never entertained.[22]

It should be clear from the foregoing why this idea was not "entertained," leaving aside the question of the fits of benevolence to which British officials were putatively prone.

The second factor explaining the relatively light burden of exploitation borne by the Malay peasantry during this period lies in the fact that the major form of exploitation in the colonial economy was directed against another subordinate class—the Chinese immigrant proletariat. This is reflected in the revenue basis of the colonial state, since it was the state, as well as Chinese mining and plantation capitalists, that benefitted the most from expropriating surplus from them. Throughout this period, the largest sources of revenue for the operation of the administrations of the Straits Settlements and of the western states of Kedah, Perak, Selangor, Negri Sembilan, and Johore were derived from taxes and profits from the consumption and production of the Chinese mining and plantation proletariat. The state possessed a monopoly on goods and services consumed by it, that is, opium, liquor, tobacco, and gambling, and imposed duties levied on its production of tin. During this entire period, in the Straits Settlements, income obtained from the sale and processing of opium was the single largest source of revenue.[23] In the states of the Federated Malay States, although annual statistics on opium revenue are not available in the first part of this period, what information is available suggests that income from opium, liquor, and tobacco, combined with the duties on tin, made up the majority of revenues of these states during the entire period.[24] In 1913, opium revenue alone provided 23.4 percent of total revenues for the Federated Malay States, and even in 1922, it was 19 percent.[25] In both Johore and Kedah, dependence of state revenues on the consumption of the Chinese proletariat of opium and other addictives continued from the precolonial period. In 1913, opium sales provided 43 percent of the total revenue of Johore, while in 1918 and 1919 these sales provided 45 percent of the total revenue of Kedah.[26] What British officials were most committed to was the solvency of the colonial state; on this their careers quite unambiguously depended; and from the addictions and physical effort of Chinese mining and plantation workers they extracted what was essential to the successful expansion of their administration: the wealth required to sustain the growing state.

In short, if colonial officials laid what appeared to be a light hand on the Malay peasantry during most of this period, this is because their attention, their interests, and their commitments lay elsewhere; they were directed toward the continuation of surplus extraction from another surbordinate class whose members suffered in the most abject misery, in large part as a result.

Appropriation of the Land, New Settlement, and Pioneer Capitalism: 1874–1905

In the first subperiod, the British administration effectively subordinated members of the precolonial Malay ruling class through military force, persuasion, civil pensions, and the creation of the Malay College at Kuala Kangsar.[27] At the same time, it set into motion extensive schemes of road and railway construction, jungle clearance, disease eradication, and the building of public works.[28]

During these three decades, as British influence and power increased throughout the western states, officials interpreted the primary objectives of the administration to be the "opening up" of the land of the western states to settlement and commercial use, and the encouragement of the Chinese tin mining industry.[29] After 1905 or so, this latter policy was to change, as the interests of British and other European mining and plantation capitalists became more important in official concerns while Chinese influence declined sharply—a change with implications for the Malay peasantry.

Crucial to "opening up" the land were changes initiated by the administration redefining the jural relationship between land and human beings that had been in effect from the precolonial period, as described in the previous chapter. Soon after treaties were concluded with Malay *raja* in each state, British officials declared through their Malay proxies that all lands were vested in an absolute sense in the Ruler. But such rights of ownership were nominal, and, in practice, were held by the British Resident or Adviser of each state. Subsequent to this legal *coup-de-main,* the lands which Malays and others had, in fact, been occupying and cultivating up to that time were then leased back to them, in the form of "titles" provided them. Lands not actually occupied or cultivated at the time of treaty were to become "State land."[30]

In the decade between 1879 and 1889, General Land Regulations based on a standardized leasehold definition of ownership were adopted in Selangor, Perak, and Negri Sembilan. Rural Malays occupying land were to be given a registered title to such land in the form of a lease from the government for 999 years or in perpetuity; in return for this, they had to pay an annual quit rent. All land not under actual occupancy at the time was deemed to be "waste land," which was to be owned by the government. In 1897 these regulations were superceded by the uniform Land Enactments for the Federated Malay States which required Malays holding "country land of 100 acres in area or under" to register their plots in a Mukim Register; these Enactments remained in force until 1926.[31] Land Enactments in Kedah and Johore, modelled closely on these, went into force in 1910 and the years immediately thereafter.[32]

With this single innovation, reinforced by the Torrens land registration system brought in from Australia, the colonial administration provided itself with a unique base for future influence over the direction of the colony's economy, a source of revenue in land rents and premia, and power over the Malay *ra'ayat* by controlling their access to their means of production—land. Above all, for British officials, this turning of the greater part of the peninsula into "State land" offered an unparalleled opportunity to make land available in the future, at the most nominal rents, to settlers and to British and Chinese capitalists for their use.[33] This outright appropriation of Malay and aborigine lands and the subsequent history of land alienation to colonial capitalists were crucial aspects in the process of primitive accumulation.

Two aspects of this process of appropriation are particularly worth mentioning. First, in addition to gaining control over land in order to allow for its "opening up," a major objective of the land regulations was to secure revenue for the government. In the early years of this period, revenues from tin and opium still remained modest, and officials were desperate for new revenues.[34] Despite peasant opposition (discussed below), the administration was determined and successful in implementing the new land rents. For instance, as the new rent scheme was put into effect in Selangor, land revenue collected in 1883 was twelve times that of 1882.[35] Second, British officials justified what was a major transformation in land tenure from the precolonial period in terms of *continuity* with "the native system of land tenure" from the earlier period. Here W.E. Maxwell, whose views I examined in the previous chapter, was the pivotal figure, an official whose interpretations and innovations in land law were influential throughout the early British administrations of the western states. Although it was demonstrated in the previous chapter that his argument that the Malay *raja* held "absolute property in the soil" could not be sustained, it was his view—grounded in a conception of Oriental despotism as a kind of Asiatic feudalism—that prevailed[36] and provided the rationale for a new tax on the *ra'ayat*. Forcing rural Malays to pay rent on what they had long valued as their own through the labor invested in it was no less than a new form of surplus expropriation.

In addition to the new land laws, another significant development of this subperiod was the in-migration of Malays from elsewhere on the peninsula to the western states, and the large-scale immigration of settlers from the Indonesian archipelago into the coastal and upland areas of the western states. Many areas of the peninsula previously under forest or swamp and occupied, if at all, only by aborigines were settled by indigenous Malays and by Javanese, Banjarese, Sumatrans, and other immigrants from the archipelago during these years. As a result, there were significant increases in the populations of these areas. For instance, between 1879 and 1884, the number of Malays in Perak increased by 164 percent; in Selangor between 1884 and 1891, they increased by 48 percent.[37] A new and more complex pattern of social differentiation among the "princes of the soil" began to emerge on the landscape.

Indigenous Malays migrated from Kedah and Perlis to the Krian, Kurau, and Selama areas of Perak; Patani Malays moved south to the upland districts of Ulu Krian and Ulu Perak in Perak; Kelantan Malays settled in Kuala Selangor in coastal Selangor and in almost every district in Perak.[38] A large increase in the non-Chinese population in western coastal Johore dated from the 1870s, when Malay and then Javanese pioneers in the alluvial lowlands cleared forest and planted coconuts, betelnuts, bananas, manioc, and fruit for their own use and for sale to Singapore.[39] Many of these Javanese settlers turned to rubber growing in the early 1900s. In these years, Javanese were brought in as contract laborers on rubber estates in southern Johore; after completing their contracts many opened land to work their own smallholdings.[40] Javanese immigrants settled in coastal areas in Klang, Kuala Langat, and Kuala Selangor; they also settled inland in the Ulu Langat valley in Selangor.[41] Banjarese from southern Kalimantan migrated to the Krian district beginning in the 1870s, drained swampland, and began intensive wet-rice cultivation there.[42] Banjarese also settled in Kuala Selangor on the coast.[43] In the 1880s and 1890s, both Javanese and Banjarese cleared the alluvial swamps of Lower Perak and the Dindings and planted coconuts and rice.[44] Sumatrans pioneered settlement in inland areas of Selangor (e.g. Ulu Langat), Perak, and northern Johore as tin miners, petty traders, and wet-rice agriculturalists.[45] The migratory flows initiated in these years between specific areas of the Indonesian archipelago and regions and districts in the peninsula continued over the next fifty years, reaching a peak during the two decades from 1911 to 1930.[46]

The process of settlement by migrants into a previously unpopulated area involved negotiations between District Officers and *penghulu*, on one side, and the leaders of migrant groups consisting of several families or related male settlers, on the other. The administration encouraged settlement by offering rent remissions, small loans, and preferential hiring of new immigrants for casual wage labor.

What information there is about the social organization of the new settler communities of immigrants from the archipelago suggests that they were fundamentally similar to the *ra'ayat* kin-ordered village community of the precolonial period, with one difference that, over time, became a source of instability and inequality—the emergence of land as a commodity and a form of private property. The settler communities appear to have had a relatively egalitarian village social order, at least initially.

In a case study of Javanese and Sumatran immigration into the Ulu Langat valley from 1904 to 1914, Tunku Shamsul found that "cooperation on the *gotong-royong* system was beneficial to all concerned and this was the common method of pioneering adopted by many of the communities in Ulu Langat." Land was at first allocated to a group's leader by the *penghulu* of the *mukim* into which it was migrating. But, after the communal work of clearance, it was subdivided into lots, and individual titles were given out, as provided for by colonial land regulations.[47] Most immigrants from Indonesia were men immigrating on their own or with male relatives and friends. After the first few years of arduous pioneering, they would go back to their natal areas for their families and then return with them to Malaya. Since the residents of a new settlement tended to be from the same village of origin, it can be assumed that within a few years the social organization of the new settlement would be one of overlapping ties of kinship and neighborhood linking households to one another.[48] The leader of the group would become the new *ketua kampong*, mediate between the new settlement and the local representative of the state, the *penghulu* or District Officer, and arrive at decisions affecting the new community through informal consultation with his fellow settlers.[49] In all these ways, immigrant settlements appear to have been very similar to the kin-ordered village communities of peninsular Malays in the early years of this period.

At the same time, however, it appears from Tunku Shamsul's account that the members of different regional groups were segregated from one another in separate villages, thus reinforcing preexisting regional differences.[50] If the findings from this case study can be generalized, then a new source of division within "Malay society" can be said to have emerged at this time—regional differences reinforced by residential segregation in distinct village communities. Nonetheless, the colonial administration treated both indigenous Malays and the new immigrants as jurally identical, and both shared Islam as a unifying perspective, the same language to some degree, and other common cultural features. As a result of these external and internal constraints and a nascent nationalist movement, there was extensive intermarriage among these groups, and a new and more inclusive "Malay" ethnic identity was to be born out of this assimilation to one another over the next two generations.[51]

Malays from elsewhere in the peninsula and immigrants from Indonesia were not the only new occupants of the land during this subperiod, however. Early British and other European efforts at plantation production in these years were only marginally successful. Between 1875 and 1900 British planters, encouraged by the success of Chinese entrepreneurs with commercial cultivation of gambier, tapioca, and pepper, were quick to invest in land. Coffee and sugar were planted according to the intensive methods used in Ceylon, Mauritius, British Guiana, and elsewhere in the empire. It is not surprising that, given the speculative approach of British planters combined with their ignorance of local climatic and soil conditions, most early ventures failed utterly after a few years. Yields were low, plant disease epidemics set in, and British planters had to compete for international markets with better adapted enterprises elsewhere.[52] Most important, European planters experienced difficulties finding and retaining a permanently exploitable labor force.[53] Chinese laborers were well organized through *kongsis* and remnants of the secret societies, and were thus costly; Javanese had a propensity to leave plantations and settle as independent smallholders as soon as they were economically able to do so;[54] and Tamil laborers from southern India were as yet unavailable in any great number. Officials of the colonial administration were deeply disturbed by these failures, for they realized that if they were to be able to attract European capital investment to the colony's agriculture—and thus ensure their own career advancement—one precondition would have to exist. There would have to be policies that would guarantee to British and other investors at nominal cost and reliably other factors of production, that is, labor and land.[55]

The Ra'ayat Kin-ordered Village Community: Colonial Rule and New Class Divisions

During this entire period, changes in the social organization of Malay *ra'ayat* village communities must be perceived "through a glass darkly," for these communities were of little interest to colonial officials except insofar as they were the objects of administration. Officials, when they interacted intensively with Malays at all, did so only "socially" with their new clients, the Malay elite—the *raja,* chiefs, and others who had been members of the precolonial ruling class. Thus the view of village communities given was provided from surveillance on high, and the relatively few sources of colonial documents available must be interpreted critically for this reason.

From the data available, it can be suggested that the *ra'ayat* kin-ordered village community began to undergo a fundamental transformation during this period. It changed from an organization without major internal class divisions to one organized in ways such that these began to emerge, particularly with respect to land ownership.

As described in the previous chapter, the *ra'ayat* kin-ordered village community of the precolonial period displayed four defining characteristics. First, it was constituted by female-centered households connected to one another by overlapping ties of agnation, cognation, affinity and neighborhood. Second, there was a large degree of communal control over the labor of residents within the village, organized by *penghulu* and *ketua kampung*. Third, and related, the village had a quasi-corporate status vis-à-vis the ruling class of the *negeri,* in that *kerah* and other exactions imposed on the *ra'ayat* applied not to individuals but to the village as a whole; similarly, the response to these impositions was that of a single village unit. Fourth, the village community was the site for the practical enactment of a peasant labor theory of value in regard to land: the rights over land of persons and the groups to which they belonged were defined in terms of the labor they expended to make the land productive. With a few exceptions land not so transformed was viewed as part of an encompassing commons.[56]

I have already suggested ways in which the new settlements of Indonesian immigrants were similar to the kin-ordered village community of peninsular Malays in precolonial years: labor for forest clearance and cultivation was organized communally, groups of kin-related households tended to settle in the same village; and new immigrant communities were founded by leaders who made decisions through consultation and consensus.[57] It is also notable that many immigrants shared with peninsular Malays a labor theory of the value of land, for Tunku Shamsul quotes a District Officer as stating that many immigrants believed that the "'person who cleared and cultivated an unoccupied piece of land had the sole right of ownership to it.'"[58] Although evidence is scanty, what there is suggests that the new immigrant settlements were fundamentally similar to the kin-ordered village communities of peninsular Malays. Therefore, in what follows, I treat both as variations on a theme.

By the end of this period, these four defining characteristics of the Malay communally-based, kin-ordered village community had begun to be transformed by the impact of colonial rule, and this village community as such began to go out of existence. Over time, in its place, there appeared a village social organization based on nuclear families holding land as private property. Within this organization, inequalities in land ownership divided relatively wealthy from poor villagers, and the emergence of land tenancy combined with petty landlordism, but was crosscut by residual ties of kinship, affinity, and neighborhood. Nonetheless, changes leading to the eventual disappearance of the communally-based village community were gradual, and what should be emphasized is the continued persistence of these characteristics of the village community from precolonial times through much of this period. One crucial implication was that, based on the organization of this village community, Malay peasants continued to employ forms of avoidance protest against the state. However, certain forms of avoidance protest became increasingly ineffective as the village community was transformed.

How did ra'ayat kin-ordered village communities come to be so radically changed by events during this period that it makes sense to speak of the beginning of their disappearance? To explain this, it is necessary to refer to the internal dynamics of such communities as they interacted with the new constraints posed by the colonial state, rather than to invoke the exogenous forces of capitalism, as world systems theory would have it. That is to say, the explanation must be a dialectical one. The new constraints on the village community set by the colonial state and the colonial economy included a new human relationship to land, changes in the position of penghulu, and the effects of the adoption of rubber as a commercial crop.

As described in this chapter, the colonial administration transformed land into a form of private property over which the "owner" possessed absolute rights, except those reserved to the state ("the Ruler," but in reality the British Resident or Adviser) by the long-term leasehold system. This made land a commodity, that is, an object that could be bought and sold on a market; both "alienation" and "sale" of land to British and Chinese mining and plantation capitalist enterprise then became possible. In the years after 1874 in the Federated Malay

States and after 1910 in Kedah, Perlis, and Johore, several institutions that buttressed this new definition of land were put into place. They included land survey, registration by title in accordance with the Torrens system, the collection of rents, and the use of "caveats" (i.e., land as collateral), to name the most important.

In his essay "The Negri Sembilan Economy of the 1890s,"[59] Gullick has given perhaps the most detailed reconstruction of what occurred, in effect, within the communally-based kin-ordered village community when the colonial state imposed on rural Malaya its new definition of land and the institutions supporting it.[60] Although the area to which his essay refers is one in which matrilineal descent groups were present at this time, the underlying processes that he points to implicitly were far more widespread, and encompassed areas without such corporate groups. He notes that "the big change was to come with the planting of rubber as a smallholder's crop in the twentieth century. Land owned by men was a disrupting element because it became a bone of contention between two groups [a man's matrilineal relatives, and his wife and children] upon the death of the owner."[61] Note that certain of a man's cognatic kin—his mother, father, mother's brother, his sisters and their children, his brothers, his mother's sisters and their children—would have had joint rights with him over land cleared and cultivated, because they would have acquired such rights through cooperative labor with him on this land as part of the production process within the female-centered household characteristic of the precolonial period and the early years of this period. This would have been true *irrespective* of the existence of a local core of a matrilineal descent group. Of course this would not have precluded his wife and children from having similar rights as household members. Therefore, Gullick's example is of far wider application than merely Negri Sembilan.

From the 1880s onward, as the British sought to institute land rents on Malay land as a revenue-raising strategy, it became essential for its success that individuals be held legally accountable for rents on the lands they cultivated. Moreover, from the 1890s onward in Negri Sembilan, rents were calculated not on a per acre basis as previously, but on the production derived from the land—5 percent of the annual padi crop. Gullick states correctly that "the general effect of the land tax was to hasten the change to individual instead of group tenure."[62] During the late 1890s and early 1900s, the owners of Malay land holdings were registered in Mukim Registers and, as land was registered, it was surveyed as well.

These developments taken together acted as a constraint to reduce the pre-existing set of complex, overlapping, and conditional rights over land held by the various members of peasant households based on labor they invested, to an im-poverished notion of individual tenure in land as private property. Or rather, to speak strictly, the reduction was accepted by some persons and not others, for here it is likely that new divergent *individual* material interests in land appeared. Certainly, it was in the interest of British officials to effect this reduction, for their district's revenues and thus, indirectly, their careers depended on the newly-created fiction.

It was also, however, for the first time in the interest of certain Malay peasants to accept and promote, at least in certain contexts, this new individualized land tenure. This was particularly true as land came to have increasing commercial value as a commodity in the rapidly expanding colonial land market as the land hunger of British and Chinese plantation capitalists grew in these years. Thus it was that disputes between rural Malays themselves —disputes now adjudicated by British officials and their *penghulu* subordinates—provided the opening wedge for the initiation of actual, rather than merely nominal, individualization and privatization of land tenure. As Gullick perceptively points out,

> it is not suggested that the entry of a name and a lot number in a book in a government office caused an immediate change from family to individual tenure. The old tenure was understood and accepted by those concerned and no doubt they continued to behave in relation to themselves and the land as before. But in those family disputes which must arise under any system of tenure, and especially in a period of rapid economic change, the one or other contestant will naturally invoke the Land Office record if it supports his cause. In this way new legal conceptions enter into a customary tenure.[63]

Gullick's insight that individual strategizing by Malays due to such legal changes led to disputes within the village community was attested to by no less an authority than Maxwell. He writes:

> the rise in the value of land occasioned by the establishment of British rule resulted in a general rush for possession, men who had long since sold their fields by *pulang belanja* ["return of expenses"] coming forward to declare that the sale was merely conditional, while in other instances conditional vendees in possession were equally ready to declare that the transaction which gave them their right was *jual putus,* an absolute sale, not *jual janji,* a conditional one.[64]

In the case of Negri Sembilan where matriclans were land-holding corporate groups (but of course with only residual rights, not those of "absolute" proprietorship), Gullick observes that similar conflict took the form of disputes between clan chiefs and ordinary clan members, as chiefs "sold" land to non-Malays:

> in Jelebu before the era of British protection clan chiefs had begun selling vacant land in lots of 3-4 acres for a premium of $8-10 but there were disputes over the sharing of the proceeds between chiefs and clan members. As

European ideas of ownership spread disputes over revenue became disputes over ownership.[65]

Thus in the context of this dispute and others like it, divergent interests over land emerged for the first time within most *ra'ayat* kin-ordered village communities, leaving aside those exceptional areas where land had already emerged as a commodity in the precolonial period, such as in the Kedah Plain. But, unlike the precolonial period, increasingly strong and growing state power in the form of the District Officer and bureaucratized *penghulu* were thrown into the balance on the side of those Malays who favored the individualization and privatization of rights over land.

Two new additional factors would have reinforced the role of the new Land Enactments and their associated institutions in effecting this change. One was the increasing distance between the *penghulu* and the village community he had previously represented to the precolonial state, at least in the Federated Malay States. In the course of the process of breaking through the barrier to penetration created by the solidarity of the village community, British officials such as District Officers clearly expected *penghulu* to seek to achieve the policy goals of revenue-generation and the regulation of subject populations through enforcing the new land enactments and their associated institutions (registration, survey, etc.). It was precisely the fact that this expectation was unrealistic that led to the replacement of the *penghulu* by the District Officer as the collector of land revenue, as described above. Nonetheless, the precolonial role of *penghulu* as front-line defender of village interests through collusion with touring higher officials, underreporting of village incomes and land holdings, and so on, was effectively compromised during these years by the British program of rationalizing the *penghulu*'s position.

In addition to the privatization of land and the changing status of the *penghulu,* a third factor contributing to the internal reorganization of the village community was the adoption in the early 1900s of rubber as a commercial crop and the technical constraints on labor cooperation created by its cultivation. Bailey has discussed these most perceptively. He observes that,

> in comparison with the more traditional economic activity of rice farming, rubber required less social cooperation. In rubber production . . . the jungle is felled, the trees planted, and the undergrowth periodically cleared while waiting for the trees to become productive. Each of these tasks can be done by an individual working alone, although in some cases small cooperative groups of six or eight men work on each other's land in turn. Once tapping is underway, however, the need for this cooperation is removed and rubber extraction becomes essentially a one- or two-person operation. Social interdependence lessens and traditional patterns of organization give way to increased dependence on the nuclear family as the primary production unit.[66]

It should be added that Bailey's point is somewhat misplaced in that technical conditions of rubber cultivation did not alone bring about such fundamental change; if it had not been for other, political, developments such as the commoditization of land, it is doubtful that it would have occurred, as witnessed by the fact that such change had also taken place in areas where rice, and not rubber, was the principal crop.

Bailey adduces another consequence of rubber cultivation which is also germane. When peasants came to rely on cash incomes from rubber tapping to purchase food rather than producing it directly, there were now uses for money other than for meeting obligations of generosity toward kinsfolk and neighbors. They now purchased not only food for their own households but also imported consumption goods or other commodities such as bicycles or store-bought cloth from local Chinese shopkeepers. Thus, in the case of Sik, Bailey reconstructs a decreasing tendency to meet the norms of generalized reciprocity toward kin and covillagers after the adoption of rubber-growing in 1910.[67] The effect of this change was that it "tended to strengthen the nuclear family at the expense of broader kin ties for the majority of Sik's residents. Material support could [only] be counted upon within the nuclear family and from such close kinsmen as one's parents, grandparents, and siblings."[68]

Thus, by the end of this period, the privatization of land, the attenuation of generalized reciprocity among covillagers, the emergence of the nuclear family as the constituent unit of village social organization, the penetration of the quasi-corporate solidarity of the village community by administration officials who created new dyadic relationships between the Malay "yeoman" and the state,[69] the abolition of *kerah* and other exactions on the village as a whole, the bureau-cratization of the position of *penghulu,* were processes that were well underway. The exceptions were the three Unfederated Malay States—Johore, Kedah and Perlis—where these changes probably occurred only in the 1920s and 1930s.

These conditions were ideal for the incipient emergence of intravillage class divisions based on differential ownership and control of land, and in some locales at least this seems already to have occurred by the end of this period. Hill writes,

paralleling these changes in social organization was a change in attitudes towards land. Where once land was "owned by Allah," and controlled by the local raja as "God's trustee," under the colonial regime land became real property and by 1910 a market in rice land had developed in most parts of the Peninsula. Rice land, even with tenants on it, was bought and sold and the tenant became a source of income, not only for the traditional aristocracy many of whose bondsmen became tenants, but also for the rich peasants.[70]

These changes within the kin-ordered village community were to have crucial consequences for Malay participation in the colonial land market and rural indebtedness in the later years of this period and the one that followed.

CHAPTER FOUR

The Emergence of Capitalism 1874–1920

Part II: Peasant Resistance, State Power, and
Rubber Cultivation

Introduction

In this chapter I continue to reconstruct developments in the political economy of
British Malaya from 1874 to 1920. I first discuss the forms of Malay peasant
resistance to the impositions of the colonial state and dominant classes. I then
turn to the second subperiod from 1905 to 1920 to consider the ways in which
one form of Malay resistance—squatting and unapproved (and often illegal)
cultivation of rubber—came to place rural Malay smallholders in a threatening
competitive position vis-à-vis European plantation capitalism by the end of this
period.

During this second subperiod, British and Chinese plantation capitalists,
with the crucial assistance of the administration,[1] adopted rubber as the major
cash crop of the colony, and it progressively came to provide one financial
underpinning of state power. The organizational weakness of the state at this
time and the diversion of concern by its officials toward both internal
administrative growth and the fostering of tin mining enterprise enabled rural
Malays to take advantage of the opportunity to cultivate rubber and thus
participate successfully in the colonial economy. They were successful despite
growing opposition to their participation during the last years of this period by
the colonial authorities and British plantation capitalists. After 1920, in contrast,
with the growth of state power, this increasingly powerful opposition became a
crucial factor in consigning rural Malays to long-term conditions of stagnation
and impoverishment. Nonetheless, what confutes the mechanistic predictions of
world systems theorists in this regard is that Malay peasants did far more than
remain passive or merely *react* to developments over this period: they
themselves took advantage of these changes, and it was their praxis that initiated
a further dynamism in the colonial economy. Rural Malays were so successful in
growing rubber, in fact, that by 1920 they were to pose a serious competitive
threat to the plantation interests of British colonial capitalism.

Forms of Resistance: Avoidance Protest Under Colonial Rule

During this period, as the social organization of the Malay village community changed in the ways described in the previous chapter, the *ra'ayat* persevered from the precolonial period in engaging in a variety of forms of avoidance protest against state exactions, to the point that some forms of protest verged on confrontation with the British colonial administration. Peasant avoidance protest centered on the British juro-political innovations in land tenure which represented new kinds of social control and surplus expropriation. However, protest was not limited to targeting the state; in certain circumstances, members of exploitative classes other than officials were the object of resistance—local landowners and non-Malay plantation capitalists and shopkeepers. Insofar as the occlusion of peasant protest brought about by Orientalist and social Darwinist assumptions in official documents can be penetrated, it is possible to reconstruct some of the major forms of peasant resistance to the state.

One kind of peasant initiative which the weakness of the colonial state during these years made possible was squatting. This involved covertly clearing and settling on forest or swamp land without to registering the land, receiving title on it or, most important, paying rent on it to the local Land Office. Wong notes that during the early years of this period,

> many other new peasant settlers, who were at that time almost exclusively Malays from outside places such as Sumatra and other Malay states, simply migrated into the country and took up occupation of land without the knowledge of the government land officers; and of course, the local Malays continued as before to clear and occupy new lands according to their customs. In the course of time, the number of native or Malay holdings, old and new, lying outside any form of land administration increased quite considerably.[2]

Tunku Shamsul makes clear the logic of the squatter's action: once he had cleared and cultivated an unoccupied plot of "state land," he would have known that it was difficult for the administration to evict him; eviction was only possible through recourse to a law court.[3] Tunku Shamsul also implies that migrants from the Indonesian archipelago continued to squat on land throughout this period and during the decades of immigration that followed.[4]

Once the British began to implement land rents in the 1880s, peasant protest to these new exactions became more overt. One form of protest was, apparently, a persevering argumentativeness that disputed the right of British officials to impose land rents. Their arguments appear to have presupposed that, prior to colonial rule, the *raja* had possessed no right to "absolute" proprietorship over the land, which the British now claimed they were merely exercising on his behalf by imposing rents and premia. W.E. Maxwell provides a classic description of what must have been a recurrent encounter between Malay cultivator and British District Officer:

> this principle [the *raja's* right to "absolute" ownership in land] has always been
> recognized in all sales of land in Malay districts in Perak which have come
> under my notice. But the Malay cultivator is always ready to claim from
> British officers, whom he may think likely to be ignorant of the real conditions
> of native land tenure, a larger interest than Malay law gives him, in fact, as
> large an interest as can be conceded. The official who hears the words "sell"
> *(jual)* and "buy" *(beli)* used in connection with the transfer of land under
> native tenure, is apt to conclude that a title to the soil has been passed by the
> transaction, and he very possibly recognizes . . . this view of the matter, and so
> people get to believe, or are allowed to assert, that their position in respect to
> the State is something quite different from what it really is.[5]

Were a British administrator to be hoodwinked in this way by the peasant,
Maxwell goes on to say, "it may cause embarrasment in administering the land-
revenue of a district."[6] Indeed, that would have been the whole point to the
peasant's crafty argument.

At times peasant protest against the new land premia and rents became
more confrontational. Wong refers elliptically to the situation in Selangor when
the rents were first imposed in the 1880s: "this attempt towards native holdings
was from the outset met with strong opposition by the Malay peasants. In some
places, the angry peasants had to be suppressed by force."[7] Unfortunately, Wong
does not elaborate, and there is little known about these episodes.

Peasant resistance was also directed against plantation capitalists and, in
areas like the Kedah Plain, against aristocratic landowners and other dominant
groups, as well as the state. I have already noted that peasant avoidance and
footdragging made it impossible for British officials and planters to recruit rural
Malays into permanent wage labor. I would add only that such resistance drew
its strength from the fact that its superficial manifestations conformed with the
European Orientalist and social Darwinist stereotype of Malays as being
"indolent." As Syed Hussein Alatas observed of Javanese peasants being
exploited by the Dutch, "the phenomenon characterized as indolence among a
section of the native population, may in actual fact be interpreted as a silent
protest. It was a form of strike, secret, collective and steady. That was their only
means of resistance; indeed it was a camouflaged resistance at that."[8] I suggest
moreover that, in many situations, rural Malays may well have ascertained that
this was, in fact, the unflattering stereotype held of them by the British *"Tuan"*
and other Europeans of the district, and would have taken advantage of this
preconception whenever possible.[9]

Peasant avoidance protest, under specific circumstances, took more
predatory forms when it was directed against rural landlords, Chinese
shopkeepers, and other relatively wealthy groups, as seems to have occurred in

the case of banditry in rural Kedah. In chapter 2, I indicated the special status of Kedah in the precolonial period: land had clearly emerged as a commodity, having been appropriated by members of the ruling class who oversaw its clearance and settlement by the *ra'ayat*. As a result, a class composed of aristocratic landlords—referred to by George Maxwell as "the *rajas*, *syeds*, and persons of good birth"—had emerged by the late nineteenth century and established itself in power in rural wet-rice-growing areas during the period under discussion here. This class, as well as Chinese shopkeepers and even Europeans, became the object of banditry by impoverished peasants. According to Cheah Boon Kheng, throughout this period and through the 1920s, "social banditry" was "endemic" to Northern Kedah, and at times of extreme peasant hardship was "epidemic" there.[10]

Cheah argues that by the early 1900s Kedah Malay peasants were a "depressed class" who, when there was drought or poor rice harvests, "found it difficult to make a decent living."[11] Prior to 1909, they had either to perform *kerah* or pay land tax or land rent—exactions from which aristocratic landowners were exempt. In 1909 with the assumption of active British administrative control of the state, although *kerah* was then abolished, officials required peasants to pay increased land rents and land taxes (collected regularly and rigorously for the first time) as well as fees for cattle licenses, forest clearance, collection of forest produce, and hunting.[12] As was true elsewhere, peasants resented these new impositions and protested by petitioning for exemptions, but without success.

As a result of these hardships, peasants turned to robbery, thefts and housebreakings. Banditry took two forms: that of a seasonal sideline and that of permanent banditry in gangs. Victims of both appear to have varied—Malay landlords, Europeans, *penghulus*, Chinese shopkeepers and padi planters[13]—but, compared to impoverished and even starving peasants, they shared the attribute of belonging to the propertied classes. As one Malay padi-cultivator remarked to Cheah, "'No peasant has enough money or padi to be robbed except this class of people.'"[14]

More specifically, who were the bandits? Cheah has found that they came from the most disadvantaged segments of the rural population: "they were drawn from peasants, farm labourers and unemployed youths who drifted from village to village, seeking odd jobs, excitement and high living. Their kind would hang around the *warong* (coffee stalls), or the homes of the village elders or landlords in the hope of getting jobs or of running errands for them."[15] The leaders of bandit gangs became legendary among the peasantry. Thus there was and still exists a long-standing oral tradition among poorer peasants celebrating the exploits of Nayan, Salleh Tui and Awang Poh, and other notorious bandits.[16] What distinguished these leaders and apparently the seasonal bandits as well was that they appear to have attacked persons *outside* their own *kampong*, and were protected by their own village communities when police pursued them.[17] At least certain of the bandit leaders, such as Nayan, were perceived as fighting for social justice on behalf of the poor against the wealthy.[18] What can be intuited is the existence of a large degree of solidarity within the peasant community with the "bandits" who belonged to it, on the basis of accepted norms for the need for peasant survival during economically difficult times, and of the moral economy of a redistributive ethic.[19]

Peasants resorted to banditry under conditions that were quite specific; they tended to adopt this form of resistance in areas far from colonial centers of power and poorly integrated by transport and communications into more inclusive administrative and political systems. Thus Kedah peasants turned to banditry in the mountainous, forested areas between southern Siam and northern and eastern Kedah, during a period when the police power of the state was deployed thinly on the ground.[20] As I show in the following chapter, such areas can be called "peripheral" in economic as well as political terms, and shown to share certain social characteristics during this period and subsequently. Thus I would suggest that similar instances of banditry as a form of protest might be found in peripheral areas elsewhere in rural Malaya during this period and afterward.

What is most crucial to note about almost all forms of avoidance protest adopted by peasants over these years is that they displayed a steady, if gradual decline in effectiveness. The *ra'ayat* disputed with British officials over land rents, but to little avail. Peasants confronted British District Officers and *penghulu* with collective protest, and were put down by force. *Penghulu* provided progressively less protection to peasants against the state, as their privileges were eliminated or supplanted by the British administration and dyadic relationships initiated between peasants and state officials. Above all, a civil war between classes *within* the kin-ordered village community had broken out, in which certain individuals and groups within it came to have an increasing stake in the exploitative legal and political arrangements established by the colonial state. The one form of avoidance protest that appears to have been effective during this period was squatting and illegal settlement. With the advent of rubber cultivation this became a crucial tactic of resistance.

Rubber, The Emergence of Plantation Capital and Peasant Initiatives: 1906-1920

In this second subperiod, the preexisting arrangement of mutual benefit between the administration and Chinese capitalists in the mining sector came to an end. In the place of Chinese *towkays* (businessmen), British mining and plantation capitalists came to occupy a favored position with officials. Much as in the earlier case of administration, British officials proceeded to encroach on, then later supplant, those whom they had at first needed as allies but initially were too weak to displace. During the first subperiod, they had encouraged Chinese mining ventures and made use of the capacity of Chinese *towkays* to control Chinese laborers in the tin mines and to fill government coffers from the opium and other revenue farms let out to them. From the 1890s onwards, colonial officials undermined the power of Chinese capitalists by adopting three measures. First, in the 1890s, they broke the rigid control by Chinese capitalists over the immigrant Chinese labor force by prohibiting the secret societies which the former controlled, by reforming the discharge ticket system with the Labour Code of 1895, and by reducing the power of the Chinese Kapitans.[21] Second, they assumed the direct collection of revenues from the Chinese proletariat by abolishing in 1909 and the years thereafter the opium, spirits, tobacco, gambling, and other revenue farms by which Chinese mining *towkays* had benefitted, and which made it lucrative for the latter to mine even on poorer-yielding tin land. Either these revenue farms were replaced with government monopolies (in the case of opium, liquor, and tobacco), or the services they taxed (such as gambling) were simply outlawed. Finally, through regulations, enactments, and informal policy, officials encouraged British mining enterprise to expand operations vis-à-vis their erstwhile allies, the Chinese mining *towkays*.[22]

The ascendance of British over Chinese tin mining capital in these years was associated with another shift—the growing importance of the European rubber plantation industry, not only as a sector of growth in the colonial economy, but also as a source of expanding state revenues. For rubber cultivation, at least so it seemed at the time to officials, was to be much more a European endeavor than an Asian one.

Thereafter the direction of the colonial economy was set not solely by British officials, who as an ideological matter enthusiastically supported European capitalist investment as the central element of "opening up" the country, but by a working partnership between British mining and plantation entrepreneurs and British administrators in the actual governance of the colony. Butcher observes that

the rubber industry was founded by European planters and . . . it continued to be dominated by them. As a result of their growing economic importance European miners and planters were able to exert greater influence within the government. The Federal Council, which first met in 1909, was in effect a recognition of their new standing. Three of the four "unofficial" seats on the council were held by Europeans, while the other was held by a Chinese.[23]

By the end of this period, rubber had replaced tin as the chief export of the peninsula,[24] and the increased political representation of British rubber planters was, at one level, only a reflection of the increased importance to the colony's economy of the commodity they owned, managed, and exported. It is interesting that the ascendance of British mining and plantation capitalists was associated with the appearance of a variety of racist institutions of exclusion and discrimination sponsored by the colonial administration and directed primarily against the Chinese, but also against Malays. It was, after all, in these years that the European-only clubs, hill retreats, and first-class railway carriages were established to service a growing European urban expatriate community.[25] It was also at this time that the image of the "indolent" rural Malay, that is to say, the peasant unwilling to work at the poorly-paid drudgery of wage labor under European plantation enterprise, first gained currency.[26]

By 1900 extensive experimentation with the Brazilian rubber plant, *Hevea brasiliensis,* had made commercial rubber cultivation feasible on the peninsula.[27] With the rapid upsurge in demand for rubber resulting from the growth of the United States automobile industry—a development totally exogenous to Malaya but having repercussions throughout not only the metropolitan countries of industrial capitalism but also their colonies[28]—the rush to establish rubber plantations was on. The international rubber booms of 1905 to 1906 and of 1910 to 1912 convinced British and other European investors beyond a doubt that Malaya was a colony where large and rapid profits were to be made.

The colonial administration responded eagerly to the interest of British capitalists by offering to alienate land to them on extremely favorable terms. To sate the land hunger of foreign investors, enormous tracts of land on the west coast and, to a lesser extent, on the east (e.g., in Ulu Kelantan) were alienated at nominal rents. Land alienated tended to be located near the main railway lines and trunk roads already in place to service the tin-mining and smelting industries. This was a crucial facility for the inexpensive transport of rubber to seaports, given the otherwise high costs due to the friction of distance in a tropical forest environment.[29] By 1908, 762,408 acres in what then constituted British Malaya had been alienated to, but not necessarily planted by, plantations; by 1912, the acreage alienated was 1,498,282 acres.[30] In 1913, for all Malaya, rubber acreage on plantations and smallholdings, either bearing latex or already planted came to 829,354 acres; of this area, 24.4 percent was located in the Straits Settlements, 52.2 percent in the Federated Malay States, 7.1 percent in Kedah, and 14.1 percent in Johore.[31]

During these several years, there appeared one of the first manifestations of the more antagonistic stance that the state began to adopt toward a peasantry whose activities grew progressively more salient and threatening to European plantation capital. Not only were European investors interested in land for cultivation, but so too were Malay peasants, either to grow padi as a food crop for themselves or to plant in smallholdings that new cash crop, rubber. In the allocation of "state land" for new commercial cultivation, officials clearly discriminated against Malay peasants by alienating superior land to foreign-owned plantations. This took many forms, the most significant being to alienate land with road frontage preferentially to plantations, whose advantages have just been mentioned.[32] Drabble notes that

> H.C. Belfield, Resident of Selangor, instructed District Officers in 1905 that land adjoining Government roads should not be alienated to smallholders without the Resident's sanction, which became general policy in the F.M.S. He stated that he was trying to concentrate this group in certain areas, discouraging occupation by them of land useful for "scientific" planting, i.e. estates.[33]

Moreover, more fertile lowland was set aside for plantation exploitation. And, in the latter part of this period, the building of new roads and drainage works were both directed toward plantations and away from peasant village lands.[34] Lim has stated that the effect of this land policy "left peasants with lands less valuable and less suitable for agriculture. . . . It also helps to explain why the peasants owned only a small proportion of the alienated land in the developed districts accessible by road and rail."[35]

Immigrant Labor, Food, and the Real Tragedy of the Commons

With the introduction of rubber and the rapid spread of plantations from 1905 to 1920, the presence of a low-paid and unskilled agricultural labor force, which could be subjected to intensified exploitation and whose size could be varied in response to changes in international demand for rubber, became critical to the development of large-scale European plantation production. In 1907, with the urging of European planters, the administration passed the Tamil Immigration Fund Ordinance under which Tamil immigration was to be subsidized by a tax on planters and overseen by the government.[36] In the years that followed, indentured and "free" Indian Tamil laborers, most from the greater hinterland of the city of Madras in southern India, were brought in in great numbers to work on jungle clearance, rubber tapping and weeding. In 1917, for instance, there were an estimated 220,758 wage laborers employed by plantations in the Federated Malay States. Of these, 148,834, or 67.4 percent, were classified as "Indian," most of them Tamil.[37]

This large proletarian population required food, and more food than could be grown locally. Plantations were almost completely dependent on outside producers for foodstuffs; estate laborers rarely were allowed even small plots to cultivate foodcrops. Moreover, the cost of food, particularly rice, constituted the largest charge against a plantation worker's wage: in 1925 purchases of rice made up 37.7 percent of the average monthly budget of an Indian plantation laborer.[38] The importation of labor thus introduced a new factor of instability into the capitalist sector: a steady and high rate of capital accumulation could occur only if the cost of food were kept low so that workers' wages would remain low and profits high against the costs of production.[39]

The new alliance between British plantation and mining capitalists and British colonial officials shaped the response that the colonial state was to make to this "necessity." This response was to establish by 1900 a policy of massive imports of rice from Burma and Thailand—one a British colony, the other an outlier of the British sphere of influence. By 1910 or so, the colony depended on imported rice as its major food staple; between 1911 and 1916 the Federated Malay States imported an average of 82 percent of all the rice consumed by the population.[40] This was no short-term phenomenon: between the years 1918 and 1957, except for the Japanese occupation, British Malaya imported between 40 and 80 percent of all rice consumed annually. Between the years 1895 and 1938, rice constituted the largest import of Malaya.[41] The percentage of rice domestically produced of the total consumed in Malaya did, however, increase over the long term as a result of the cyclical policies of pressures and inducements placed on Malay rice cultivators to increase production by the British colonial state (see pp. 98–102): from an average of about 32 percent during the decade from 1921 to 1930, to an average of about 38 percent in the decade from 1921 to 1930, and an average of about 49 percent in the postwar decade from 1946 to 1955.[42] The long-term significance of such imports here in encouraging the administration to relegate the Malay peasantry to the poorly rewarded padi sector cannot be overstressed. Moreover, the program of importing rice to feed the workers of the plantations and the mines precipitated further instability in the evolving colonial economy.

Kratoska has argued that during this period British officials, under their conception of Malay society as unchanging and feudalistic, did not seek to constrain rural Malays to cultivate padi for the consumption of the immigrant proletariat, although they pressed them to do so after 1930.[43] In this respect, he reinforces the view of Sadka, who argued that, through 1900, British officials not only did not attempt to force Malay peasants to grow rice, but even occasionally encouraged them to produce commercial crops. According to Kratoska, even in 1930 and the years thereafter, at a time when "a policy was adopted promoting commercial rice cultivation in Malaya," British officials' attempts to relegate rural Malays to the role of indigenous cultivators of rice to be consumed by the immigrant labor force came about only as an incidental side-effect of their paternalist conception of Malay society and out of deference to Malay elite wishes to preserve padi cultivation for Malays alone and not for immigrant Chinese or Indian farmers.[44] Nevertheless, against Kratoska's position, there is evidence that British officials placed pressure on Malay peasants to cultivate padi by the end of the period under discussion (by 1919 and 1920) as part of their strategic concerns at the end of World War I.

In any event what needs explaining is not merely why the British chose Malays rather than Chinese or Indian immigrants to cultivate rice. It must also be asked why it was at some times and not others that officials sought to impose the burden of cultivating rice for the use of the immigrant proletariat on Malay foodcrop cultivators, and how it was that the paternalist views about Malay society held by British officials were related to such efforts. As I demonstrate in the next chapter, changes in official British attitudes toward rural Malay wet-rice cultivation, during the period under discussion as well as later, were cued for solid material reasons to the colonial capitalist business cycle. Moreover, it is entirely consistent with their ideology of paternalism, with its sentimental nostalgia for an Asian feudalism, that British officials viewed the Malay *ra'ayat* as a subordinate class from whom they could justifiably appropriate rent, taxes, and the labor-power crystallized in padi cultivation, on terms set by the administration. On this last point, there is no argument with Kratoska's position.

With the onset of the rubber boom in the early 1900s, local Malays began extensively to clear forest land near their *kampong* and plant it in rubber trees, and then "sell" it to plantation capitalists or their land agents. At this time, immigrants from the Indonesian archipelago who had settled in areas where rubber trees could be planted began to do likewise. In passing it is worth reflecting on the question of why Malay and "Malaysian" peasants acted in these years in what appears to be a self-defeating way, for such actions were taken as prima facie evidence for the "impulsiveness" and "lack of foresight" which, given the assumptions of British social Darwinist thought, were supposed attributes of the "Malay race."

I have already discussed the appearance of divergent material interests over land among rural Malays within the changing village communities of this period. What is important here is that, in their strategizing, peasants would have in some contexts accepted as being to their advantage the new legal definition of land as something individually "owned" e.g., when "selling" land to non-Malays. In other contexts they would have found themselves favoring earlier conceptions of land as part of a more inclusive commons, e.g., when clearing forest land and cultivating rubber trees on it. In other words, the logical distinction that modern scholars perceive between the two radically differing conceptions of land—a precapitalist labor theory of value, and a capitalist notion of value as determined by market price—follows from latter-day knowledge of the antagonistically distinct set of social, cultural and political institutions in which these two conceptions were embedded. Such is the advantage of hindsight; it was not available to the Malay *ra'ayat*. Therefore it cannot be assumed that because peasants were by this time (whether they wished be to or not) committed to individual land "ownership" as reflected in their registered titles, surveyed plots, and annual quit-rents, they fully understood the operation of a land market under the conditions of capitalist expansion. Most peasants simply had little or no experience with the cultural practices of agrarian and petty finance capitalism. It cannot be said, therefore, that they were merely engaging in "normal" capitalist speculative behavior, but doing it incompetently by recklessly "selling" their land, as British officials and some historians have claimed. As a result, many Malays must have regarded transactions with British and Chinese planters and land agents as no more than remuneration for the labor they expended in clearing forest and planting rubber trees, within a more inclusive process of circulating lands of a common, lands which they viewed as, in the course of time, necessarily returning to the commons.

It is a clash between two cultures which lies underneath the "short-sighted" actions of peasants: peasants "sold" the land they had cleared to British and Chinese planters, or charged land as collateral to moneylenders, and then applied to the administration for more land to be alienated to them.

But with the full emergence of land as a commodity and the appearance of a market in it, the rules of the game had radically changed. Under these conditions, because of the high demand from plantations, rapid increases in the price of land no doubt provided rural Malays with an inducement to "traffick" in land, although at this time they did not comprehend the full significance of doing so. This also persuaded Indian Chettiars and other moneylenders to accept land as collateral for loans.[45] Rural Malays were quick to lose their lands to planters and land agents who regarded land as a commodity to be purchased for speculation or long-term investment, and to moneylenders eyeing its market value as collateral when peasants defaulted on their loans. Because rural Malays had little in the way of cash incomes to redeem their loans (based as these were on the inflated value of land charged as collateral), and because of very high interest rates, it was extremely common for peasants to default. Moneylenders were then prompt to seize the land charged. The result was that, by 1915 or so, many peasants were threatened with the loss of land and were extensively in debt to moneylenders.

It was this process of loss of Malay land by sale and seizure which led officials to fear that the rural Malay would become, in the words of one District Officer in 1910, "at best a day labourer and at the worst, a vagabond," and to excoriate rural Malays as "improvident" and "thriftless."[46] Because of such apprehensions, in 1913 the administration of the Federated Malay States passed the *Malay Reservations Enactment* which set aside land in each state exclusively for Malay ownership. Very similar enactments were put into effect in Kedah and Johore in subsequent years.

The *Malay Reservations Enactment* and the *Rice Lands Enactment* should thus be seen as both the salvation and the great loss of Malay peasants: their salvation in that had land not been reserved to them and thus protected from the capitalist land market, they would have rapidly become a landless proletariat. But these enactments were their loss as well, in that their passage ensured an important necessary condition for their relegation to the status of producers of rice for the immigrant labor force, as I show below—a move entirely consistent with British paternalism. Moreover, the Malay Reservation policy further promoted class division within *ra'ayat* village communities by making it impossible for non-Malay merchant capitalists, particularly Chinese, to hold land. In addition, it restricted land purchases within the Reservations to Malays and Indonesian immigrants (and in Kedah, to Siamese), thus artificially deflating the price of land and making it available at low cost to an emergent class of Malay rentiers in the years that followed.

Nonetheless, during this period their cultivation of rubber and other cash crops provided them with the means by which to engage the capitalist economy, without being fully implicated in capitalist relations of production.

Peasant Practice and Rationality and State Power

Even as the *Malay Reservations Enactment* and *Rice Lands Enactment* were being passed, rural Malays were enthusiastically planting rubber whenever and wherever they could—in newly alienated forest, in what had been their padi fields, in their fruit orchards. British stereotypes "that Malays are as apathetic as they are distrustful of changes" notwithstanding, peasants demonstrated by their activity from about 1909 onward that they were well aware of the economic advantages of rubber cultivation. Consider the state of Selangor in that year: "the rubber craze was said to have permeated every class of cultivators, including those holding land on temporary licenses in which cultivation of a permanent nature, including rubber cultivation, was prohibited. It was also observed that practically every garden or orchard was planted with a number of rubber trees."[47] Compared to padi cultivation, furthermore, rubber growing in succeeding years proved to be far more economically rewarding for those rural Malays who had a choice between the two.[48] Rubber planting continued at an intense pace from 1909 to 1916, and then slowed thereafter to 1920. By 1921 there were no less than 415,799 acres of peasant rubber "smallholdings" in the Federated Malay States, comprising 33.4 percent of the total planted rubber acreage.[49] And by 1920, 27 percent of all Malayan rubber production was recorded as coming from smallholdings of less than twenty-five acres.[50]

The venture of the peasantry into rubber planting did not, however, occur without growing opposition by the British administration during the last years of this period. This opposition took many forms. In the state of Selangor, officials enforcing the *Malay Reservation Enactment* restricted the kind of cultivation that Malays could undertake on the land, and specifically prohibited rubber as a crop. Rent schedules which favored padi and coconut growing and discouraged rubber planting were adopted throughout the Federated Malay States.[51] The *Rice Lands Enactment* of 1917 stipulated that *all* Malay land which had originally in name been alienated for padi production had to be cultivated in padi. The legal penalties were confiscation of the crop and money fines.[52] Even these official efforts to prevent the further dispossession of Malays from their land were shaped by a new bias against Malay rubber smallholding cultivators. Moreover, peasants were denied the technical assistance and information given eagerly to plantation capitalists by the Department of Agriculture. As a result, as Lim Teck Ghee put it, "early peasant knowledge of the plant was only painfully gathered, through emulation and trial and error."[53]

Plantation capitalists were given loans from the Planters' Loan fund; peasants were ineligible for them. Officials refused to alienate land to peasants who stated their intention to cultivate rubber, and "no rubber" restriction clauses were placed on land alienated. Peasants lost their lands planted in rubber on Temporary Occupation Licenses in some areas; other peasants discovered to be cultivating rubber had to cut down their trees or were required to pay increased rents. By 1917, with the passing of the *Rice Lands Enactment,* these measures had slowed the pace at which peasants were planting forest, padi, and orchard land with rubber trees, but they had by no means stopped the trend.

Two questions need to be asked at this point. First, why was it that the administration began to oppose Malay peasant rubber smallholding only at this time? Second, why was it so ineffective in doing so during the final years of this period? The first question may be answered by referring to the growing political influence of British rubber planters, both through their representatives within the Federal Council and through their interest group, the Rubber Growers Association, with the Colonial Office in London, in the years before, during, and after World War I. Rubber was viewed as a "strategic" commodity in wartime, and the views of rubber planters in Singapore, Kuala Lumpur, and London began to be of far weightier account than previously to both Malayan officials and the Colonial Office. At the same time, planters faced downward pressure on prices as Great Britain entered the war because the loss of German business, American import quotas, and restricted imperial shipping capacity available for rubber exports led to local overproduction.[54] Thus, restriction of the output of Malay smallholders to such quantities "as may be considered reasonable" became the objective of British rubber planters in the last years of this period.[55] The arbiters of rationality for Malay peasant behavior were, as usual, to be British.

The answer to the second question—why was opposition to Malay rubber smallholders generally ineffective—is more complex. First, according to Mills, before World War I some officials believed that Malays should be allowed to plant rubber, since elsewhere in the empire padi could be grown more efficiently and then imported cheaply and reliably into Malaya: "a strong body of opinion among civil servants and unofficials considered that the economic position of the Malays could best be improved by encouraging them to plant rubber and to leave the less profitable rice to the Burmese and Siamese."[56] Empire-wide consider-ations, therefore, have to be taken into account during the initial years of the century. However, this appears to have been a minority opinion and, with the events leading to the rice scarcity of 1917 to 1921, it rapidly disappeared, and was not voiced in subsequent years.

More important, during this period the colonial state was simply too weak, in terms of its organizational basis and the power it could exert, to follow through systematically on the ad hoc measures many officials had taken against the actions of Malay peasants who planted rubber. Officials were few in number, and yet concentrated in the most urbanized areas: in 1915, for instance, there were only 236 Malayan Civil Service officers for a combined population in excess of 1,900,000 for the Federated and Unfederated Malay States.[57] Admin-istrative duties also increased during this period. As a result, officials in many instances were either ignorant of specific violations by Malays of regulations against planting rubber or unable to do much about it. This allowed the Malay peasants' strategy of squatting on "state land," clearing it, and planting it in rubber without official knowledge or approval to proceed in many areas with few obstacles. They could also convert to rubber on lands they already cultivated in other crops such as padi, where ecological conditions allowed.

Moreover—and this proved to be most crucial in the long run —despite the temporary overproduction crisis of wartime, during most of these years, the rubber market was booming. Powerful interest groups like the Rubber Growers Association simply had no reason to pressure the Malayan government or the Colonial Office to take more extreme action against a competing peasantry. Thus, at this time the administration was neither fully committed to blocking independent peasant initiative, nor was it in any position to do so. At times it could impede such initiative and experiment with strategies for more effective regulation in the future.

Under these conditions peasants evaded the provisions of the laws, kept officials in ignorance about their activities, and, on occasion, defied officials *en masse*. For instance, in 1911 "one officer ruefully commented that he could not prosecute when all the inhabitants of a whole *mukim* joined hands in defiance of the padi rules."[58] During the subperiod from 1905 to 1920, then, at least one form of Malay peasant avoidance protest—squatting and "illegal" settling of "state land," and covert conversion of lands already cultivated in other crops to rubber-growing—continued to prove effective. In this period the Malay peasantry provided an illustration of the adage that where and when state power is weak, peasant power is strong.

Nonetheless, by the end of this period state administrative power over the *ra'ayat* had grown greatly, and the design of policies interfering more actively with the processes of peasant production was already underway. In the following phase of colonial capitalism and colonial rule—a period of consolidation—the design was put into effect, with devastating consequences for the peasantry.

CHAPTER FIVE

Colonial Capitalism Triumphant

The Consolidation Phase of Malayan Capitalism: 1920 to 1941

The years from 1920 to 1941 covered in this chapter were the dark years for the Malay peasantry in more than one sense. They were "dark" in that the colonial state accomplished the fundamental reversal of the successful participation of rural Malays in the colonial economy; but "dark" also in that very little is known for these years about the social organization of the Malay village community or Malay popular resistance, at least in rural areas of the western states. In general, what can be intuited is a continued decline in the effectiveness of peasant avoidance protest against state officials and their actions, while the confrontation protests by peasants during these years, such as the 1928 uprising in Trengganu, proved markedly disastrous. Nonetheless, we can assume that class differentiation increased within many Malay village communities, while peasant avoidance protest persisted but took such covert forms as squatting on land, illegal planting and tapping of rubber; and evasion of taxes, rents, and permanent wage labor about which the historical record is least informative.

During this period there was a continued consolidation of formal British rule and influence throughout the peninsula, which occurred despite the considerable sound and fury of the "decentralization" controversies during the administrations of Guillemard in the 1920s and of Clementi in the 1930s.[1] In 1937, while noting obstacles and limitations, Emerson pointed clearly to the general trend toward expanded British administrative standardization and control across the different states, when he wrote that "there can be little doubt that the future will witness, as has the past, a gradual but continual encroachment on the autonomy of the several administrations," and that "a large measure of uniformity has in fact been attained."[2] Associated with administrative consolidation was a routinization of the Malayan Civil Service, as its members came to share a common and exclusive cultural background. According to Yeo, "while the nineteenth-century Residents hailed from a wide variety of social backgrounds, their successors were now drawn from the narrow middle-class of British society. With a common public [i.e., private] school and university background, the Residents shared a high degree of uniformity in values and outlook."[3] In a bureaucracy that promoted from within, this became increasingly true of District Officers as well.

Within this framework, moreover, British official power continued to override unambiguously that of the Malay rulers in the Federated Malay States where European economic interests were concentrated. But this official power was reinforced, checked, and tempered by the influence of representatives of British plantation and mining enterprise, as "Unofficials" on Federal and State Councils. As important as this formal representation were the informal mechanisms of consultation, discussion, and lobbying between British officials on one hand, and European commercial, mining, and plantation capitalists, their pressure groups, and the media they controlled, both in Malaya and in London, on the other. Such mechanisms both relied on and reinforced the racially exclusive enclave character of British Malayan colonial society which was fully established by 1920. Both formal and informal channels of European capitalist influence were to be decisive in forming official and "unofficial" animus toward Malay rubber smallholders in the events of this period.

By the 1920s peasant rubber producers began to pose a formidable competitive threat to the position of plantation capitalism in Malaya. No less an official than the Under-Secretary for the Colonies, Ormsby-Gore, concluded from his survey of the Malayan rubber industry in 1928 that

> Native rubber production . . . introduces an element of competition which is destined to put the European estates, with their high overhead charges and costly management, to an increasingly severe test. It appears at first sight, indeed, that rubber production may quite conceivably follow the example of the coconut industry and become a predominantly native crop. . . .The native is already a serious competitor.[4]

Indeed, a good case can be made for the "natural superiority" of the peasant producer vis-à-vis the plantation system of production. "Natural," that is, prior to the exertion of effective state power against the peasant producer, a part of the primitive accumulation process.

For smallholders with all labor needs met by members of the Malay family, capital requirements were minimal and far below those of the European or Chinese rubber plantation. On many Malay smallholdings, unlike plantations, other cultigens such as fruit, coconut trees, and low-lying annuals were intercropped with rubber stands. Rubber stands were often discontinuous, and undergrowth was allowed to remain. In contrast, on plantations, rubber stands were continuous, and undergrowth was cleared. In peasant smallholdings, not only did intercropping and undergrowth provide a curb on *lalang* grass (various species of *Imperata*), but they also slowed erosion and provided a layer of humus essential to growth in the laterized tropical soils. Plantations on the other hand were chronically plagued with *lalang* invasions, and arsenite herbicides had to be used.[5] Due largely to the various laws against Malays using reservation land for rubber cultivation and to the artificial land scarcity brought about by the opposition of the administration to alienating lands to Malays for rubber, peasant rubber plots were quite small, less than five acres as an average.

The Malay rubber cultivator compensated for the smallness of the plot and the scatter or rubber stands within it by planting a high density of rubber trees per acre. A smallholding might have an average of more than 250 trees per acre compared to a plantation density of 80 to 100 trees.[6] The density of planting on smallholdings prevented soil erosion and the spread of plant root diseases, which had been a severe problem with plantation rubber.[7] Consequently, in this period average yields per acre from mature smallholdings were far greater than for plantations— according to Lim, "at least 50 per cent."[8]

In many respects, then, Malay rubber smallholdings shared the advantageous characteristics of swidden cultivation in Southeast Asia, noted by Geertz and others. These included the imitation of a generalized ecosystem, a high proportion of nutrients in plants relative to those in the soil, and a "closed cover" forest canopy, but without the "land-eating" tendencies of prolonged slash-and-burn cultivation in much of upland Southeast Asia.[9]

Peasant rubber producers were also, in general, well adapted to dealing with fluctuations in the market price of rubber, that is, their production behavior showed a high degree of price elasticity.[10] When prices were high, peasants tapped their holdings frequently, perhaps, rain permitting, every day or two. When prices fell, they tapped their trees less frequently. In times of prolonged depression in rubber prices, they would then reallocate labor to padi, coconut, and other subsistence crops, engage in small cash crop production (e.g., fruits), and work as casual laborers, hawkers, fishermen, or timber cutters.[11] Only when peasants had no options for raising cash through their labor other than rubber production would they proceed to "slaughter tap" their trees by tapping more latex as prices declined.[12] But this behavior would have depended on specific conditions (e.g., family financial emergency, falling rubber prices, and lack of alternative income sources) which rarely coincided and were extremely exceptional during this period.

In distinction to peasant rubber smallholdings, plantations had high fixed overheads, required high minimal levels of production for their operations to be economical at all, and were thus relatively sluggish in their response to market prices, that is, relatively price-inelastic. In attempting to react to international rubber prices, planters had to try to balance off several factors against one another—current and projected production, the size of their resident immigrant labor force, wage levels, and the importation or local purchase of rice. Further, politico-economic changes elsewhere in the world capitalist system and the

British empire determined many of these factors: the international rubber market was uncertain; labor migration was affected by events in India and China; the price of imported rice, by harvests in Burma and Thailand and by demand elsewhere in the British empire. Thus the instabilities of capitalist operation were many and the interaction effects only partially predictable or controllable.

If ever there was an instance where "small is beautiful," the Malay rubber smallholder in the 1920s may have been it. The fears of Ormsby-Gore, other officials, and European planters were well-founded: the competitive position of the Malay peasant sector was potentially formidable.[13]

This contradiction between the "needs" of capital accumulation in the capitalist sector and the competitive vigor of the peasant noncapitalist sector was not to be resolved by the "invisible hand" of free market competition, as capitalist ideology would have it, but by the application of colonial state power against the Malay peasantry. For, during this period, colonial officials served the interests of the British capitalist class by their gross appropriation of the surplus product of Malay rubber producers on behalf of British and other large-scale plantations. There is no little truth in Caldwell's claim that "far from British enterprise rescuing a richly endowed land from stagnation and galvanising a torpid population from slumber, it was British enterprise itself which had to be rescued from vigorous local competition by British political intervention designed to nullify it."[14] If we are not merely to assume the functionalism of an extreme "world systems" model, (holding that somehow British officials, Malay peasants, and all other colonial classes functioned teleologically to support the needs of capital), then it must be considered why this should have been so, a matter I discuss briefly below. Nonetheless, by the end of this period, despite peasant initiative and resistance, the deployment of state power had affected the social relations of production in peasant villages to the point that the preconditions for the lowered productivity, landlessness, and proletarianization evident among Malay peasants after 1946 were firmly established. The principal mechanisms of appropriation were the rubber restriction schemes and the administration's policies that dictated that rural Malays cultivate padi. It is during this period, then, that the critical events of the primitive accumulation process occurred.

Spatial Location and Constraints on Peasant Action

By the early 1930s, the vast majority of Malay peasants participated actively in the commercial production of commodities in demand in the colonial economy. However, this by no means implied their extensive involvement in capitalist relations of production, that is, in their sale or purchase of labor-power depending on whether they owned private productive property. A crucial corollary of this is that their actions can be understood only in terms of their spatial location within those distinct regional economies which had, by this time, emerged throughout colonial Malaya. Where peasants lived implied their differential access to trading networks and to means and facilities of transport and communication, which in turn *constrained but did not determine*, their participation in cash-crop production.[15]

It is first necessary to consider rural Malays living in the "core" areas of the northern, central, and southern regions of the Malayan peninsula. These areas were densely populated and relatively urbanized, with cores being centered on towns built near tin fields and the offices of colonial administration, and with reticulated road and rail systems. These core areas constituted what has come to be called the peninsula's "rubber belt" extending all the way from southern Kedah in the north to southern Johore. (See Map 1.) In these areas, rural Malays planted rubber trees whenever they were able to get away with doing so, and continued to tap trees when these were already planted and secreting latex.[16] Generally, over this period, peasants substituted rubber tapping for padi cultivation as a means of livelihood. The presence of developed networks of roads, railways, and trails in these core areas upon which rural Malays could conveniently carry sheet rubber to dealers or dealers could transport rubber to higher-level wholesalers, as well as the presence of the dealers themselves, were crucial to the growth of rubber smallholding.

In areas outside the cores of the northern, central, and western regions, rural Malays found themselves facing constraints markedly different from those for peasants in core areas of the peninsula. These non-core areas were of two kinds, and peasants' actions varied accordingly. The first kind consisted of what I refer to here as "semicore" areas: lowland alluvial areas drained of swamp only in the nineteenth century or twentieth century through this period, and settled by peasant pioneers (the Kedah Plain, Krian, and coastal areas such as Tanjong Karang and Sungei Manik which would be opened to cultivation only after 1930 [Map 1]).[17]

These semicore areas had come to be densely populated by padi cultivators. However, these areas were far less urbanized, and road and rail networks were far less developed than in core areas. Even as late as 1951 in the Kedah Plain, according to Dobby, "there are only some 85 miles of road to serve the 800 square miles and quarter million population of the Plain."[18] In these areas, Malay peasants grew padi both for commercial sale and for their own consumption, but little or no rubber. In the case of northern Kedah and Perlis, British officials opposed the alienation to Malays of State lands for new rubber planting on the grounds that they might be attracted away from padi cultivation.[19] Moreover, a cycle of rural Malay indebtedness to Chinese shopkeepers and rice millers, who obtained depressed padi prices from

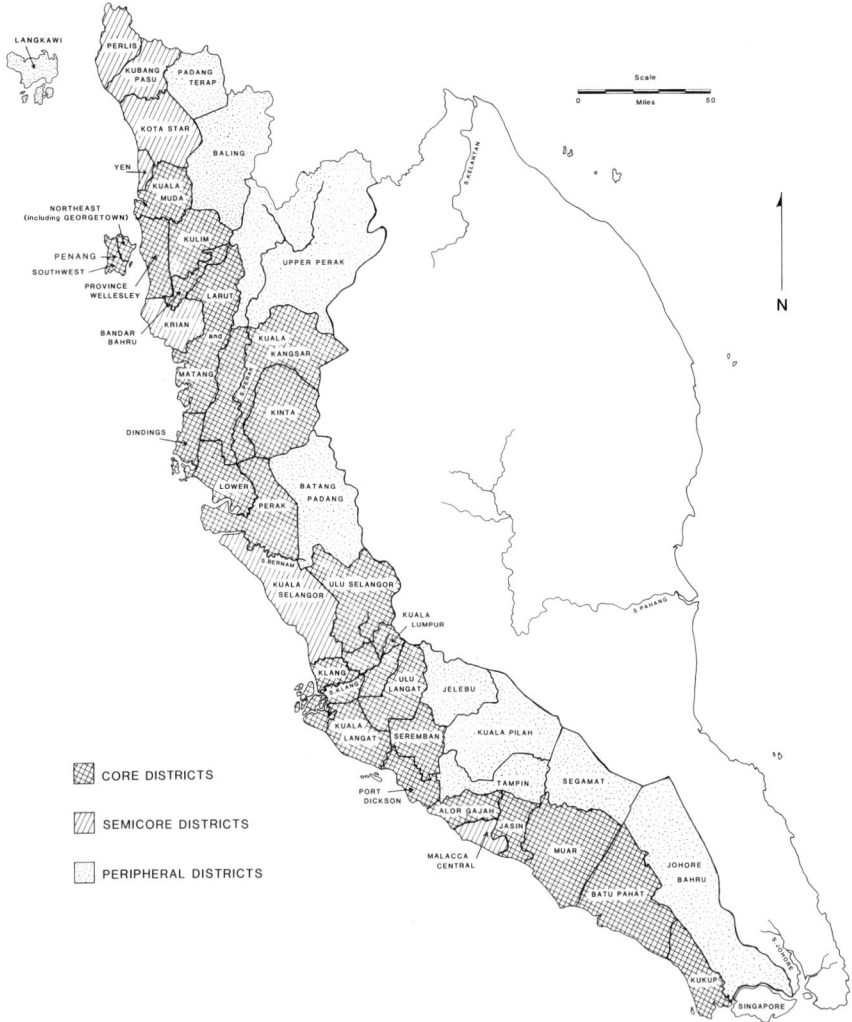

LANGKAWI

PERLIS

KUBANG
PASU   PADANG
         TERAP

Scale

0   Miles   50

KOTA STAR

BALING

YEN

KUALA
MUDA

NORTHEAST
(including GEORGETOWN)

KULIM

PENANG

SOUTHWEST

UPPER PERAK

PROVINCE
WELLESLEY   LARUT

N

KRIAN

BANDAR
BAHRU   KUALA
                   KANGSAR

MATANG

KINTA

DINDINGS

LOWER   BATANG
PERAK   PADANG

BERNAM

KUALA   ULU SELANGOR
SELANGOR

KUALA
LUMPUR

KLANG   ULU
          LANGAT   JELEBU

KUALA
LANGAT   SEREMBAN   KUALA PILAH

▨ CORE DISTRICTS

▨ SEMICORE DISTRICTS

▨ PERIPHERAL DISTRICTS

PORT
DICKSON   TAMPIN   SEGAMAT

ALOR GAJAH

JASIN

MALACCA   MUAR   JOHORE
CENTRAL   BAHRU

                   BATU PAHAT

KUKUP

SINGAPORE

cultivators through the notorious *padi kuncha* (or *padi ratus*) arrangement, also contributed to the persistence of padi cultivation in these areas. Despite official and Malay elite claims to the contrary, exploitative Chinese merchants were by no means the only beneficiaries of this practice when viewed within the more inclusive context of political economy discussed in this book. Chinese shopkeepers and millers practicing *padi kuncha* were, in this respect, no more than de facto "on the ground" agents of the rice policies set by the colonial state, and not the primary creators of it.[20] In any event, therefore, because of insufficient transport facilities, legal obstacles, and cycles of rural indebtedness, peasants in the northwestern "rice bowl" remained locked into commercial padi production during this and the following period. In contrast, in southern Kedah, especially in Kulim and Kuala Muda districts, British and Chinese entrepreneurs were allowed to open rubber plantations from 1905-1906 onward, and Malay peasants in these districts soon followed suit. These districts belonged to the core area of the northwestern region.

Outside of Kedah, in coastal alluvial areas cleared of swamp by the colonial administration, notably the Krian district, British pressures on peasants to cultivate padi were strongest, and the presence of irrigation and drainage facilities made relatively higher yields possible. Further, large proportions of the Malay population who settled in projects in Krian, Tanjong Karang, and Sungei Manik before and during this period were immigrants from the Indonesian archipelago. They had cultivated padi prior to immigration and, being relatively impoverished, were compelled to do so after moving to these projects.

Thus it was in the semicore areas of the Kedah Plain, Perlis, in Krian, and the new coastal areas which were to be developed after 1930, that rural Malays were most receptive to the commercial cultivation of rice. As the Director of the Department of Agriculture stated in 1936, "in Kedah, in the Krian district of Perak and in Malacca, padi is a commercial crop."[21] More important, the alternative of rubber smallholding was simply not feasible in these areas, and, after the implementation of the International Rubber Restriction scheme in 1934 with its prohibition on new rubber planting, it became moot in any event.

The other kind of noncore areas were peripheries consisting of the upland and mountainous margins on the western sides of the mountain ranges to the east of the coastal plains in the northern and central regions of the peninsula.[22] These were essentially the areas generally referred to in Malay as *ulu* ("up country" or "up river"), located within the higher catchment zones of rivers debouching on the west coast, such as the Sungei Kedah, Sungei Muda, Sungei Perak, and Sungei Selangor (Map 1). Malays living in these areas were remote from centers of population, population densities were extremely low, roads and trails were sparsely distributed and in poor condition, and traders in provisions and other commodities extremely scattered. In such areas, Malays cultivated padi — "dry" padi under swidden regimes on mountain slopes and "wet" padi in mountain valleys — and other food crops for their families' consumption. They also herded buffalo and cattle, hunted, fished, and gathered forest products. They neither cultivated padi commercially nor in most areas tapped rubber; both activities were precluded by the lack of roads and trading facilities. An example of such an area was the Sik district in northeastern Kedah before World War II, described by Banks as follows:

> People prepared and cultivated as much land as they needed. A family made up of a man, his wife, and small children only cultivated about two *relung* of paddy land, although they could cultivate two or three times that many. There was little cash and long periods when there was little to buy. Families sought self-sufficiency. Rice yields in Sik were low by coastal standards. . . . Since there was no alternative source of livelihood, people did not think about maximizing the productivity of their fields.[23]

The remoteness of peasants in these peripheries during the interwar period rendered them marginal, literally, to major developments in the colonial economy. Since the Japanese occupation the opening of new roads has increasingly brought them, by way of a lowered friction of distance, closer to the core areas of northern and central regions of the peninsula. Since then they have adopted rubber cultivation widely, as in Baling and Sik districts.

Rural Malays in the cores and semicores of regional economies therefore produced commodities in demand in the colonial economy, albeit under different constraints, for a major part of their livelihoods. At the same time, those in upland peripheries produced foods and other crops for their own use, and in this sense (but only in this sense) did not participate in the colonial economy. This tripartite differentiation among regional cores, semicores, and peripheries, and the constraints that residence in each set on peasant livelihood, have been noted, if implicitly, by historians and other scholars. R.D. Hill, in his history of rice cultivation, for instance, has discussed the west coast region of the "Northern Malay States" as follows:

> By 1910, therefore, well-marked regional contrasts had developed. The Kedah-Perlis plain was the centre of a largely commercialized, export-oriented economy [of padi production] of which the social and especially the entrepreneurial basis was still "traditional" in nature. . . . Flanking this region was another to the north-east, east and south which was sparsely inhabited and still largely subsistence in economy though doubtless with some local market orientation. The third economic region was discontinuous and represented modern mining and rubber estate interests, the latter clustered in blocks along the Singgora road in Kubang Pasu district and in the Kuala Muda and Kulim districts to the south.[24]

It was of course in the southern areas of this "third economic region," (part of the northern regional core), that the extensive transport and commercial networks available first to rubber estates later made rubber smallholding among rural Malays possible. And it was in this area that Malay smallholders were most active in this period and subsequently. In the passage quoted above, then, Hill distinguishes nicely, in order, between the semicore, periphery, and core of the northern region.

It is in light of their differing locations within colonial regional economies, therefore, that the constraints placed on the livelihoods of Malay peasants by changing social and economic conditions and the shifting policies of the colonial state can best be understood for the period from 1920 to 1941 and subsequently. Nonetheless, it is necessary to add that many peasants fought at great cost against the constraints posed by their spatial locations, that there was a long-standing Malay tradition of *merantau*, "wandering," in search of new opportunities for livelihood or seasonal employment, and that, in general, peasants were highly mobile.[25] Therefore, spatial position never determined but only set limits on peasants' actions, and it is always crucial to distinguish the spatial stage from the historical players who performed upon it.

Rubber Restriction; Who Paid, Who Benefited

From 1922 to 1928 and again from 1934 to 1940, rubber production in Malaya was not determined by the price vagaries of an international market, but by two rubber restriction schemes organized by agreements between large capitalist producers and colonial states. Despite its relative weakness, the British colonial state was able to implement these schemes by law and enforce them through its *strategic* use of coercive and economic power.

The aftermath of World War I brought on a major recession in the colonial economy, lasting from 1920 to 1922. Depressed demand by United States industrial consumers sent the price of rubber plummeting. As the perturbation spread, the plantations, as was true for other sectors of the Malayan economy, were hard hit. In an attempt to bolster rubber prices, the Rubber Growers Association — the major interest group of British proprietors of rubber plantations operating in Malaya and Ceylon — sought in London to have the Colonial Office impose restrictions on Malayan rubber production and to negotiate a restriction agreement with the government of the Netherlands East Indies, where there was a large rubber industry. In 1921 the Stevenson Committee was appointed in England, and in 1922 its recommendation that the Colonial Office unilaterally restrict rubber production in Malaya was accepted and put into effect.[26]

Under the Stevenson scheme, Malayan rubber production was limited by law. Plantation and smallholder production in the year 1920 were to serve as the

"Standard Production," a base for setting each year's export quotas for both sectors as percentages of this base figure. Each year, quotas were set according to the prevailing international price for rubber in the preceding twelve months.[27]

The determination of the "Standard Production" required an assessment of the yields of mature rubber by each producer in the year 1920. This assessment was carried out quite differently for the plantations and the peasant smallholdings. For plantations, the figures from production records for that year were accepted as the "Standard Production." For peasant and other smallholdings, an arbitrarily drawn-up measure, the "Duncan Scale," was used to set the "Standard Production."[28]

It has been observed that through this method the yields, and thus the allowable production under the Scheme, of peasant smallholders were grossly underassessed, and those of plantations proportionately overassessed.[29] As mentioned earlier, average rubber yields per acre from mature peasant smallholdings were at least 50 percent higher than from plantations, because of the far denser planting on smallholdings. Despite this, the authority on Malayan rubber production restriction, P.T. Bauer, has estimated that peasant holdings were, in fact, assessed at about *half* the yield per acre of plantation holdings.[30]

Though peasants were found to have no less than 31.33 percent of the total area of rubber holdings in 1921, in the first three years of the Stevenson scheme they received only 27.1, 26.0, and 26.47 percent respectively of the total allowed production, despite the much denser planting on their holdings.[31]

Malay smallholders by no means placidly accepted the inequitable assessments mandated them by the Duncan Scale. In 1922, within a few days after the introduction of the Stevenson scheme, rural Malays in rubber areas protested violently against restrictions on the sale of their rubber, perceiving correctly that this was a direct threat to their livelihoods. According to Lim Teck Ghee, "peasant discontent spread rapidly throughout the country and violence broke out in various parts of Perak and Johore as peasants, unable to sell their rubber, reacted desperately to what appeared to be moves to break their rice bowls."[32] The desperation of peasant smallholders at this time was evident in the extreme form of protest to which they felt forced to resort. In response to these protests, the administration hastily convened a committee of inquiry to reconsider the rates of assessment of smallholdings under the scheme. As a result of its findings, it increased very moderately the Standard Production allocated to smallholders. Nonetheless, serious inequities remained.[33]

Lim has estimated that as a result of this systematic underassessment and forced restriction on production, for the seven years of the Stevenson scheme (1922 to 1928) the loss to the peasant smallholding sector amounted to $173 million Straits Dollars, or about sixty pounds sterling per smallholding acre for this period, and the Federated Malay States alone.[34]

The loss to the peasant sector was a proportionate gain for the plantations. From 1923 onward, despite the restriction scheme, the "Standard Production" for plantations was set at a figure *greater* than the average maximum sustained yield they were capable of producing, which was about 375 pounds per acre annually. Though in 1921 plantations (which were defined by the authorities as those rubber holdings over 100 acres) formed 63.57 percent of the total rubber acreage, in the first three years of the scheme they were alloted 66.25, 67.38 and 66.81 percent of the total production quotas.[35] Thus the Stevenson scheme ameliorated the lot of plantations under restriction while it depressed smallholder production; and the lost income of the peasantry went into the pockets of European planters and their companies' shareholders.

How did such inequitable assessments come about and, equally important, how did the administration have the power to carry them out against peasant smallholders? As I have suggested, the British administration, although weak in bureaucratic manpower, nonetheless was able to use what power it did have strategically through its control of the rubber export process by allocating coupons and licenses to producers. Moreover, understaffed British officials — District Officers and officials from the Department of Agriculture — sought the assistance of British plantation managers and owners in assessing the "Standard Production" of peasant smallholders.[36]

British planters showed themselves to be prompt in taking advantage of their quasi-bureaucratic status. Many pretexts were employed to allot peasants a low assessment: smallholdings were untidy, there were diseased trees, there were fruit trees intermixed with rubber, trees were heavily wounded by bad tapping, there was a lack of drainage.[37] Whether such complaints were in the least justified is beside the point, although the evidence is overwhelming that peasant techniques of rubber production did not adversely affect yields.[38] Planters saw peasant smallholders as a competitive threat to plantation production and profits, and acted in their own best interests. The Stevenson scheme and the active collaboration of colonial officials provided them with an opportunity to "rectify" the situation.

It should be noted that no conscious and functional "master plan" to deprive Malay smallholders of their livelihood need be invoked. Shared cultural assumptions about the laziness, waywardness, and childlike incapacity of rural Malays, and of the rightfulness of the aims and methods of European plantation enterprise held by British officials and planters, are sufficient to explain the inequities of underassessment, and the rigor with which strategic state power was deployed. Or, another way of stating this might be that when a culture of imperialism exists, there need not be conspirators in order for there to be a conspiracy.

During the Stevenson scheme from 1922 to 1928, the administration continued to favor the plantations over the peasantry in its land alienation and use policies. For instance, between 1926 and 1930 in the Federated Malay States, 56,000 acres of State land were alienated to rural Malays for rubber production, while plantations were alienated 174,000 acres.[39] In some cases, the provisions of the *Malay Reservations Enactment* and other laws prohibiting rubber planting on Malay land were enforced by evicting peasants or forcing them to remove their trees. In other instances, peasants were punished with increased rents and premia although the trees were allowed to remain.[40] Despite these disincentives, Malay peasants continued to plant new rubber trees where they could get away with doing so.

In 1928 the Stevenson scheme was rescinded because nonparticipation by the Netherlands East Indies had allowed its rubber industry to gain a greater proportion of the international market than before. Malayan rubber production was unrestricted from 1929 to mid-1934, and the full measure of the threat posed by peasant smallholders to the European plantation sector became apparent during this interlude. Even with the onset of the world depression in 1930, the yields for peasant smallholdings were an average of 7 to 31 percent higher than for plantations for this period. By 1930, smallholdings produced about 45 percent of all of Malaya's rubber.[41]

World Depression and the "Problem" of Peasant Competition

By 1930, however, advanced industrial capitalism was spiraling down into the worst depression of its modern era. With the collapse of the auto industry in the United States, the demand for Malaya's two major export products, rubber and tin, fell precipitously. The incomes of all producers of these commodities decreased steeply, the administration's revenues were lost, and the colony faced its gravest economic crisis. (At the same time, one major source of government revenues continued to provide the administration with a buffer against these shocks —its exactions on the Chinese proletariat through the sale and distribution of opium, and taxes on liquor and tobacco. Li observes that during the depression, in the years when there was a government deficit, "the shortage was never serious, and it was balanced by the tremendous surplus [from the Opium Reserve Replacement Fund] previously accrued." With the exception of a few years, notably during the depression, the government operated at a surplus due to these revenues over this entire period.)[42]

In response to these conditions, plantation capitalists again sought to stabilize rubber prices by lobbying the Colonial Office in London to restrict production outputs. In mid-1934 a new rubber restriction scheme was implemented by the colonial administration, and was to last until the Japanese occupation of Malaya in 1941. An International Rubber Regulation Committee was appointed to oversee the program. Aside from price stabilization, it had a second major goal that can be termed its subagendum. According to Andrew McFadyean, a high-ranking member of the Committee and the official historian of the scheme, "one of the primary objects of the Rubber Control Scheme was *to protect European capital in plantation companies in Malaya, Borneo and the Netherlands East Indies from competition arising from the production of rubber by the natives at a fraction of the cost involved on European-owned estates."* [43]

The conditions of the International Rubber Regulation program were similar to those of the Stevenson scheme. Base production quotas, derived from 1929 to 1932 export figures, were calculated for each participating country and for the smallholder and plantation sectors in each. Each year the actual quotas for plantations and smallholders of each country were set by starting from the base quota and adding to it an allowance for newly-maturing trees coming into productive age.[44]

From 1930 through 1941 there was a total ban on alienation of land for rubber planting, and, after 1934, the planting of rubber on land already alienated was prohibited except for the year 1939-1940 when five percent of such land could be replanted — pointless for smallholders.[45] However, between 1934 and 1938 *replanting* was allowed on up to 20 percent of all acreage in production since 1934, and after 1938 it was allowed on almost all rubber acreage.[46]

In his definitive study of the International Rubber Regulation scheme, *The Rubber Industry* and in other works,[47] P.T. Bauer has demonstrated how successful the scheme was in achieving its second major goal — the protection of European plantation enterprise from competition from the peasant rubber sector. This goal was attained in two ways. The first was through a continuation of past practice — the gross underassessment of peasant smallholding production and the corresponding overassessment of plantation production. Some insight into the drastic change of fortune for the Malay peasantry can be obtained from Table 2 which details the relative shift in production under the conditions of rubber restriction after 1934.

Whereas in the five and one-half years prior to regulation, plantations produced an average of 53.8 percent and smallholders an average 46.2 percent of total annual production, under the restriction scheme plantations produced an average 63.8 percent and smallholders an average 36.2 percent. Bauer has estimated that the loss of income to smallholders brought about by the forced limitation on production in the years 1934 to 1940 came to $85 million Straits Dollars, or ten million pounds sterling. This figure is based on the sale of the 400,000 tons which would have been produced by smallholders, most of them peasants, given 1929 to 1932 production figures, if restriction had not occurred. And this loss to smallholders, as in the previous period, represented an equivalent gain to European and Chinese plantation capitalists.

Table 2

Colonial Malaya: Rubber Tonnage and Shares of Production,
Plantations vs. Smallholdings, 1929-1940

Year	Plantations (> 100 acres)		Smallholdings (≤ 100 acres)	
	Tons (1,000s)	As % of Total Production	Tons (1,000s)	As % of Total Production
1929	246	55.2	200	44.8
1930	236	54.6	197	45.4
1931	240	55.1	197	44.9
1932	240	57.6	177	42.4
1933	240	52.2	221	47.8
Jan. - May 1934	102	48.3	107	51.7
REGULATION INTRODUCED				
June - Dec. 1934	160	59.7	108	40.3
1935	243	64.0	137	36.0
1936	233	63.9	132	36.1
1937	314	62.4	189	37.6
1938	246	68.1	115	31.9
1939	245	67.7	117	32.3
1940	334	60.8	215	39.2

Source: Bauer 1961b:247

Bauer describes how the complex methods of assessment of yields militated against equitable assessments for smallholdings, while proportionately overassessing plantation holdings. As in the Stevenson scheme, British officials called on European planters to assist in setting smallholders' allowable production, and peasants were not represented on the various committees that created restriction policy under the new scheme.[48]

It was precisely those Malay peasants living in the core areas of the northern, central, and southern regions who, because of their dependence on rubber smallholding, were most hard hit by the restrictions of the Stevenson and International Rubber Regulation schemes. Peasant smallholders in semicore areas were also adversely affected but not as severely, since they were far more dependent on padi cultivation for their livelihoods than on rubber, the great majority exclusively so.

Even so, peasants in core areas persisted in tapping their rubber smallholdings under the conditions of restriction, although when rubber prices were lowest not as intensively as otherwise. Both P.T. Bauer and Lim Teck Ghee have argued that it was economically advantageous for peasants to tap rubber, rather than grow rice, even during the most difficult years of rubber restriction. Their observations apply most accurately to peasants in the core areas of these regional economies. According to Bauer, even during the depression of the 1930s, with world demand for rubber very low,

> rubber was still the most profitable crop among the available alternatives, except for those producers who were furthest from the principal markets, or whose holdings were particularly poor-yielding. The price of rice and padi also fell sharply after 1929, and throughout the depression the great majority of the rubber-growing smallholders could obtain more rice with the proceeds of rubber than by growing it direct.[49]

As support for this claim, Bauer amasses data to argue that during the years from 1929 to 1933, both net incomes from rubber for smallholders and net amounts of rice purchasable would have greatly exceeded those of commercial padi cultivators, for each acre of land in use. Calculated from his figures, the net cash income difference in favor of peasants' growing rubber over cultivating padi for these years was at least 35 percent higher (in 1932), with a modal value of about 227 percent higher during these years.[50] Similarly, Lim's comparison of the economic returns for peasants in the Krian area of growing rubber versus cultivating padi per acre of land in use for the years 1922 to 1938 shows that the yearly gross incomes of peasants from rubber growing would have exceeded those from padi growing by a minimum of 14 percent, with an average difference of 195 percent and a modal difference of 147 percent.[51] That is, on the average, peasants could expect about three times as much income from rubber growing and tapping than they could from commercial padi cultivation. A more important inference from Bauer's and Lim's findings is that because as a rule Malay peasants, like peasants elsewhere, were far more concerned that the margin between subsistence and starvation be assured every year rather than maximized as an average, peasant experience over these years would have shown that at no time did income from rubber fall below that for padi cultivation in these areas, and that incomes from rubber were therefore highly reliable — something that could not be said for padi.

Nonetheless, although Bauer's and Lim's conclusions on the basis of microeconomic factors alone are illuminating and probably applicable for most peasants in regional cores, they by no means state the whole matter. First, no doubt some smallholdings were so unproductive that Bauer's and Lim's assumptions would not apply, and this would have been exacerbated by underassessment. Second and more important, Malay peasants would have been more concerned with ensuring and maintaining their livelihoods and a culturally-prescribed minimal standard of living than in "maximizing returns" in accordance with abstract calculations of gains over losses. In short, most peasants —as distinct from capitalist farmers engaged in risk-taking for profit — were and are extremely cautious, because their families' livelihood and survival were at stake, year by year.[52]

This no doubt explains what the circumstantial and anecdotal accounts of peasant actions during these years strongly suggest that Malay peasants did in fact do. They diversified by growing several crops including rubber, instead of specializing in rubber alone — they fished, produced handicrafts, worked as peddlars and hawkers, and occasionally engaged in wage labor. When rubber prices were most depressed, peasants tapped less frequently or not at all, and then resumed more frequent tapping when prices rose. Rubber tapping, therefore, remained one albeit crucial element in their overall strategy of not putting all one's eggs in one basket. Bauer himself observed that

> when the present writer visited Malaya in 1946 many smallholders were asked how they had managed to make a living during the great depression of the early thirties when the Singapore price of rubber at one time declined below 5 Straits cents . . . per lb. The answer was generally that as the cost of living, especially the price of rice, had been very low at that time, it had been possible to make ends meet, though in some instances it had been necessary to rely to a greater extent than before on other activities such as fishing or hawking, or the production of *rattan* to supplement the income from rubber. But among smallholders, as distinct from unemployed or under-employed labourers, there was apparently little hardship even in 1931-32. The smallholders were unanimous in saying that they were glad to possess a rubber holding, and that in spite of its violent price fluctuations, rubber had proved a very satisfactory crop, highly suitable to their requirements.[53]

At times, peasants did not tap their smallholdings merely because the coupons they were issued quarterly as part of the restriction scheme could be sold separately (i.e., without rubber) at high prices. This was because an informal market in coupons had emerged among lower-level rubber dealers, who sought to buy coupons to match with the rubber, unaccompanied by coupons, that they had previously purchased on speculation from smallholders.[54] Peasants also sold their coupons to large estates, and in this way a portion of their market share passed over to plantations, while smallholders without coupons ceased tapping.[55] In any event, diversification appears to have been the "name of the game" when rubber prices were depressed during this period, as it has been subsequently when rubber prices have been low.[56]

A Note on State Power and the Culture of Imperialism

In the course of a counterattack against those who have applied a "world systems" approach to colonial Malaya, Kratoska has recently made two important claims that bear on the issues of colonial state power and the culture of imperialism discussed through my reconstruction of the events of this period.[57] These two claims are in part valid, but are incomplete as they stand. An assessment of these claims will be valuable for a more dialectical, and less functionalist Marxist analysis of Malayan colonialism than that provided by "world systems" theorists. First, Kratoska has argued that "the colonial administration was committed in a general way to promoting the interests of the Malay population, cast by British officials in the role of a yeoman-peasantry: independent, self-sufficient small landowners."[58] Thus, through the *Malay Reservation Enactment* of 1913 (discussed above) and its 1933 amendments, British officials sought to create "a protected arena for Malay economic development."[59] Without the *Enactment* and similar legislation, Kratoska states, there would have resulted "displacement of the Malays from their land and the creation of a landless rural proletariat."[60] This is consistent with the findings of this study as presented in the previous chapter. He goes on to argue that, although the original intent of the *Enactment* was to "protect" Malays from incursions on their lands by non-Malays (including Europeans), in fact, however, the *Enactment (*combined with the policies introduced after 1930 to stimulate domestic rice production) "tended to promote" the incorporation of rural Malays into the colonial economy as food producers for the immigrant labor force.[61] Therefore, colonial land law and the Reservation Enactment "produced unforeseen consequences,"[62] contrary to the paternalist, if benign intentions of colonial administrators. Rural Malays became relegated to the role of low-cost food providers for the plantation and mining proletariats of immigrant Chinese and Indians.

Kratoska's second but related point is that the colonial state was simply too weak to carry through on those policies and programs which, according to "world systems" and dependency theorists, brought about the impoverishment and proletarianization of the Malay peasantry: "the fallacy of the model, however, is more than these factual errors. It is the mistake of crediting the British administration with having controlled, or with having been able to control, the economic behavior of the population. Britain ruled Malaya by suffrance, not by fiat."[63] Kratoska's emphases on the open-ended and contingent quality of the colonial administration's policies toward the peasantry, on the cultural and ideological factors (e.g., benign paternalism) mediating state policies, and the state's lack of power to at times fulfill its (theoretically-defined) "function" of promoting the capital accumulation of colonial capitalists, are congenial to the approach taken here.

Nevertheless, there are shortcomings in these two claims which lead to a picture of colonial rule that misrepresents the history of the primitive accumulation process. First, it is important to point out that, as noted above, British officials and the managers and owners of colonial enterprises — at least those at higher levels — shared both a common class and ethnic background, and a class-based and British-centered cultural perspective.[64] Arenas for the validation and elaboration of this cultural perspective included exclusive social clubs and hill stations frequented by the wealthiest and most influential Europeans in the colony.[65] Associated with this common class-based and ethnic-based culture were institutions of interest aggregation and expression and of political influence which were almost exclusively European in character. Except for the formal participation of the "unofficial" representatives of British commercial, mining, and plantation enterprises on Federal and State Councils, most of these institutions were informal, and existed both in Malaya and at the imperial level in London. Yeo has nicely described these institutions in his treatment of the "decentralization" controversy of the 1920s. His portrayal of them is equally relevant to rubber restriction, and is worth quoting at length:

> the British *modus operandi* in Malaya . . . always sought to have policy accepted through discussion, conciliation, and co-operation with interested parties who mattered. This was effected through private consultation with leaders in the confidence of the government and through public discussions in the various legislatures and Malayan newspapers. It offered European commercial interests, *the best organized and most articulate lobby in the FMS,* considerable scope to influence official policy. Their demands were voiced through many commercial organizations such as the Rubber Planters' Association of Malaya, through their representatives in the Federal Council, through the Malayan English newspapers, and through the Association of British Malaya. In this connection their close social ties with the British administration and their political ties with the British Parliament proved highly useful. . . . In all this the commercial interests gained a receptive ear from British officials because upon them depended the realization of the government's central goal of economic development in Malaya.[66]

If this was true during the relatively prosperous 1920s, it was even more so as European enterprise suffered the manifold shocks of the depression. These institutions and the cultural perspective they perpetuated provided a certain overall integration of worldview, purpose, and aim. The events leading to the drastic underassessment of the yields of Malay smallholders by British officials working in tandem with plantation managers, described above, illustrate this nicely.

Moreover, this shared class- and ethnic-based culture and its institutions contrast clearly with the cultural multiplicity of those who were colonized — the Malay *ra'ayat* and the Malay elite; immigrant Indonesians; Chinese differentiated by class, China native-place, and occupation; south Indians working on plantations and for the government, but divided by caste; the Sikhs of the colonial army and police; and many other groups. British attempts, when successful, to direct the members of specific ethnic groups into certain occupations and not others in the colonial division of labor, reinforced these cultural divisions. "Divide and rule," whether deliberate or not, should be seen as a force with a crucial cultural dimension.

Second, it must be pointed out that the material interests of many senior British officials and those of British tin miners and rubber planters coincided, for the former frequently retired to join the boards of directors of London-based rubber estate management agencies and mining companies.[67] As Allen put it,

> "Big Business" meant tin and rubber; neither industry required a particularly large number of Europeans on the spot, and it is difficult to resist the conclusion that there was some sort of alliance between the M.C.S. [Malayan Civil Service] and the London Boards which found expression in the number of top administrators who retired to join these boards, and which was symbolized by the British Malaya Association founded in 1920.[68]

Moreover, many British officials, both senior and junior, while still in service invested their capital in, and speculated with, shares in Malayan tin and rubber companies during this period, and even earlier.[69]

Third, although, as Kratoska points out, the colonial state may have been "committed in a general way" to furthering the welfare of rural Malays, when British capitalist interests were threatened in any serious way by the actions of Malay peasants —or as the subsequent history of the "Emergency" was to show, by the behavior of immigrant Chinese or Indians — then British officials and European planters and tin mine owners and managers joined together to override any official sympathies toward those being colonized. Despite the conflicts and contradictions within the colonial state, a condition of cultural "closure" emerged which suppressed these antagonisms during times of crisis. Here again, the history of rubber regulation during the years of the world depression serves as an excellent illustration. One central feature of such "closure" was that British capitalist interests were able to appeal directly to and lobby for their interests with higher levels of the imperial bureaucracy (the Colonial Office or colonial governors). These latter would direct their occasionally wayward subordinates within the Malayan Civil Service to conform to higher policy. The successful pressure of the Rubber Grower's Association on the Colonial Office, recounted above, can provide an example. The Association of British Malaya represents another.

Fourth, although as Kratoska claims, the British colonial administration was weak on the ground and its power circumscribed accordingly, its coercive and economic power could be, and was, brought to bear strategically at certain "choke points" in the colonial economy. These included its control and administration of import and export trades, of immigration, of land alienation, and in its issuing of permits and licenses. Here again, the coupons required of Malay smallholders to be able to sell their rubber during the years of rubber regulation provide a good example.

Thus, a common class- and ethnic-based culture grounded in formal and informal institutions, shared material interests, cultural closure in times of crisis, recourse by European colonial capitalists to higher levels of imperial administration, and the strategic use of limited colonial state power provided mechanisms which, on the side of the colonizers, promoted the process of primitive accumulation.[70]

While hardly representing the kind of monolithic colonial state power predicted by "world systems" theorists, these mechanisms do imply the existence of means for a far more potent imperialist rule than that implied by the nominalist perspective put forward by Kratoska and others.

The Devolution of Peasant Rubber Production and State Policy

Other than systematic underassessment and over-restriction of Malay smallholding production, the most deleterious effect of the International Rubber Regulation scheme for the Malay peasantry lay in the consequences of prohibiting new planting of rubber while encouraging replanting of rubber acreage already alienated. One cannot assume that British officials fully foresaw the outcome for rural Malays of these provisions of the scheme — though some elementary reflection on the comparative economies of scale for plantation versus smallholding production were certainly not beyond their capacity — or that the provisions were implemented with this outcome in mind. Instead, it appears that the scheme was designed with the interest of the large-scale plantation sector in stabilizing production, prices, and markets as the uppermost aim, while the implications of these provisions for Malay smallholders were simply not considered. Why should they be, in a sense, when Malay smallholders had no representation in the establishment of the scheme, and when, to begin with, European production methods were judged the most "reasonable" by officials and British planters alike? In any event, officials' prohibition of new planting while promoting replanting led to a long-term decline in the (yield) productivity of peasant rubber growing and to the loss of their competitive position vis-à-vis the European and Chinese plantations. How did this come to pass?

The effective economic life of the rubber tree is thirty to forty years. It cannot be tapped until six or seven years after planting. Latex secretion reaches a peak at fifteen years and declines steadily thereafter.[71] Thus, by its fortieth year, the yield of a tree may be so low that, even with extremely low labor costs, it is not worthwhile economically for the producer, even a peasant producer using family labor, to tap the tree. By the thirtieth year or so, the rubber producer should plant a new area with trees, or replant the original area, if he wishes to receive continued minimally sufficient yields in the future.[72]

The provisions prohibiting new planting but allowing replanting thus had critical effects on the reproductive process by which rubber producers maintained their yields over the long term. These provisions had different consequences for peasant smallholders and for plantations. As discussed above, Malay rubber holdings possessed a very high density of trees per acre. In contrast, plantations had relative sparce stands of rubber and vast areas of unplanted land for future cultivation.

It was impossible for most Malay smallholders (with by far the smallest of smallholdings) to replant, as the scheme allowed them to do. Full replanting would have led to a loss of their incomes during the six or seven years after replanting, during which the young rubber trees yielded no latex and could not be tapped. In the economic depression few, if any, could afford such a situation. Partial replanting was also not feasible because of the small size of Malay rubber holdings: from two to five acres, for the vast majority. Further, the administrative procedure for applying to replant was too complicated and unfamiliar for most peasants to understand. The only way for them to regenerate their rubber holdings and maintain their incomes was, paradoxically, to expand them by planting rubber trees on newly alienated land. But this was just what the scheme prohibited.

Unlike most smallholders, plantation managers sought to increase rubber yields by maximizing the yield *per tree* with fewer trees, rather than by maximizing the yield per acre with more trees. There were solid economic and political reasons for their preference, and these favored extensive replanting by plantations. Unlike smallholders, plantations had vast areas with few trees, and thus had no need for more alienated acreage. Instead, the provisions of the scheme allowed them to replant areas of the oldest and least productive rubber stock with high-yielding, bud-grafted trees, while not noticeably affecting total revenues because of the uninterrupted yields in the acreage not yet replanted. Replanting was thus a gradual process, imposing a minimal shock on estate production and incomes.

Not only were plantations allowed to replant, but economic events during the depression encouraged them to do so, unlike the situation for smallholders. The largest component of plantation production costs were, predictably, wages. With the onset of the depression, plantations were "required" to lay off laborers (many of whom were repatriated to India and China at government expense) and to cut wages severely, so as to trim production costs.[73] In a period when world demand for rubber was slack, plantation managers were able to reallocate part of their reduced labor force toward replanting, and away from production. The low wages also enabled plantations to carry out replanting at minimal cost.[74]

Over the long term, replanting with high-yield stock allowed plantations to increase their productivity *per laborer,* since much tapping time consists of going from tree to tree, making a tapping incision, and later emptying the latex cups on each tree. Faced with a depression of indeterminate length and the problems and expenses of importing labor, plantation proprietors and managers sought by replanting to lessen their dependence on immigrant labor, and thus to lower the proportion of wages in the total cost of production. In so doing, plantations were also able to improve their competitive position vis-à-vis peasant producers.

The cumulative effects of the International Rubber Regulation scheme thus undermined peasant rubber production even as they advanced the productivity of the plantations and furthered capital accumulation within the capitalist sector. As a consequence, by 1952 no less than 67 percent of all acreage in rubber held by Malay peasants was in trees more than thirty years old; and 27 percent was in trees older than forty years.[75] That is, two-thirds of all peasant acreage was already or was rapidly becoming economically useless.

Thus the situation of the 1920s had been completely reversed by the 1960s: whereas in 1921 the yields of smallholdings were at least fifty percent greater than those of plantations, by 1960, in contrast, smallholding yields were an average two-thirds of those for plantations, and falling. As one commentator has concluded, "the serious outcome of the planting provisions [of the scheme] was to destroy the long-term competitive ability and prospects of the peasant smallholders and correspondingly to enhance that of the plantation producers."[76]

The Capitalist Business Cycle, Colonial Rice Policy, and the Peasantry

Government measures against peasant rubber producers in this period complemented the other prong of the adminstration's attack on relations of production within the peasant sector: its increasing effort to relegate rural Malays to padi production to feed the immigrant labor force. Viewed statically or from afar, the colonial administration's policy toward Malay rice producers appears to be a contradictory and incoherent mixture of indifference and activism. But what we discover is that British policy closely followed the vagaries of the world capitalist business cycle as these impinged on the Malayan economy.

In times of economic growth, with high tin and rubber prices and, thus, high government export tax revenues, rural Malays were allowed to go their own way. They were neither given encouragement nor severely penalized for not cultivating padi. This was entirely consistent with the custodial ideology of the British regarding Malay society. At these times, British administrators and colonial capitalists alike saw rice imports from Burma and Thailand as sufficient and satisfactory sources of food for the Indian and Chinese laborers of the tin mines and plantations. Massive rice imports kept the costs of the workers' food bill low, thus ensuring low wages, while depressing the price of local padi.

However, in times of recession or depression, as in the years immediately after World War I and again in the 1930s, government export revenues fell, the loss of foreign exchange was decried,[77] and officials and capitalists alike expressed fears that rice imports at a low price would be insufficient, and that food riots would occur among the immigrant labor force. At such times, administrators adopted an aggressive stance toward Malay padi cultivation. Government committees convened to investigate local conditions for padi growing; the recognized Malay elite — members of royal families, *penghulus* and officers of the Malay Administrative Services — were mobilized to persuade peasants to cultivate padi; the laws prescribing padi cultivation on lands alienated to Malays were enforced; and irrigation, drainage, and other projects were started—all with the aim of increasing rice production. (It was only in 1939 at the end of this period that minimum domestic padi price levels were set by the administration. To British officials and the Malay elite, the maintenance of padi cultivation as a "way of life" for Malays far overrode such crass considerations as raising farmers' incomes through price controls.)[78] During these periods of crisis, the price of local padi would rise to a peak for several months or a year; but as the crisis passed, it would then fall again when rice imports were resumed at previous levels. As administrative concern and alarm slackened, the subsidies for irrigation and drainage and for cooperative credit and marketing schemes would then be reduced or abandoned, the regulations requiring padi cultivation less strictly enforced, etc.

Observers have commented previously on the existence of such a cycle, although its close linkages to state policy and the process of primitive accumulation have not been sufficiently recognized. For instance, according to *The Area Handbook on Malaya,*

in the early 1930's, when the terms of trade were adverse, the costs to the economy for the importation of food needs dictated a modification of the exclusive concern with the export sector. As the trade situation was improved, concern with smallholder food production became less, and there was a tendency for enthusiasm for food production to wax and wane with the trade in rubber and tin.[79]

In an historical study of the rice industry of Malaya, Cheng Siok Hwa has remarked of British colonial officials that

> [their] concern with rice production was due partly to the natural desire of any country to grow some of its food requirements, if not all; and partly to the policy of preserving the Malay traditional way of life which is closely associated with padi growing. This interest was more pronounced during trade depressions when Malaya's revenue and income from rubber and tin were seriously reduced and during times of world rice shortage and high rice prices.[80]

During the period from 1920 to 1941, administrative policy toward padi producers passed through two such cycles, the first a minor, the second a major one. In the subsequent postwar period, discussed in the following chapter, yet a third policy cycle is discernible beginning in the years immediately after the Japanese occupation. Cheng has noted precisely the *peaks* of these three cycles of administrative activism:

> The work of these Departments reflects the policy of the Government to attain self-sufficiency in rice as far and as soon as possible. The policy was always there but was intensified during periods of world shortage and high prices, like the period near the end of the First World War, the Great Depression of the early 1930s, [and] the early 1950s during the period of the Korean War boom.[81]

The first cycle, a relatively minor one, occurred during the years from approximately 1917 to 1922. In the war years from 1917 to 1918, officials became alarmed because the wartime shortage of shipping meant that imports of rice would have to be curtailed. With the end of World War I, the price of rubber fell sharply, and from 1918 to 1920 famine in India and drought in Thailand caused rice imports into Malaya to drop steeply. In Malaya, the price of rice rose rapidly. In response British officials set out actively to stimulate domestic padi production. State land was alienated to peasants for padi cultivation, members of the Malay elite were called on to press peasants to increase production, and seed distribution and credit schemes were planned.[82] Due to the increase in price as much as to these strategems, rural Malays increased their production of padi in the Federated Malay States to its highest point in 1920 by opening new padi fields, and, in some cases, returning fields planted to other crops back to padi.This is noted for Krian, Kuala Kangsar, and Lower Perak districts, and for Kuala Pilah, Rembau and Tampin districts in Negri Sembilan.[83] Even so, in order to meet the rice shortage, the government finally imported rice at its own expense in order to feed the plantation and mining populations, depress wages, and maintain profits for colonial enterprise.[84]

By 1922 however, the government had resumed massive imports of rice at low cost. The price of padi fell accordingly, Malay peasants in these areas withdrew from padi production, while government programs to meet the peasantry's needs for credit and for irrigation and drainage facilities fell to a nadir of activity. The outcome was predictable: from 1921 onward, wet padi production declined in the Federated Malay States, reaching its lowest point in several years in the 1926-1927 season.[85]

With the onset of the world depression in 1930, the second cycle of the administration's rice policy began. Based on the experience of the rice import crisis of 1918 to 1920, officials' fears about rice sufficiency again rose to a peak. In 1930 a Rice Cultivation Committee was formed, and it made the first comprehensive report on Malaya's padi production. In 1932 a Department of Drainage and Irrigation was set up that immediately began programs to maintain old irrigation and drainage schemes in established padi areas, while opening up new padi land through large-scale schemes elsewhere. In 1933 a revised *Malay Reservations Enactment* was passed to further prevent non-Malays from owning or acquiring land in Malay Reservations. During the 1930s, more than 350,000 additional acres, much of it highly productive padi land in semicore areas, were declared Reservation land in the Federated Malay States alone.[86] The administration even went so far as to impose an import duty on rice from 1933 to 1935, and used the revenue to finance the new irrigation schemes. At the same time, the laws requiring Malays to plant padi on lands designated for its cultivation were strictly enforced.[87] The "carrot" and "stick" were effective when applied together, for, by the 1936-1937 season, the padi harvest in the Federated Malay States again rose to a peak — 219 percent of the 1926-1927 production. In Kedah it was at its highest for several years in the 1935-1936 season.[88]

By 1935 or so the Malayan economy had at least partially recovered from the depressed tin and rubber prices of five years earlier. At this time, again, official activism toward Malay rice cultivation began to flag, and Malay peasants began to decrease their padi production. The second cycle in the administration's policy (but not the policy itself) toward rice producers came to a close — a cycle abruptly ended by the Japanese Army's invasion of the Malayan peninsula in 1941.

So far as the sparse and aggregated data of the period allow us to determine, rural Malays responded differently to these shifting policy cycles depending on their location in core, semicore, and peripheral areas of the west coast. Malays living in core areas, where they had access to rubber smallholdings, appear to have responded to the complementary pressures and inducements of price changes and government policy shifts by reverting to rubber planting (when they were able to get away with it) and tapping, and to shift their labor out of padi production when these lessened in intensity. Malays in semicore areas where intensive wet-rice cultivation prevailed had fewer options. They increased both wet padi acreage and, when weather permitted, padi production steadily from 1932 onward. It is noteworthy that the major increases in both padi acreage and production for Malaya over these years are those for Kedah and Perak, presumably in Krian and Lower Perak, where the Sungei Manik irrigation project was underway.[89] In these semicore areas, rural Malays were most affected by the government's irrigation and drainage improvements and schemes and by its diffusion of high-yield variety padi seeds. Because other options were limited, they committed themselves to maintaining these enhancements to padi production even when official enthusiasm flagged. At the same time, however, they were those rural Malays who were most victimized by the administrations' overall determination to maintain low padi prices to feed the immigrant proletariat and thus assure colonial capitalist accumulation at whatever cost to the Malay peasantry. Lastly, rural Malays in the peripheral areas of the west coast regions were least affected by these policies, since their remoteness from the main lines of the domestic rice trade made their exploitation as commercial padi producers as unrewarding as it was unlikely.

Taken together, the colonial state's efforts to limit peasant rubber production and curb the competition it posed to European plantation capitalism, combined with policies toward Malay rice cultivation — fluctuating as these did with the business cycle — relegated poor peasants to the conditions of low productivity observed in the postwar period. Malay peasants in core areas found themselves the losers of the rubber restriction years, and yet they had little if any long-term motivation to plant padi, as the administration periodically desired. Peasants in the "rice bowl" semicore areas were held down by the state's commitment to low rice prices, even as its officials cajoled, pressured, and induced them to produce more rice. Peasants in peripheral areas were simply ignored as developments in these years mostly passed them by. The impoverishment of rural Malays was not primarily a result of greedy and exploitative middlemen or moneylenders, though these certainly did exist at times, rather, adverse terms of trade were in the first instance set by the colonial state.

It is not surprising, then, to find the rural Malay peasantry of the postwar period in a state of semipermanent stagnation, migrating extensively from underproductive rural farms to newly-settled lands (such as new irrigation schemes and later FELDA settlement schemes). Nor is it surprising that, when political events made it possible, as during the 1950s and later, they took wholesale flight out of padi production.

CHAPTER SIX

Vicissitudes of Dominion: Japanese Occupation and the Postwar Years, 1941-1957

The fall of Singapore to an invading Japanese army in February 1942 marked the end of the era of unchallenged British political dominance in Malaya. After the end of the Japanese Occupation in 1945, it became clear to Europeans and non-Europeans alike that a new period leading to decolonization and eventual "self-governance" had begun. The divisive issues concerned the timing of the decolonization process, the economic and political conditions under which self-governance would occur — who would benefit, and at whose cost — and the nature of the postcolonial state and its social order.

The spectacular events of these years — a cruel Japanese occupation, Allied victory, demonstrations by Malays against the Malayan Union, labor militance, the insurgency of the Malayan Communist Party (MCP), the declaration of the "Emergency," the forcible resettlement of more than 500,000 rural Chinese into "New Villages," and the formal Independence of Malaya from British rule in 1957 — have obscured those transformations that most greatly affected rural Malays, particularly when viewed in terms of the ideology of the Cold War. They have also hidden the ways in which Malay peasants reacted to, and in several respects, resisted those changes adversely affecting their livelihoods.

British imperial objectives in these years were, first, to defeat the Japanese and regain control of Malaya. After 1945, the goal was to prepare for a smooth and gradual transition to an independent Malayan state — one that would ensure unimpeded capital accumulation for British mining, plantation, and commercial enterprise. Obstacles to achieving these objectives were great.

During the immediate postwar years after the defeat of Japan, there emerged two major blocs opposed to continued British rule. One was composed of a militant Malayan Chinese and Indian working class led by the Malayan Communist Party and hostile to both British political dominance and capitalist exploitation. The other was a congeries of Malay nationalist groups, all seeking independence, but otherwise split into two camps — one composed of groups antagonistic to European (and Asian) capitalism, and the other constituted by the United Malays National Organization (UMNO) and other groups quite willing to accommodate to it through the institutions of bourgeois parliamentary democracy. A triumphal history of decolonization from the British perspective would emphasize the military defeat of the "Communist" bloc during the Emergency and the neutralization of anti-capitalist Malay groups—portrayed as "extremists," "subversives," or even "communists." It would point to the cultivation of a new interethnic Malayan elite dominated by UMNO leaders, followed by the successful transition to independence, political stability and continued economic growth in which British enterprise still played a part.

Nonetheless, another kind of history also needs to be written — a history of the victims of these triumphs of the postwar years.These victims were not only those repressed by the state during the Emergency, for instance, thousands of New Village Chinese who were, in effect, forcibly reintroduced to capitalist "industrial discipline."[1] They were also poorer rural Malays, who suffered from combined neglect and discrimination by state functionaries and, for the first time, direct capitalist exploitation in the waning years of British colonialism. During the postwar years, it was these poorer rural Malays who cultivated the smallest and most unproductive parcels of padi land and rubber smallholdings, who were forced by their low incomes to curb consumption to a bare subsistence level, and who engaged in seasonal or part-time wage labor. It was they who, after Independence, became marginalized in the countryside as increasingly desperate cultivators-cum-laborers. And it was they who began to migrate in great numbers either to cities and towns, where most became full-time wage laborers, or to the new FELDA land resettlement schemes, as described in the next chapter.

The years from 1941 to 1957 can of course be divided into the period of the Japanese occupation from 1941 to 1945 — almost four years of deprivation and subsistence survival by rural Malays — and the postwar period from 1945 to 1957. In what follows, after describing the occupation years, I make several points about the postwar period that bear crucially on the history of rural Malays and their interaction with the late colonial state.

First, during these years, British policies toward rural Malays must be viewed within the context of a strategic response to the threat to British interests posed by the labor militance of the immigrant proletariat and the struggle for independence of the Malayan Communist Party.The British attempted successfully to have Malay peasants act in a variety of ways that supported British rule against this threat, as strikebreakers, police, and army soldiers, and as padi cultivators continually increasing production.

Second, a popular nationalist movement among Malays appeared in these years, one that forged a new and distinctive "Malay" ethnic identity. However, this movement was characterized by contradictions between the differing class elements composing it. These contradictions were overcome by the forcible intervention of the colonial state on the side of the movement's conservative elements — the UMNO leadership — against those that were more progressive.This intervention shaped both the future manifestations of this ethnic identity, and policies toward the peasant sector; thereafter, the latter presupposed a general pro-capitalist orientation toward the serious problems confronting this sector.

Third, the accommodation reached between British officials and UMNO leaders after 1946 to share power in the late colonial state meant that there was a marked policy shift toward rural "development." This shift toward "development" in turn led to the promotion of increased production of peasant cash crops —padi, rubber, and others — as essential for enhanced rural welfare.

After a brief description of the Japanese occupation, I discuss these major features of the postwar period to Independence.

Dominion Lost: The Japanese Occupation, 1941–1945

The Japanese occupation affected the lives of rural Malays in a number of ways — by the disappearance of an international market for rubber, by the exactions of the Japanese on their labor and agricultural products, by the inflation, speculation, and deteriorating conditions of life brought on by war-time scarcity and distress, and by their participation as police and petty officials in the military administration of the Japanese.

For most rural Malays, the fall of British colonial rule in early 1942 and the ascent of Japanese military administration must, at first at least, have seemed to have been a mere change of masters at several removes from the exigencies of day-to-day peasant livelihood. Because the Japanese military administration recognized the Sultans as guardians of Islam in each state and extensively employed Malay aristocrats and other leaders in positions of authority as District Officers, police chiefs, and other middle-level bureaucrats, the Malay *ra'ayat* at first found few differences arising from the change of regime.[2] The Japanese occupiers in general did not interfere with the practice of Islam or Malay village customs.[3]

However, as the war progressed, Japanese demands on rural Malays increased. Rice was requisitioned by "rice policemen" or *mata-mata padi,* labor drafts of *kampong* Malays were instituted, and Japanese-controlled *kumiai* or "syndicates" increasingly monopolized the sale of rationed food items.[4] The loss of income from rubber production, the inflation brought on by a black market, the scarcity of goods, and increased personal violence directed by Japanese soldiers against rural Malays, all combined to lead to dissatisfaction with Japanese rule, to a falling level of consumption, and extensive misery among peasants.[5] Insufficient food, nutritional-deficiency and other diseases, and the lack of Western medicines led to a high mortality rate, at least in some areas.[6] All

the same, preexisting status differences among Malays appear to have been
muted by an equality of deprivation; one local study observed what was no doubt
a far more widespread phenomenon: "society was more egalitarian than ever
before because wealth was not really an advantage owing to the scarcity of
goods."[7]

As the guerrillas of the largely Chinese-manned Malayan Peoples Anti-
Japanese Army (MPAJA) resisted Japanese rule in rural areas, the Japanese
military administration began to employ and train many rural Malays as an
auxiliary army and police force against the resistance movement, eventually
using several thousand altogether.[8] However, according to Cheah, most Malays
saw themselves as being caught in the middle between the Japanese and the
MPAJA forces, "like the proverbial mousedeer between two fighting elephants."[9]

Regardless of this, in the interregnum of late 1945 MPAJA guerrillas in
Johore took violent retribution against those Malay officials, soldiers, and police
whom they viewed as collaborators with the Japanese. In revenge and self-
defense, rural Malays formed the armed Sabilillah movement that attacked rural
Chinese settlements.The movement then spread beyond Johore to other states.
Altogether several hundred people, almost all Chinese, were killed in a variety of
clashes between Chinese farmers and MPAJA guerrillas, and armed Malays.[10]
The experiences of these conflicts were a major source of the generalized
animosity between Malays and Chinese in the immediate postwar years, an
animosity which has shaped both political practice and discourse along ethnic
lines up to the present.[11]

During the occupation, for a minority of Malay intellectuals, who in 1938
had formed the *Kesatuan Melayu Muda (KMM)* or "Young Malay Union," the
anti-British sentiments of the Japanese were congenial to their nationalist and
populist aspirations.[12] According to Roff, the *KMM* was "vaguely Marxist in
ideology, and reflected both a strong anti-colonial spirit and opposition to the
'bourgeois-feudalist' leadership of the traditional elite."[13] Before the occupation,
it had been a small organization advocating independence from colonial rule and
the unification of Malaya and the territory of the Netherlands East Indies within
one Malay "nation," *Indonesia Raya,* or "Greater Indonesia." A large number of
its members were vernacular schoolteachers who were graduates of the Sultan
Idris Training College in Tanjong Malim.[14]

With the invasion successful, in 1942 the Japanese administration sought
out and managed to coopt the leaders of the *KMM,* in particular Ibrahim Yaacob,
into the occupation government. *KMM* leaders were accorded special privileges
denied other Malays, including the Sultans and the aristocratic-administrative
elite, and became patrons to Malay peasants by extending them protection.
Although the *KMM* was disbanded by the Japanese later in 1942, its leaders were
allowed to continue to play a major role during the occupation period in calling

for the independence of Malaya from Britain and the unification of Malaya and Indonesia in *Indonesia Raya*.[15] Ibrahim Yaacob and other *KMM* members were recruited by the Japanese to lead the *Giyu Gun*, "Volunteer Army," known in Malay as *Pembela Tanah Ayer* or PETA. PETA was to be employed as an auxiliary force to defend Malaya against the British; they eventually commanded a contingent of 2,000 soldiers, almost all Malays.[16] In early 1945, as the Japanese war position deteriorated, Ibrahim Yaacob and other *KMM* veterans came to an agreement with the military administration to allow them to organize a new association for pan-Indonesian independence against the British and the Dutch, known *as Kesatuan Rakyat Indonesia Semananjung* or *KRIS*, "Union of Peninsular Indonesians."[17] In early August, 1945, one week before the Japanese surrender, *KRIS* members met in Malaya with Sukarno and Hatta, leaders of the Indonesian independence movement, to prepare for the declaration of an independent state based on *Indonesia Raya*. A meeting of *KRIS* leaders and members of the Malay aristocratic elite was held, but the sudden Japanese surrender and the unilateral declaration of Indonesian independence without Malaya undercut the base of support of *KRIS*, and the organization was disbanded.[18] As to the significance of the *KMM*, and one could apply the same point to *PETA* and *KRIS*, Cheah states that "its single major contribution was no doubt the resurgence of Malay nationalism."[19]

Dominion Regained: The Postwar Years Through Independence

For the years between 1945 and approximately 1950, British policies toward rural Malays must be viewed as part of a strategic response to the threat to British imperial and capitalist interests posed by the labor militance of the immigrant proletariat and by the struggle for independence by the Malayan Communist Party. These should be seen not only as they challenged the viability of Malayan capitalism per se, but also the attainment of more inclusive imperial goals, in particular, the maintenance of sterling area balance of payments vis-à-vis the United States. Within this overall strategy, Malay peasants, like their leaders, were co-opted as political and military allies in the state's campaigns against both Communist insurgency and non-Malay working-class militance, while — at least in "rice bowl" areas — they increased their cultivation of padi, and otherwise were left to their own devices.

Colonial Capitalism in Crisis and Policies Toward The Peasantry

The postwar years from 1945 to 1947 were marked by the most serious challenge ever posed to capitalist domination in colonial Malaya. This included the widespread and well-organized strikes, demonstrations, worksite occupations, and clashes with police, and formation of trade unions mounted by a militant and unified labor movement of Chinese and Indian laborers led by the Pan-Malayan and Singapore General Labour Unions and, through these, the Malayan Communist Party.[20] Stenson, Gamba, and others have described the sources of popular grievance among both urban and rural immigrant laborers which led them to adopt these extreme actions.[21] What appears to have been at issue were violations by employers of implicit agreements between capital and labor over just wages and benefits in the face of a drastically increased cost of living, extreme rice scarcity, and the failure of employers to increase wages and other benefits correspondingly.[22] From 1945 to 1947 employers were forced to make large wage and other concessions to militant Chinese and Indian laborers, who were coordinated in their strike actions by the General Labour Unions throughout Malaya and Singapore. According to Stenson, the Pan-Malayan General Labour Union represented a "genuinely popular movement" whose strikes led to a "major improvement in wages, conditions and benefits" for Chinese and Indian workers.[23]

For the British Military Administration (BMA) which assumed power upon the Japanese surrender, and for British employers alike, the immediate postwar years were a time of great crisis. The labor movement organized by the MCP was strong and broadly based, European prestige had suffered a severe blow from the ignominious defeat by the Japanese in 1941, British military and administrative power were weak and too widely deployed on the ground, and the militance of labor toward employers was reinforced by a severe labor scarcity. In contrast to the weak positions of both the government and employers, the MCP, through its organizational and ideological support of the Federations of Trade Unions as well as its reputation as the core of the MPAJA resistance movement during the occupation, had attained its apex of power and influence. Seeing the immigrant proletariat as the revolutionary class, Communist leaders were committed to the overthrow of British rule, the establishment of a "Malayan Peoples Republic," and the socialization/nationalization of European-owned private enterprise. These objectives were well known to British officials through their police intelligence.[24]

In the immediate postwar years and the years of the Emergency that followed (1948-1960), the overriding concern of the successive colonial administrations (the BMA, the Malayan Union in 1947, the Federation of Malaya from 1948 onward) was to establish the order and stability — the "security" — required to quell the demands made by a mobilized immigrant working class. In addition, they sought to destroy the power of the MCP and return to the superficially placid conditions of labor exploitation of the *status quo ante bellum,* but within the new framework of eventual decolonization and "self governance."

One of the first concerted measures taken by the colonial state from 1947 to 1948 was the repression of the MCP and its front organizations (the Federations of Trade Unions, the Malayan Democratic Union, the MPAJA Ex-Service Comrades Association, and others) by the banning of the Party and its organizations, and by the arrest, detention, and later banishment of MCP leaders, by raids on organization offices, and seizures of property. The response by the Party to these actions was the initiation of an insurgency against the British state and against British plantation, industrial, and mining enterprise.[25] This, in turn, led to the declaration by the colonial state of the "Emergency," the publication of its draconian Emergency Regulations, and the initiation of counterinsurgency measures.[26] In addition to the MCP and its front organizations, one of the first targets of these actions was the anti-capitalist wing of the Malay nationalist movement, described below, as parties and associations such as the Malay Nationalist Party, API, and AMCJA-PUTERA were banned and their leaders arrested and jailed.[27]

British policies toward rural Malays in these years were shaped by these events and the strategic British response to them, as well as by more encompassing imperial concerns. British officials called on rural Malays to act as strikebreakers against the militant actions of immigrant laborers.They co-opted *kampong* Malays into the counterinsurgency campaign by employing them as police and army soldiers to fight the MCP guerrillas. They promoted anti-Communist and anti-Chinese sentiments (since most MCP guerrillas were Chinese) among Malays through their propaganda, thereby consolidating a hostile buffer zone of Malay villages between the mountain- and forest-based MCP guerrilla units and their military and industrial targets.[28] Above all, British pressured rural Malays to increase their cultivation of rice, for several reasons, both domestic and imperial.

Subaltern Classes Divided: Malay Peasants, Chinese Squatters, Indian Laborers, and Counterinsurgency

During the years from 1947 onward, British officials and employers provided rural Malays with wage-labor opportunities at a time when, as discussed below, poorer *kampong* residents grew increasingly desperate in their attempts to find seasonal and temporary employment to sustain their livelihoods; at the same time, the employment provided buttressed both the anti-labor efforts of capitalist employers and the counterinsurgency campaign of the administration. This ironic connection between the emergent crisis of livelihood among rural Malays and the reactionary strategies of colonial capitalists and officials has had consequences that have lasted up to the present.

Beginning in 1947, British and Malay colonial officials recruited rural Malays as non-unionized strikebreakers to defeat the militant Indian and Chinese labor unions on plantations and elsewhere.[29] As Stenson has pointed out, this confluence of "supply" and "demand" in the colonial labor market had profound long-term implications for the possibility for unity among the diverse ethnic fractions of Malaysian subaltern classes:

> the mid-1940's witnessed the beginning of a trend that was to be of major long-term significance, the entry of increasing numbers of Malay peasants into the industrial labor force. After 1948 there was never again to be widespread employer concern about labor shortages. The effect was two-fold: first, to reduce the bargaining power of the existing labor force, and second, to delay indefinitely the formation of a truly united, self-conscious working class.[30]

Kampong Malays also began to join government employment in substantial numbers in this period, in positions supporting the counterinsurgency effort. Malays were recruited as "Special Constables" and army soldiers to fight the MCP guerrillas. Other rural Malays became general laborers, truck drivers, and postmen for the administration.[31] In this way, the antagonisms toward Chinese recently reinforced in Malays by the violent retribution against "collaborators" by the triumphant MPAJA guerrillas in 1945 and by the armed clashes between Malays and Chinese that followed were exploited to the full by the colonial administration. Thus, paradoxically, rural Malays bore a disproportionate burden of the cost of this campaign, even though they had been driven in large part to seek government employment because of the long-term effects of policies toward the peasant sector. Again, the colonial state had succeeded in dividing one ethnic fraction of a subaltern class off from another, for the main supporters of the MCP guerrillas were rural Chinese workers, farmers and squatters, and Indian estate laborers. Their repression and demoralization became the principal task of the counterinsurgency forces, of whom large numbers were Malays.

Of Padi Farming, Labor Militance, Low Wages, and Balance of Payments

One major preoccupation of officials in the early years of the Emergency was to assure a supply of rice on the domestic market sufficient to prevent a recurrence of the widespread militance among Chinese and Indian laborers of 1945 to 1947 which had occurred in part due to widespread rice scarcity. In addition, they wanted to maintain low prices, and thus low wages, in the plantation, mining, and urban industrial sectors.

This was, indeed, quite explicit in the statement of colonial officials and employers.[32] In 1948 the Secretary of State for the Colonies commissioned two Labour Party trade unionists to investigate the situation of labor and trade unions in Malaya, in order to advise on policies that would lead to "responsible" (i.e., compliant) trade unionism. According to the report of S. S. Awbery and F.W. Dalley, "in all our discussions we got back sooner or later to the same point. 'If only', said employers, workers and officials alike, 'there was a sufficient supply of rice at a reasonable price, industrial troubles would be solvable.'"[33] And one of the trade unionists' major recommendations was that:

> So far as Malaya is concerned the increase of rice production . . . is clearly of the first importance. We understand that a special investigation is now being made. We can only stress its urgency and reiterate that the solution of many, if not most of Malaya's industrial troubles depends on the availability for consumption of more and cheaper rice.[34]

The actions and policies of the colonial administration vis-à-vis the Malay peasantry were inextricably intertwined with this goal: while the Chinese and Indian proletariat was to be forcibly returned to the conditions of exploitation of the prewar period, rural Malay cultivators were to play their part, when needed, to assure a reliable supply of rice at low cost to this proletariat, thus making possible both low wages and industrial harmony.

In the years from 1945 to 1950, British policies toward rural Malays were also shaped by imperial concerns. One of these was the problem of the Sterling area's balance of payments with respect to the United States, in light of Great Britain's accumulated debt servicing from World War II, and of its continuing current balance of payments deficits. During these years, Malaya was *the principal* earner of American dollars for the sterling area comprised of Great Britain and its colonies, and itself had a positive balance of payments with respect to the United States. Rubber and tin in turn were the major sources for this positive balance.[35]

The economic and strategic value of Malaya to Great Britain goes far toward explaining the ferocity with which the British administration attacked the labor movement of the postwar years and prosecuted its counterinsurgency campaign during the Emergency as means of protecting vital British plantation, mining, industrial, and commercial interests. In addition, similar considerations about balance of payments for Malaya itself reinforced official commitments to Malayan rice self-sufficiency for the domestic reasons just noted. According to Rudner, "the dominant agricultural policy objective imputed to the DDP [Draft Development Plan for 1950-1955] was to lessen Malaya's dependence on imported rice through increased domestic production. . . . Sterling area balance of payments interests impelled the British to try to minimize imports of foodstuffs."[36] However, in order to understand the causes of formation of state policies and practices toward the Malay peasant during these years, it is necessary to go beyond *British* Malayan and imperial official concerns. For during these same years, as the British sought to guarantee an "orderly transition" to "self-governance" while quelling labor discontent and Communist insurgency, they had to come to terms with a growing and increasingly powerful

Malay nationalist movement. They had to come to share power with the leaders of this movement — but with only those who, like them had an appreciation of the colonial private enterprise system.

Malay Nationalism, Repression of the Malay Left, and British-UMNO Accommodation: Constraints on State Policy Toward the Peasantry

During the late 1940s, a popular nationalist movement among urban and rural Malays emerged that led to the formation of a new "imagined community"[37] based on a distinctive "Malay" ethnic identity. But this movement was characterized by contradictions between the differing class elements composing it. In part an outcome of social and political processes underway during the interwar period, this movement had its immediate origins in opposition to, on one hand, continued British rule, and to the perceived imminent threat of non-Malay political dominance embodied in the Malayan Union proposals, on the other.

From these years onward, this movement provided the political, cultural, and religious institutions and ideologies that sustained a new social identity among "Malays." For the first time, this new identity within the national political arena overrode the disparate and, at times, antagonistic identities that had arisen from the colonial experience among Malays in different regions of the peninsula. Examples of these contrastively defined identities were Perak Malays vs. Johore Malays; indigenous Malays vs. Javanese, Menangkebau, Banjarese or Achenese; *anak negeri* ("children of the *negeri*") vs. *anak dagang* ("outsiders"); *Melayu Jati* ("true Malays") vs. *Jawi Peranakan* (Muslims of mixed Indian-Malay descent), some of which have been discussed in previous chapters.[38]

Thus an outcome of this movement was the appearance of a new self-conscious identity placing a claim on all Malays as followers of Islam, subjects of the Rulers of their states (that is, being in a condition of *kerajaan*), speakers of the Malay language and those acting in accordance with Malay custom. This new identity was one which was opposed at the most encompassing level to the identities of all non-Malays, but particularly the Chinese, who were seen as "overrunning" Malaya economically and now it was feared, with the Malayan Union proposals, politically as well.

The postwar Malay nationalist movement was not unitary, but rather was riven by what was, in effect, a struggle between two classes. With respect to the Malay peasantry, the history of conflict within this movement is important because its outcome was one that institutionalized the generally pro-capitalist policies that the late colonial state, and after Independence the contemporary Malaysian state, imposed on the peasant sector. Moreover, the rapproachment between the British and the UMNO leaders who emerged triumphant from this struggle explains changes in policies toward rural Malays — changes that ostensibly began to emphasize their welfare — in the last years of colonial rule. What were the two classes contesting for control of the postwar nationalist movement? On one side, there were Malay-educated intellectuals who were descendants of peasant *ra'ayat,* who were committed, albeit at times only vaguely, to socialism, to a pan-Indonesian Malay national identity, and to a strong anti-colonial and even anti-"feudal" position. On the other side, there was the Malay administrative-aristocratic elite, who showed strong sympathies for British rule and colonial capitalist enterprise, and vested Malay political and religious interests in the Sultan or Ruler of each state. This struggle was, in effect, resolved by the British, who favored members of the latter class, the leaders of UMNO, as their heirs to political power in the transition to "self governance." They repressed the anti-capitalist elements within the nationalist movement, in particular members of the former class who led and supported the mass movement represented by the Malay Nationalist Party. Thus the path that the postwar Malay nationalist movement was to take was determined negatively by British actions. This was true also, in a broad sense, for subsequent policies toward the peasant sector, policies which shied away from fundamental land reform and redistribution, and promoted instead capitalist "market-oriented" solutions to the problems of this sector.

The first popular manifestation of Malay nationalism appeared in 1946 with the demonstrations by Malays against the Malayan Union plan which had just been imposed on the Rulers by the McMichael Mission. The proposals of this plan gave new citizenship rights to Chinese and Indians, curbed the sovereignty and many of the traditional privileges of the Sultans and other royalty, and initiated a widespread administrative centralization designed to integrate more efficiently the governments of the Straits Settlements, the Federated Malay States, and the Unfederated Malay States.[39] In early 1946, thousands of Malays in Kedah, Johor, Selangor, and in the eastern states protested vigorously against this plan. For Malays, the Malayan Union scheme violated previous understandings given by the British to them; as Funston put it, "Malays believed that beyond the special position the British had till then given them, lay recognition that the British were dealing with a nation *(bangsa)* not a community, whose homeland was *Tanah Melayu* (Land of the Malays)," and it was this that the scheme transgressed.[40] The origins of the different nationalist movements that these protests unified, however temporarily, lay in the activity of various Malay groups in the years before the war.

Roff and others have analyzed in detail the sources of Malay nationalism during and before the interwar period.[41] According to Roff, by the late 1930s, there were three contending streams of Malay nationalism, each composed of organizations founded and organized by a specific intellectual elite: "the 'Arabic'-educated religious reformists," "the largely Malay-educated radical intelligentsia" of the *Kesatuan Melayu Muda,* and "the English-educated administrators recruited mainly from the traditional ruling class."[42]

The interests of the "'Arabic'-educated religious reformists"were primarily cultural (through the newspaper *Saudara* and the literary association *Sahabat Pena,* "Friends of the Pen").[43] The latter two elites came from different class backgrounds, had contrasting orientations toward both capitalism and European rule, and contested for leadership and control of the mass-based movement arising from the protests against the Malayan Union.

"The radical intelligentsia" were vernacular-educated schoolteachers and journalists, many of whom were graduates of the Sultan Idris Training College in Tanjong Malim founded by the British as the only Malay-language teachers' college in the interwar period.[44] According to Roff, Sultan Idris students "were drawn by competitive examination from village vernacular schools — the sons for the most part of peasant farmers and fishermen."[45] The establishment of and participation in *KMM* by Ibrahim Yaacob and other graduates, and later during the Japanese occupation, in *PETA* and *KRIS* have been described above.

In late 1945, radical intellectuals who had been members of *KMM-KRIS* joined with others, including Malays belonging to the MCP, to form the Malay Nationalist Party (MNP)[46]. If Ahmad Boestamam's account is to be believed, founders included he himself and another associate with *KMM-KRIS experiences,* several friends on the staff of the Ipoh daily newspaper *Suara Rakyat* ("Voice of the People"), and Malays in the MCP led by Mokhtaruddin Lasso.[47] Like its *KMM* predecessor, the MNP advocated socialism and a "vehement anti-colonialism,"[48] and supported the Indonesian independence movement and a Malay identity based on a "Greater Indonesia." In 1946 this party joined the United Malays National Organization (UMNO), the broad-based coalition of opposition to the Malayan Union. But three months later the MNP left UMNO in opposition to the conservatism of its leaders.[49]

During the next five years of struggle against UMNO and its accommodation with British rule, the MNP gained much support among Malays. According to Funston, "it has been widely accepted that MNP and its offshoots did not gain a popular following, but the available evidence suggests a different conclusion. Membership, variously estimated at between 60,000 and 100,000, may well have been similar to that of UMNO."[50] The MNP became a major partner in a loose coalition of left-wing Malay groups called PUTERA, which in turn became part of the joint front of all major leftist organizations (including those of non-Malays) opposed to British-UMNO cooperation — the All-Malayan Council of Joint Action-PUTERA front. The AMCJA-PUTERA front carried out a nation-wide general strike in October 1947.[51] The MNP also formed a close alliance with the *Majlis Agama Tertinggi Se-Malaya* (MATA), or Pan-Malayan Supreme Religious Council, led by Islamic reformists.Thus, according to Funston, "the post-war years then saw a coming together of the left-wing and Islamic reformist streams of Malay nationalism."[52]

Arrayed against the MNP as a contender for the leadership of the postwar nationalist movement was the English-educated administrative-aristocratic elite, about whose origins much has been written.[53] By 1941, participation by educated Malays in the upper levels of the colonial bureaucracy had reached its highest level with approximately 150 Malays throughout the peninsula, and ninety in the Federated Malay States, occupying official posts in the Malay Administrative Service and at the lowest rungs of the elite Malayan Civil Service as district officers, magistrates, and land officers.[54] Most were of "gentle birth," *anak baik-baik,* being the descendants of the royal families or of the precolonial aristocracy, though a few fortunate *ra'ayat* were admitted. Almost all those from the Federated Malay States were recruited into the bureaucracy after graduation from the Malay College at Kuala Kangsar, where they received an English-language simulacrum of a British elite "public school" education. The College was known variously as the "Eton of the East," or as *Bab-ud-Darajat,* "The Gate to High Positions."[55] Most of those from Kedah and Johore, also *anak baik-baik,* were recruited directly into the state bureaucracies without benefit of this education, although there were a few exceptions, the most famous being Dato' Onn bin Ja'afar.[56]

In the late 1930s, members of this administrative-aristocratic elite had been the founders and key members of the *Persatuan Melayu,* or "Malay Associations" that formed in each state. The objectives of these associations were to pressure the British to continue to act as the guardians of Malay rights, to assure the sovereignty and privileges of the Sultans, to cooperate with other state Malay associations in efforts to benefit the Malay "race," and to support Great Britain in the early war effort[57] —objectives that reflected, in large measure, the material interests of this elite.

In 1945, after the McMichael Mission sought to impose the Malayan Union plan upon the Sultans, it was this elite — led by Dato' Onn bin Ja'afar — that provided the vanguard of Malay opposition to the scheme; its interests, after all, were those most threatened by the plan, after those of the Sultans. Dato' Onn and his supporters lobbied British officials against the plan, pressured the Sultans to resist British blandishments to accept it, and convened a Congress of all Malay associations opposed to the plan in Kuala Lumpur in March 1946. At the Congress, UMNO was founded.[58]

Informal lobbying and threats by UMNO leaders of impending Malay violence against the British, UMNO-sponsored demonstrations, direct protests by the Sultans, and intensive pressure by retired British administrators in London on Parliament, memories of violent conflicts between rural Malays and Chinese during the interregnum, and the militance of the Communist-led labor

movement, all seemed to have entered into the British Colonial Office decision
to rescind the Malayan Union scheme. By late July 1946, British representatives
had begun to meet with UMNO leaders to draft the agreement for what became,
after the interlude of the Malayan Union, the Federation of Malaya from 1948 to
Independence.[59] Under this agreement, the sovereignty and privileges of the
Sultans were reaffirmed and UMNO political supremacy was, in effect, ensured
through the establishment of a "Working Committee" that the British were bound
to consult. In addition, the British gave promises of independence in the near
future, and citizenship requirements for non-Malays, although liberalized from
the prewar period, were made far more strict than under the Malayan Union
scheme.[60]

     One of the conditions imposed by the British as part of the accommodation
between the colonial administration and UMNO was that there be constitutional
guarantees in the Federation that non-Malay economic activity — that of British,
Chinese, and Indian private enterprise — would remain unimpeded. In the years
that followed, the British also made it clear to UMNO that one precondition of
independence was the establishment of extensive cooperation between UMNO
leaders and the wealthiest Chinese and Indian capitalists, who were also the
recognized leaders of these "communities" — cooperation that would take the
form of active consultation between these elites and coordination of electoral
campaigns. With the founding of the Malaysian Chinese Association (MCA) in
1949, controlled by wealthy Chinese capitalist interests, and the UMNO-MCA
coalition leading to electoral victories in the Kuala Lumpur municipal elections
in early 1951, a successful formula for converting political necessity into mutual
electoral advantage through elite interethnic cooperation was found. Under
Tunku Abdul Rahman this arrangement was formalized as the Alliance, the
ruling coalition composed of UMNO, MCA, and the Malayan Indian Congress,
which dominated electoral politics until the declaration of independence in 1957.
Thus it was that members of the Malay administrative-aristocratic elite, who by
the early 1950s began to share direct executive power with the British through
the "Member" system, came to regard both European and Asian capitalist
interests as close to their own. This was an attitude that was to change after the
ethnic riots of May 13, 1969 and the inception of the New Economic Policy in
1971, as discussed in chapter 8.

     It is important to observe, however, that UMNO dominance of the Malay
nationalist movement and the defeat of the Malay left in the years between 1945
and 1950 did not come about as a mere reflex of UMNO's popularity as the
future midwife of Malayan independence under the Federation agreement,
although no doubt British promises of independence through UMNO did draw
off some supporters from Malay leftist organizations. All the same, as mentioned
above, in the late 1940s, the number of MNP members was about the same as

UMNO's. Rather, it was state repression of various organizations on the Malay left that provided UMNO with a clear field on which to accommodate to British terms for decolonization. In 1947, API (*Angkatan Pemuda Insaf,* "Generation of Aware Youth"), the youth wing of the MNP led by Ahmad Boestamam, was banned; in 1948, with the declaration of the Emergency, so too were many of the organizations belonging to the PUTERA side of the AMCJA-PUTERA alliance. At that time, large numbers of PUTERA officials were arrested and detained. The MNP was itself banned in 1950.[61]

It is of course impossible to know what would have been the outcome of the struggle within the Malay nationalist movement if the colonial state had not repressed the left wing of this movement. And, even if the left had emerged victorious, it is by no means clear what views on the causes of Malay peasant poverty were held by the leaders of the MNP and other leftist groups, much less would have been implemented within a power-sharing arrangement with the British. According to Ahmad Boestamam, the MNP did form a peasant division called *Barisan Tani Sa-Malaya, (BATAS),* the "All-Malaya Peasant Front," and "BATAS did arouse a kind of awareness — awareness of the need to unite, to organize, to love one's people and homeland, and so on."[62] But he also adds that BATAS did not achieve the same popularity as other MNP divisions. And he gives no description of what MNP policies toward the peasant sector were like — whether they would have called for fundamental land reform or collective peasant production, for instance. A plausible speculation is that, had MNP been allowed to survive, this would have been the case. Nonetheless, what can be stated with more assurance is that the defeat of the Malay left wing almost certainly *precluded* the possibilities of land reform, communal rural production, or similar transformations as options within post-colonial Malaysian society.[63] In any event, it can be said without fear of contradiction that these have not, as yet, ever occurred on the Malaysian landscape.

An indigenous Malay radical tradition created in these years which could be drawn upon endured through the 1950s, and has shown new manifestations periodically — whenever and wherever state power has allowed — in the four decades since then. The heirs of this tradition have varied in their orientations. Some leftist Malays joined the Malayan Communist Party and participated in the ongoing guerrilla insurgency, which ended only in 1989. Those in PAS, the Pan-Malayan Islamic Party, combined rural Malay populism with ideas of Islamic reform[64]; PAS gained control of the government of Kelantan state in the 1950s for several years, and has contested UMNO electoral hegemony off and on since then. One of PAS's presidents was Dr. Burhanuddin Al-Helmy, a founding officer of the MNP. The Partai Rakyat Malaya joined Marhaenist (Sukarnoist) populism with a socialist program, and cooperated with a non-Malay working-class party, the Labor Party, in the Socialist Front from 1957-1965; the first president of Partai Rakyat was Ahmad Boestamam of the MNP and API.[65] In the 1970s, a revived Partai Rakyat challenged UMNO electoral supremacy in the eastern state of Trengganu.

The triumph of an overall pro-capitalist orientation toward the peasantry and peasant production, and the cultivation by the British of the UMNO leaders as their heirs to rule meant, given the parliamentary electoral system that the British sought to install, that as UMNO power became entrenched, state policies and programs seeking manifestly to improve the welfare of the peasant sector became more frequent and salient. Thus, toward the late 1950s and into the post-Independence period, there was a general shift within the state and its bureaucracy from "custody" goals to "development" goals.[66] This change may have been eased by a new generation of British officials in the late 1940s, "thinking themselves possessed of a brief to prepare Malaya for self-government," and with specialized administrative training. They replaced many of the previous generation of Oxford and Cambridge graduates, gentlemanly generalists as most were, who had been interned during the occupation, and retired prematurely.[67] It was certainly reinforced by the influential World Bank Mission to Malaya of 1954, whose report provided the basis for the First Malayan Plan from 1956 to 1960.[68]

The shift toward "development" led to the promotion of increased rural production of cash crops — of increased padi output and increased yields in rubber smallholdings through replanting — which was viewed as essential for enhanced rural welfare. This was in line with the notion, beloved by World Bank consultants and mainstream development economists, that growth in aggregate rural production would somehow lead to increases in incomes for the entire rural population, and thus to overall improvements in rural welfare.

Paradoxically, "development" goals towards Malay padi production were completely consistent with previous "custody" goals of the early Emergency period — in both cases the call was to increase output. At the same time, in the case of rubber, the new policies aimed at replanting smallholdings, which by these years had devolved into underproductive holdings due to the restriction schemes of the interwar period, eventually reversed the previous market dominance by European plantations.

In return for rural Malay electoral support, the "new men of power" — the leaders of UMNO — and thus the British also, sought to respond to what they viewed as the needs of Malay peasants, albeit within the general framework of capitalist growth. During these years, at national and regional levels, these needs tended to be interpreted in terms of a lack of physical infrastructure — roads, schools, irrigation, etc. The provision of such infrastructure became a major goal of development programs, and was seen as providing rural Malays with evidence of the government's concern for their welfare.[69] However, ethnographic evidence from Malay *kampong* suggests that underlying UMNO popularity at the local level was a patronage system in place by the 1950s. Thus UMNO leaders ensured that their peasant followers would vote as directed for UMNO or Alliance candidates in return for various spoils that these leaders could provide —favors in gaining access to government programs or jobs, but also sharecropping and wage labor work provided directly and indirectly by these leaders.[70] Related to this patronage system were specific redistributive practices in Malay villages, discussed in the next chapter.

Expansion of Padi Production, Policy Cycles, and Rural Destitution

Within the framework of accommodation between the British and UMNO favoring economic growth under capitalist conditions of "development," the late colonial state sought to stimulate the expansion of padi growing among rural Malays from the late 1940s onward. In these efforts it was largely successful, for, by 1960, padi farmers had more than doubled their volume of padi production from its figure in the late 1940s.[71] This occurred despite clear evidence that padi growing was the least remunerative agricultural activity among the major subsistence strategies available to rural Malays. And, during this period, yet a third policy cycle by the state toward the padi-growing sector — activism followed by indifference manifested in government actions — can be inferred. As in the previous two policy cycles, peasant response to government policies depended on their location in Malayan regional economies: in general, peasant livelihoods in the "ricebowl" semicore areas were those most negatively affected.

During the postwar decade of 1945 to 1955, the administration sought to attain rice self-sufficiency and to expand peasant padi production in two major ways. First, it reinstituted a Guaranteed Minimum Price offered to peasant rice cultivators;[72] and second, it implemented schemes both to improve irrigation and drainage in preexisting areas of commercial rice cultivation (i.e., semicore areas) and to open new land to cultivation by constructing irrigation facilities.[73] As well, from 1945 to 1949, rice was rationed to consumers and a maximum retail price was set.[74] Under the Draft Development Plan of 1950, the ambitious goals of improving the irrigation facilities of 300,000 acres already in padi production, and of opening an additional 100,000 acres for padi, were set.[75] Finally, with rice imports still scarce and prices high, the administration convened a Rice Production Committee in the early 1950s to investigate the causes of Malaya's poor padi yields, and to propose ways in which yields could be increased. Most members of the Committee were either British officials or representatives of the UMNO leadership.[76]

Under the conditions I have described, rural Malays in semicore areas sought to make the best of a bad situation by responding to the relatively high

(high relative to earlier years, that is, not to prices for other commercial crops) prevailing market prices for rice of the early postwar years and took advantage of government programs, when they could. In the new areas opened by government irrigation and drainage schemes, Malays planted new padi fields; in established padi areas improved by the irrigation schemes, they also increased padi production. Relative to total wet padi acreage planted in the 1939-1940 season, peasants expanded their acreage by an increase of 13.6 percent in 1950-1951. They increased their total wet-padi production by a peak increase of 29.5 percent, using the same two seasons again for comparison.[77] Padi imports were still scarce, with demand reaching a peak in 1950 and 1951 due to the Korean War.

However, by the end of this decade in 1955, as rice imports at low prices became assured and the financial costs of the new schemes became obvious, initial administrative enthusiasm for stimulating domestic padi production began to wane. The goals set in the Draft Development Plan for amounts of acreage to be improved or opened for padi cultivation through government-financed schemes for irrigation and drainage were discreetly lowered, while "this reduction in irrigation targets reflected the shifting economic priorities of the colonial government as the 1950s progressed, away from the output goals previously assigned to foodcrop agriculture."[78] The administration's achievements, in terms of acreage improved or opened by new irrigation and drainage schemes, proved to be even more modest than the reduced goals of the plan.[79] Rudner summarizes the administration's perspective in 1953 on padi cultivation at this time as follows:

> although official rhetoric regularly attached great importance to increasing domestic rice production, in practice public investment in foodcrop agriculture tended to be systematically subordinated to other claims on public finance. Agricultural policy, as conceived, suffered a lack of funding and the absence of any real sense of urgency.[80]

By the end of this period, the slackening of administrative efforts to encourage domestic padi production had become evident. The crucial shift in government policy was revealed in 1955, when the prevailing wholesale market price of imported padi fell below the minimum figure which Malay padi farmers *expected* to be offered by the government on the basis of past years' practice. The market price for imported padi fell due to large surplus padi harvests in Burma and Thailand, with imports into Malaya being unrestricted. Administration officials, having foreseen this eventuality, instead of announcing a price comparable to the Guaranteed Minimum Price of $17 per pikul at the mill door offered peasants the previous year, postponed setting the price until the 1954-55 padi planting season had already begun in Malaya. For their part, Malay padi farmers in semicore areas planted large areas in anticipation of a guaranteed price at least equivalent to that offered by the administration the previous year. However, when an official price of $12 per pikul was announced late in the season, padi cultivators suffered severe losses. Rural tenant cultivators, in particular, were caught up short because of rents owed — which, as mentioned above, were increasing annually at a high rate — and suffered serious hardships.[81] In reaction, padi farmers protested vociferously, as I discuss in chapter 7.

The slackened official commitment to rice self-sufficiency was evident in the government's rationale for manipulating peasant expectations while lowering the Guaranteed Minimum Price, which Rudner describes as follows:

> official attitudes towards rice agriculture took on a curious ambiguity: on the one hand, the lowered price guarantee was justified as an indicator to marginal rice producers to shift into more gainful occupations, notably rubber tapping . . . on the other, it was insisted that "the easing of tension in international rice affairs . . . give no grounds for complacency, and the intensification of local production . . . is still the policy of government."[82]

As in previous periods, early official activism gave way to the subsequent luxury of such ambivalence, and to the indifference to the welfare of the padi sector it reflected. Through the 1950s and into the 1960s, the government's Guaranteed Minimum Price to padi farmers remained above the world market price reflected in the price offered for imported padi, which steadily decreased in proportion over this period. But was this price an "effective subsidy" to Malay padi growers as one commentator[83] has claimed, in addition to the irrigation, drainage, and other facilities provided by the state to farmers during this decade?

What is most important here is that the Guaranteed Minimum Price and the irrigation and drainage facilities provided by the state represented a set of economic constraints *against* rural Malays moving *out of* padi production into alternative, more economically rewarding occupations. At the same time they neither redressed major problems (such as the extremely small size of farm plots which would have required both land reform and the opening of government Reserves to unrestricted Malay settlement), nor provided a guaranteed price sufficiently high to offset the rapidly increasing cost of living *and* expenses of production for padi farmers, such as rising rents and labor costs. Irrigation and drainage facilities just being constructed during these years, in combination with UMNO propaganda directed toward padi farmers, *promised* them increased incomes, because the ideology of the state favoring capitalist growth made the expansion of production equivalent to increased rural welfares. In these circumstances, the Guaranteed Minimum Price and new irrigation and drainage schemes can only be viewed as an "effective subsidy" to padi farmers if what is meant is that these were "effective" in achieving the state's development goal of increasing domestic padi production and approaching national self-sufficiency in rice. As for being a "subsidy" from the state to Malay padi cultivators, it is more accurate to state that the "subsidy" in question was one provided by padi farmers to the late colonial state.this becomes obvious when one considers that the Guaranteed Minimum Price failed to provide a margin of income to most small farmers sufficient for more than bare subsistence, if that, while the expansion of padi production combined with violent repression played a large part in maintaining industrial harmony and low wages for urban workers.

What then was the trend for the padi farming sector in the years from 1947 to Independence? Lim summarizes it as follows:

> in 1947, total Malayan rice production came to about 252.2 thousand tons, and the average price per kati was 55 cents, making a total value of about $237.7 million. Fourteen years later, in 1960, rice production increased to 560.2 thousand tons, an increase of about 118 per cent. Price, however, decreased to 28 cents per *kati,* a drop of 53 per cent, making a total value of $244.7 millions, only 3 per cent higher than that in 1947.But the general purchasing power of money in 1960 is about 12 per cent lower than that of 1947. Thus if we express our comparison in terms of real income, the 1947 position was in fact better than the position in 1960. In other words, expressed in terms of 1947 prices, the real income of the rice sector was $252.2 million in 1947 but decreased to $215.3 million in 1960. There was therefore economic decay in the rice sector.[84]

Malay peasants were by no means backward in getting the message. They took the opportunity to flee from the oppressive conditions of declining incomes and worsened living standards, and from the depredations of landlords, shopkeepers, and grain dealers. In these years, Malays left rice production in massive numbers: total employment in rice production decreased nationally from 470,692 in 1947 to 398,295 in 1957, an absolute decline of 15.4 percent.[85] Those who remained in padi production —particularly those cultivating the smallest plots — were forced to tighten their belts, seek out more land to rent in, to leave the villages seasonally for agricultural wage labor elsewhere, and to seek out opportunities for transplanting and harvest wage labor within their local areas. In short, they were engaged in an increasingly desperate struggle to gain a minimal subsistence. Their economic survival depended on a precarious balance of livelihood strategies, which was to be tipped further toward proletarianization and marginalization by events in the post-Independence period discussed in chapter 8.

State Policy Toward Rubber Smallholders, Devolution, and Revival

By the early 1950s, as a consequence of the rubber restriction schemes of the Depression years discussed in the previous chapter, Malay peasant rubber smallholdings were in a state of devolutionary decline; and even the estate sector was said to face "dilapidation,"[86] although still far more productive than the smallholding sector. Yield figures from the postwar period suggest the extent to which by then the prewar competitive advantage of Malay smallholders vis-à-vis the rubber estate sector had been decisively reversed by the anti-peasant policies of the colonial state. As is evident from Table 3, through the 1960s, smallholder yields were below those of estates, and remained static. Yields of estates continued to increase, as their budgrafted trees replanted during the interwar period came into their years of maximum yield.

Table 3
Rubber Yields in Pounds Latex per Acre, per Year,
Plantations vs. Smallholdings, 1948-1964

Pounds Latex per Acre, per Year

Year	Plantations	Smallholdings
1948	462	467
1950	n.a.	n.a.
1952	480	450
1954	480	441
1956	496	486
1958	586	461
1960	676	461
1962	745	497
1964	818	333

Source: Calculated from yield figures, Dept. of Statistics 1963:30, and Dept. of Statistics 1970:6.

Despite the devolutionary condition of the smallholding sector at this time, the state's pro-growth policies, combined with accommodation between the British and UMNO during these years, began to favor the expansion of production by rubber smallholders. An additional concern to administrators and plantation managers was the competition facing Malaya's natural rubber industry from synthetic rubber, which had begun to be produced in the United States during World War II when access to supplies of natural rubber were cut off. Not only was natural rubber production to be increased, but the productivity of tappers was to be increased so as to enhance the competitive efficiency of natural rubber vis-à-vis synthetics.

Taken together, these factors generated a renewal of the state's efforts to promote the replanting of rubber trees with high-yield stock for both estate and smallholding sectors. Substantial replanting on estates during the 1930s and in the late 1940s went part way toward meeting this objective, but further replanting with the latest high-yielding stock was considered necessary. What is qualitatively new in the postwar years were programs designed specifically to assist smallholders to replant.

In 1952 the administration initiated a novel scheme for replanting rubber for both estates and smallholders.[87] The Rubber Replanting Scheme lasted from 1952 to 1955; in 1955, a revised replanting scheme was put into effect, and lasted until 1961. Still, up to 1958, the planting of *new* rubber trees was strongly discouraged by means of bureaucratic obstacles to alienating land for rubber to rural Malays.[88]

During these years, rubber estates were provided with outright grants by the state for replanting on a per-acre basis. Assisted by these grants, estates continued their replanting efforts which had begun in 1946; by1954, estates had replanted 353,000 acres out of a total 2,018,000 acres land held.[89] For the smallholding sector, as was true for estates, replanting was subsidized by a special export duty, a "cess," levied on all rubber producers, and grants for replanting were made on a per-acre basis.

There is a difference of opinion about the capacity of smallholders with different-sized holdings to replant during these years, and thus to take advantage of the benefits of the Scheme. On one hand, Rudner has argued that those smallholdings that were, in fact, replanted from 1952 to 1961 proved to be the largest — generally those between 25 and 100 acres composing less than twenty percent of total smallholding areas in 1952.[90] He states that, for the vast majority of smallholders (poorer Malays with plots of two to five acres), replanting regulations were too stringent, the replanting subsidy provided was far too niggardly, and they could least afford to lose income for the six years during which young rubber trees matured and could not be tapped. Larger smallholders, both Malays in Malay Reservation areas and Chinese and Indians elsewhere, thus benefited at the expense of smaller smallholders.[91] Rudner concludes that the replanting cess proved to be a "regressive form of taxation on the whole smallholding sector to subsidize approved replanting on a few, mainly larger holdings,"[92] and that the two replanting schemes "served as a redistributive mechanism for transferring the compulsory savings of poor smallholders to further replanting on better-off medium holdings. As a result, inequalities within the smallholding sector increased, with the weakest smallholdings left in a deteriorating position."[93]

On the other hand, Gibbons has recently claimed that from the 1950s onward, even the poorest Malay rubber smallholders were able to replant, and that this led indirectly to their general prosperity by the 1970s and 1980s. According to Gibbons, by 1973 the Rubber Industry (Replanting) Board

had supervised the replanting of 493,000 hectare of smallholder rubber, just

over two-thirds (67.1%) of the land that had been under smallholder rubber in
1946. . . .Even more important, from our point of view, is the fact that the
replanting programs had reached a substantial proportion of poor smallholders.
. . . the participation rate of the very poor (bottom half of the poverty group) at
70.8% was virtually identical with that of the non-poor. Admittedly these
findings come as somewhat of a surprise, given previously held beliefs that the
participation rate would be less among the poor smallholders (because they
could not afford to forgo the income from the old trees for the six years that it
would take for the new trees to mature).[94]

During the years that the poorest smallholders received no income while their
replanted holdings matured, they — like other less poor smallholders — were
able to find sharetapping and temporary or casual wage-labor employment both
within their villages and beyond them, in nearby rubber estates and other
worksites. "Most of these poor smallholders and their wives had to resort to a
variety of such heavy, part-time work to make up the lost income."[95]

To complete his story, Gibbons argues that after their replanted trees
matured, rubber smallholders were then able to use the additional income
brought in by their more productive holdings in the 1970s to subsidize their
childrens' secondary and tertiary educations. This in turn allowed their children
to take advantage of the new opportunities for well-paid employment in the
manufacturing sector and in the government from the 1970s onward. Once
employed, their children began and continue to remit money to them in their
villages.[96] This led to a significant reduction of rural poverty.

To some extent, this difference of opinion may depend on semantic
ambiguity. Whereas Rudner's focus was on those smallholders with the *smallest*
holdings, that of Gibbons is on the poorest smallholders. But someone who may
have been regarded as "poor" in the late 1970s may not have been so in the
1950s if at the earlier time he or she was a child of parents owning an *undivided*
smallholding — that is, not one of the smallest holdings to which Rudner's
argument applied. Or it may be that Rudner's and Gibbons' studies are not
completely comparable in terms of the years covered, since Gibbons refers to the
years from 1953 to 1980, whereas Rudner considered the early 1950s only, when
the employment opportunities of the 1960s and early 1970s for rural Malays
were not yet available. Or it may be that the findings of Gibbons' study, which
was located in two *mukim* in Negri Sembilan (Rantau and Pantai), cannot be
generalized to other areas of the peninsula. On the other hand, Rudner's
conclusions do not appear to be derived from local empirical studies at all, but
rather from the analysis of national-level tax revenue and government
expenditure data,[97] and, in this sense, are less substantiated than are Gibbons'.

As things stand, it is impossible to resolve the issue definitively. What can
be asserted with some confidence is that government policy toward smallholder

replanting promoted class differentiation in the Malayan countryside by favoring wealthy smallholders over the poorest. To the extent that this policy was resisted, this was due to both the resourcefulness and hard effort of the poor.

Although there is controversy about the proportion of *smallholders* who were able to replant during these years, the fact that a majority of smallholding *acreage* came to be replanted during this period and the decade after Independence is incontrovertible. According to Barlow, the revised replanting scheme put into effect in 1955 was the beginning of extensive replanting of smallholder acreage: "by 1960 a good start towards renovating the capital of the industry had been made. By 1973 the task was over three-quarters completed. . . . On the smallholdings 559 800 hectares, or 67 per cent of the original 1946 rubber land, had been dealt with."[98] This change came about as a result of the rural development programs implemented by the Tun Abdul Razak administration from Independence onward, with its emphasis on building new rural infrastructure and increasing productivity in the rubber smallholding sector.

What is perhaps more surprising is the fact that, by the early 1970s at latest, the profile of the rubber industry as a whole had changed: in terms of area planted, it was predominately a smallholding and no longer an estate industry. By 1973, only 35 percent of all rubber acreage was held by estates, and the remaining 65 percent held by smallholders.[99] Divestment by European firms and government subdivision of their estates into smallholdings, planting of new rubber smallholdings in the FELDA schemes, and conversion of less profitable rubber estate lands into oil palm plantations reinforced the "rejuvenation" of the peasant smallholding sector to bring about this remarkable change.

The question of internal differentiation among rubber smallholders leads to the issue of class relations among rural Malays in the postwar period. I turn to this in the following chapter.

CHAPTER SEVEN

Changes in Malay Villages, 1945–1957

In this chapter, I discuss internal changes in Malay *kampong* which reflected the postwar nationwide developments discussed in the previous chapter. I make three major points. First, during these years preexisting stratification within the rural Malay *kampong* was intensified by the emergence of a new, relative wealthy rentier class whose members purchased land while their covillagers became increasingly destitute, depending on a fragile and insecure combination of extremely small-scale cultivation of their own land, employment in full-or part-time sharecropping, and wage labor both within and beyond the village.

Second, nonetheless, full-blown differentiation between rentiers and their poorer covillagers failed to develop because of the existence of a peasant subsistence ethic accompanied by specific redistributive mechanisms, which muted local social differences. Redistributive mechanisms provided poorer rural Malays in particular with marginal livelihoods within the villages, but these were livelihoods all the same. The existence of these mechanisms during these years demonstrates that, during this postwar period, fully capitalist relations of production had not as yet appeared in the village setting. Moreover, these mechanisms were interwoven with the political patronage system within UMNO. Thus political support of local UMNO leaders became the unstated *quid pro quo* for many poorer Malays whose survival depended on the provision of local resources—notably sharecropping opportunities—by these leaders.

Third, resistance by poorer Malays to exploitation and neglect on the part of the state, their wealthier covillagers, and to an extent, colonial capitalism itself, continued during these years. This took the form of illegal squatting and of pilferage against village rentiers. At the same time, the delicate combination of subsistence strategies open to them, supplemented by redistributive mechanisms within the village, still provided them with a measure of protection against full proletarianization. In these years the alternatives of cultivating their own extremely small parcels, sharecropping for covillagers, and working seasonally doing a variety of wage-labor work, provided them with a bargaining leverage barely sufficient to avoid having to enter the permanent wage-labor market operating for plantation, industrial, and other capitalist enterprise.

Intensification of Class Divisions in Malay Villages

How were the political and economic changes at national, regional, and local levels addressed in the previous chapter reflected in developments within Malay *kampong* during this period? As I suggested in chapter 3, stratification differences within *kampong* had emerged by the 1920s and 1930s based on individual ownership of land, the weakening of generalized reciprocity among covillagers, and the emergence of the nuclear and extended families to become basic units of village social organization. It is likely that the degree to which such inequalities existed depended most critically on the location of a village within regional systems as these were affected differentially by the extension of state administrative power and commercialization of agriculture; thus villages in peripheral areas showed less inequality in land ownership than those in core or semicore areas.

In the postwar years these preexisting differences among residents of the rural Malay village community were intensified by the appearance there of two new class fractions: a government salariat and a commercial elite of shopkeepers, rice mill owners, and moneylenders. These joined with "traditional" landowners to become a new, relatively wealthy rentier class, and both purchased land from other villagers. At the same time, more and more of their poorer covillagers sold off land. They came to depend on a combination of extremely small-scale cultivation of their own land, employment in full-or part-time sharecropping, and seasonal or part-time agricultural or other wage labor. From what can be inferred from ethnographies, not only did these "objective" differences in wealth intensify, but also these inequalities were socially recognized, but euphemized by Malay village etiquette and discourse.

In chapter 1 it was noted that, during the immediate postwar years from 1946 to 1950, rural Malays for the first time began in great numbers to seek employment as wage laborers in the capitalist sector. In addition, the proportion of Malays becoming wage laborers both within the *kampong* setting and beyond it, in the rubber estates and for the government, increased greatly in every state of Malaya in the decade from 1947 to 1957 (see Table 1). As Silcock and Aziz observed in 1953, "*until the last five years* the Malays have been unwilling to work regularly on estates or mines" [emphasis added].[1]

In these years a relatively small proportion of rural Malays engaged in full-time, permanent wage labor. No doubt most Malays in estate, mining, and government employment regarded themselves as being (and in fact were) temporary workers. Nonetheless their appearance at this time hint at an increasing need for poorer Malays to seek out employment opportunities beyond the village itself. This need would have been greatest for young Malay men with relatively little access to agricultural land. They responded by engaging in the traditional practice of *merantau,* or "wandering," working as temporary wage laborers in worksites far from their natal villages.

On one hand one can infer a process of dispossession in which poorer Malays lost land sold to the new class of landlord-rentiers. On the other there was the partial failure of redistributive mechanisms, such as landowners allocating sharecropping opportunities to fellow villagers, to compensate completely for these changes. The matter of redistributive mechanisms is addressed in the next section.

The emergence during the late 1940s and the 1950s of a consolidated class of village rentiers, whose holdings by Malay standards were relatively large, has been commented on extensively in the ethnographies cited above and elsewhere.[2] Systematic evidence on the emergence of this rentier class is lacking, but there is sufficient information available to support two claims. First, its emergence indeed did take place during the postwar period. Second, most new rentiers were of one of two groups. They were either Malay moneylenders, shopkeepers, and rice wholesalers who became relatively wealthy in this period by taking advantage of preexisting conditions of impoverishment and capital shortage among Malay farmers and fishermen. Or they were lower-level government officials, schoolteachers, and other members of the Malay salariat that came into being during the postwar years prior to Independence in 1957. Others were fortunate to inherit large holdings of land from the prewar years. Husin Ali observed for three *kampong* he studied in the 1960s, that "the main form of accumulation is through the purchase of land. . . . There are at least three groups of people who are in the position to accumulate land: (a) those who manage to save in spite of limited resources; (b) those fortunate enough to inherit or own a large amount of land; and (c) those in business, e.g. shopkeepers, or in the government service."[3]

How did "those in business" arise? It appears that in the postwar years in many villages, enterprising Malays came to occupy the roles of moneylender and of shopkeeper-cum-rice-wholesaler held by non-Malays in the prewar period. Increasingly rigorous enforcement of the enactments against the acquisition of Malay land by Chettiar moneylenders, combined with the self-repatriation of Chettiars fleeing the Japanese to India in 1941,[4] provided the opportunity for better-off Malays to become moneylenders after the Japanese occupation. The persecution of Chinese by the Japanese during the Occupation and the forced relocation of rural Chinese during the Emergency led to the flight or withdrawal of local Chinese shopkeepers from some areas. This role was assumed by resident Malays after the war, although most shopkeepers and rice wholesalers remained Chinese. In any event, by the late 1950s and early 1960s, the existence of Malays acting as moneylenders and as shopkeepers-cum-rice dealers in rural villages was commented on extensively.[5]

In addition to new moneylenders and shopkeepers, a second group of wealthier rural Malays appearing for the first time in the postwar period were members of an expanding Malay salariat employed in government service—particularly schoolteachers and clerks. In most cases, they were the clients of regional or local UMNO leaders, and they came in increasing numbers during the 1950s to occupy the middle and lower rungs of the government due to the largesse of their patrons. This salariat still resided in, or at least still identified with, their natal *kampong* in rural areas of colonial Malaya.[6]

For the new Malay moneylenders, shopkeepers, rice dealers, and members of the government salariat, several factors encouraged their purchase of land, both in rice and rubber, in Malay villages. The *Malay Reservations Enactments,* still in force, ensured that non-Malays could not purchase land in most rural areas where Malays lived; this provided newly wealthy Malays with monopsonistic buying leverage in these areas, and thus lowered the price of land. Because of Chinese control of middle levels of the trading and distribution system and of small-scale industry, members of the salariat were discouraged from investing their capital in these other sectors of the colonial economy. Rudner, moreover, argues that there were strong economic incentives for the newly wealthy to purchase agricultural land: "accelerated post-war agricultural commercialisation . . . invoked the formation of new classes of agrarian entrepreneurial and *rentier* landlord interests."[7] As a sign of the increased market value of land, it was observed by the Rice Production Committee in 1953 that in areas with commercially valuable padi crops—Kedah, Penang Island and Province Wellesley—the previous ten years had witnessed steep rent increases, the conversion from rent in kind to cash rents, and a high turnover in tenants who could not pay the increased rents.[8]

Most crucially, however, the agricultural economy of rural Malay peasants had been decisively weakened by the processes of state interference and attempted regulation of peasant production documented in previous chapters. Malay peasants were in no position to fend off their wealthier covillagers seeking to purchase their lands. Some peasants sold land to meet extraordinary expenditures, such as the cost of weddings or of curers for serious illness.[9] Others appear to have indebted themselves to wealthier covillagers, and, having pledged their land as collateral through the *jual janji* arrangement,[10] lost it when they could not repay.[11]

As a result of these developments, Husin Ali noted, in his study of three *kampong* on the west coast in the 1960s, that "in the three areas, the land-owners and the shopkeepers tend to be the same persons."[12] James Puthucheary referred in 1960 to the existence of Malay moneylenders, and stated that "more and more land is transferred to the ownership of well-to-do Malays."[13] And Swift observed for the postwar decade that "civil servants frequently use their savings for the purchase of village property, especially in an area where they have kinship connexions. Until recently it seemed the major goal of most Malay civil servants to acquire enough land while in the service to permit a comfortable retirement to their village of origin."[14] And he pointed, as well, to the general process taking place: "there is another aspect of the process, the passing of village land into the hands of an upper class who invest their savings in land. To this upper class agriculture is not their sole, or even their main, source of wealth."[15]

As poorer Malay villagers became landless, then, they rented in land as tenants, labored as sharecroppers for wealthier villagers on their padi fields or rubber smallholdings, worked as day laborers on nearby rubber estates, or left the village setting entirely, either to work as seasonal resident workers on rubber plantations, or to take up government employment as policemen, soldiers, laborers, truck drivers, and so on. Thus, as Rudner put it, "the poverty associated with heightened inequality tended to aggravate the relative deprivation of the bulk of the peasantry, impelling the beginnings of an outward flow of manpower from the rice economy while fomenting internal unrest."[16] The sources of the conditions found in rural Malay villages circa 1960, and described above thus become clear. (See pp. 10-16.)

What can be discerned at this time is not, however, a full-blown cleavage between a small number of landlord-rentiers and a large majority of tenants and rural laborers. Rather one sees an increasingly differentiated village setting in which only a few were landlords and some were pure tenants or laborers. But most struggled to get by on minute farm plots, cultivating their own land and renting in land as they could to farm, or working as sharecroppers, and engaging in seasonal wage labor. All this was done under the prevailing conditions of low productivity set by the events of the prewar period, but now exacerbated by a rapidly growing rural population.[17] Husin Ali described the complex situation of the Malay village of the 1960s as follows:

> there are the owners whose land is operated by others through the sharing and/or renting system; and there are also the individuals who only operate the land for others without owning any themselves. Yet in between there are the owner-operators, namely those who operate the land which they own. To complicate matters further, there are also people who operate only part of their own land, and others who for a living work partially on other people's land and at other times they are engaged in different types of odd jobs available in the village.[18]

Sama Senasib ("In the Same Fate"): Redistribution and the Subsistence Ethic

Ethnographic and other evidence from the 1950s and 1960s is admittedly not as extensive as one would like. Still it strongly suggests that what buffered most poorer rural Malays from social marginalization and proletarianization during these years was the existence of a subsistence ethic and extensive mechanisms of redistribution that assured them access to a subsistence livelihood, albeit a minimal one often on the edge of destitution. By "subsistence ethic" I refer not only to a morality that predicated that all villagers were entitled to a basic subsistence despite the differences in wealth that so obviously distinguished rich and poor, but also one that was grounded in a discourse and etiquette of "euphemization."[19] This morality was supported by informal sanctions against violators, and made covillagers act toward one another *as if* these differences did not exist or at least did not matter in a fundamental way. Thus this discourse was one in which class differences were systematically misrecognized, being coded in terms of "mutual help" and "charity."

This subsistence ethic in turn buttressed various practices that had the effect of redistributing resources vital to survival among covillagers, especially from rich to poor. Among these redistributive mechanisms was the providing of agricultural land by inheritance or nominal rent by elder to younger family members and other kin. Another was the giving of sharecropping and wage-labor employment by relatively wealthy rubber smallholders and padi landowners to their less well-to-do fellow villagers, who were often their kinsmen and neighbors. Additional mechanisms included cooperative labor exchanges variously known as *berderau*, *gotong royong*, or *meminjam* for padi planting and harvesting; *kenduri* or feasts, which had the effects of distributing food from wealthier families more widely to others within a neighborhood and reinforcing solidarity among extended family members and neighbors on whom survival depended; and *zakat* and *fitrah*, two forms of Islamic charity, given to the village poor. Given the scarcity of land, the most important of these were the transfer of farm land to family members and the provision of sharecropping or wage-labor opportunities. But the operation of all these mechanisms had the effect of retarding the marginalization and proletarianization of the poorest villagers.

At the core of the subsistence ethic and village mechanisms of redistribution was the obligation of parents to provide adequate farm land for their children's economic survival. According to Banks, "fathers should be able to bequeath land and other tangible properties to their sons and daughters as part of their social inheritance. This gift of land and wealth between the generations was the symbol *par excellence* of the primary kinship bond between generations."[20] Thus parents were expected to arrange the marriages of their grown children, and to establish them in viable households with enough land to be self-sufficient in rice by local standards.[21] Islamic law and *adat temenggong* ("custom" in areas of bilateral kinship) alike supported the fulfilling of this obligation by requiring that parents divide their property among sons and daughters, with the exact proportion depending upon which of the two forms of "law" was locally in effect, instead of allowing for or enjoining impartible estates. In the case of *adat perpatih*, ("custom" applied in areas of matrilineal kinship), daughters were the expected inheritors of "ancestral land," *(tanah pusaka)* generally padi land, and sons of "acquired land," *(tanah charian)* most commonly rubber smallholdings and fruit orchards.[22] Irrespective of the "law" or "custom" applied, both sons and daughters acquired de facto rights over inherited land through their spouses.

One comparison of the degree of land concentration on the Kedah plain in the late 1950s with the situation twenty years later has shown that the long-term effects of inheritance of land from parents to children has been to *lessen* the concentration of land. Thus this scarce resource was distributed more evenly across the farming population, even though the degree of land concentration still remained high, and the more equal sharing by farmers of land was one of an "equality" of deprivation rather than of plenty.[23]

While parents with grown children still lived, they provided their children and children's spouses with land to cultivate, frequently without rent, or at nominal rents only. A finding from Gibbons, Lim et al. for the Muda region for the late 1970s no doubt reflects in general an earlier period as well: slightly greater than 71 percent of all parcels of padi land operated by someone other than their owners were operated by the kin of owners; and of these kin-operated parcels, 22.5 percent were operated by the owners' children.[24] The work of Gibbons, Lim et al. also suggests that rural Malays have provided scarce padi land to cultivate not only to their children, but also to other kin, including brother and sister, "nephew/niece," and "cousins," who were not likely to inherit the land.[25] This practice was not unique to the Kedah Plain; for instance, in the case of Negri Sembilan in an area where *adat perpatih* was practiced, Swift wrote that "a man with more land than he needs is under strong pressure to allow his wife's poor relatives to use it. The land is their inheritance too; it belonged to their grandmother as well as his wife's."[26] Gibbons, Lim, et al. conclude that "a padi land owner who for whatever reason does not want to operate all or part of his land will tend strongly to give a kinsman access to it, regardless of whether or not that kinsman is a likely inheritor of the land."[27] Given the longstanding scarcity of padi land in the Kedah Plain, it is almost certain that this conclusion can be applied retrospectively to the 1950s as well. Finally, the passing down or giving/renting out of land for use by Malay farmers to family members and kin were not confined in these years to padi land, but extended also to rubber smallholdings, fruit orchards, and other cropland.[28]

Of course, parents with no land were unable to fulfil this obligation. The lack of land to inherit would be one reason for young men to "go wandering," (*merantau*) far from the village seeking seasonal or temporary wage-labor or sharecropping opportunities, when these were not available to them locally.

Providing land for cultivation to family members and close kin as a redistributive mechanism shaded insensibly into another, which was practiced by relatively more wealthy village residents. This involved offering opportunities to poorer and less close kin, neighbors, and villagers, to sharecrop or sharetap the padi, fruit, rubber, or other lands that they owned, through the *bagi dua* or *bagi tiga* arrangements. Whatever the social distance between the landowner and his sharecroppers—whether between family members or close kin, at one extreme, or between remote kin, neighbors, or covillagers, or even between "original people" and "outside people" from beyond the village[29], at the other extreme—their relationship could be expressed as *tolong menolong,* or "mutual help." *Tolong menolong* was an extremely ambiguous yet thereby useful phrase that conflated the relationships between close family members with that between landowners and their tenants. In short, it was a rhetorical device for the euphemization of the economic dependency of the sharecropper inherent in this relationship.

Nonetheless, *tolong menolong* cannot simply be dismissed as a polite hypocrisy when applied to sharecropping, for it possessed a potentially subversive cutting edge. The rural Malay subsistence ethic dictated that *tolong menolong* be conceived of as a more or less equal relationship, in which the sharecropper or sharetapper "helped out" the landowner. This, I should point out, is consistent with the Malay peasant labor theory of value from the precolonial period, which accounted a person's labor invested in a resource—land—as at least a partial just claim on the proceeds of that resource. A wealthy landowner's provision of land to a covillager to sharecrop was not merely a favor, but also expressed a need for labor that the sharecropper or sharetapper could provide. Wan Hashim, for instance, writes of a village in Upper Perak district in the mid-1970s:

> in terms of social relationships between landlords and sharecroppers or tenants, the relationships are based on the traditional Malay value of *tolong menolong* (mutual help). . . . Both landlords and sharecroppers consider themselves as *sama senasib* (in the same fate) especially when their economic well being is equally affected by the changing seasons and the changing price of rubber. The relationship between the two social groups is one of mutual dependency and, to a certain extent, of reciprocity.[30]

And Wilson wrote of sharetapping on the *bagi dua* arrangement in a village in Ulu Langat district, Selangor, that:

the use of the term *tolong menolong* to describe a relationship between a coolie and a landowner indicates that though there may indeed be an economic discrepancy between the two, their social status is nominally equal. The mutual agreement to employ and to work is an agreement between equals, a factor also indicated in the sharing of the proceeds. The term *tolong menolong* is most commonly employed within the domestic context. . . . The idea of doing each other favors and of helping each other in times of need *(tolong menolong)* is an integral part of kinship and friendship between people, and is at the same time a sign of respect and equality. When applied to coolies, it implies that the relationship is first and foremost a personal one, analogous to a kinship relation in which each partner is rendering the other a needed service.[31]

Similarly, *tolong menolong* was used to describe related families assisting each other in the preparation of *kenduri*.[32] It was used also to refer to the mobilization of neighbors into a work group to assist in cultivating the fields of a man whose wife was sick.[33]

Irrespective of the rhetorical use of *tolong menolong,* the sharecropping relationship to which it referred was one which appears to have been essential in material terms to enable poorer Malays to pursue a livelihood within the villages in which they lived during these years. For the villagers of Ulu Langat studied by Wilson, almost exclusively dependent on rubber, no less than fifty-two persons from twenty-two households (out of a total of 108 households)—all landless or nearly so—worked regularly as *bagi dua* sharetappers under *tolong menolong;* the several landowners for whom they worked owned rubber smallholdings of an average thirteen acres in area.[34] Banks noted for the Sik area in Kedah that the expansion in rubber smallholdings after World War II brought with it landless peasants from outside the village to work as *koli,* "coolie," sharetappers for smallholders under *bagi dua,* and that these newcomers constituted "a good percentage of the proportion of population growth other than by natural increase."[35] M.G. Swift observed that of a total thirty-five households in one village in Jelebu district, Negri Sembilan, the heads of twelve households were sharetappers. More sharetappers would have been counted had unmarried adult sons of these heads been included.[36]

Similarly, in the case of padi cultivation, tenants and sharecroppers made up a very large proportion of all farmers; it is difficult to distinguish the two clearly because of the general change from rents based on a proportion of harvested padi to combined cash rents and rents in kind during this period.[37] According to one census of padi farmers in the Kedah Plain in 1955, no less than 42.1 percent of all farmers were pure tenants, as were 45.1 percent of farmers operating farms less than four *relong* in area, and 41.7 percent of farmers operating farms between four and ten *relong* in area.[38]

Relatively wealthy landowners owning padi lands, as well as other sources of income, also provided their poorer kin and neighbors with wage-labor employment. Poorer villagers were hired to transplant padi and to harvest and thresh it. For his Jelebu village, Swift described how this was negotiated. His description reveals well the discourse and etiquette of euphemization in terms of "mutual help" and "charity" overlaying the wage-labor nexus:

> for harvesting labour is frequently hired because of the need for speed. As the harvesters produce their own reward payment is not a problem. . . . There are, however, also people who want rice and welcome an opportunity to increase their supplies. A man known to be a surplus producer will be approached by these people and asked whether he needs help. The wife of a wealthy man is likely to be approached by her kin; they are sorry to see her with so much work to do, and offer their assistance (paid of course). . . . Rich men even employ relatives and dependent families as a form of charity. Their work is lessened, and the crop is got safely into storage more quickly, but the notion of helping the needy is also a factor in their decision to hire labour.[39]

Owners of fruit orchards employed fellow villagers as pickers and transporters.[40] Proprietors of cattle, sheep, or goat herds provided other village residents with a few animals to raise, and divided the resulting progeny with them.[41]

Altogether, the two redistributive mechanisms within Malay *kampong* just discussed—the passing down or lending of land for use to younger family members and the provision of sharecropping or wage-labor opportunities to poorer villagers—therefore represented major bases of subsistence for a very large proportion of the less wealthy rural population. These allowed resourceful but increasingly desperate peasants to survive at a low standard of living, by hook or crook, within the village setting. Despite the use of phrases like *tolong menolong,* it must have become transparent to Malays on both sides of the rural class divide that the shared dependency of the poor and wealthy had become increasingly one-sided; "mutual help" was transformed into the outright subordination of one side to the other, as a matter of social and economic survival.

Other redistributive mechanisms were each relatively minor but, in aggregate, no doubt gave a measure of added relief to impoverished rural Malays. Swift discussed a phenomenon of "dependent families" who attached themselves to wealthier families, and borrowed from the latter when in need without having to repay. In return, these dependents were expected to "help" when requested by their patrons for *kenduri,* odd jobs, and support in village factional disputes.[42] In times of padi crop loss, landowners were expected to reduce their rents or shares in order to provide tenants or sharecroppers with sufficient padi to survive.[43] Poorer villagers asked wealthier neighbors for small "loans" that the latter knew would never be repaid.[44] Cooperative work groups based on reciprocal exchanges of labor, known variously as *berderau, gotong royong, tolong menolong,* or *meminjam,* have long been reported for Malay villages. By this period they appear to have been a means by which small-scale padi land owners, who were kin or neighbors or both, ensured that their heavy labor needs over a short period of time could be met without resorting to spending cash to hire wage labor.[45]

An extremely interesting form of resource sharing were *kenduri,* or ritual feasts held on the occasion of rites of passage in the life cycles of family members. According to McAllister, in contemporary Negri Sembilan,

> *kenduri* provide an important mechanism for economic redistribution. . . . It is my impression that in many cases there is a substantial counter-flow of resources *into* the host family. This may take the form of wealthier segments of an extended family network or matrilineage contributing to the household of poorer relatives to help them put on such a ritual occasion. Such contributions are often quite substantial and stretch well beyond the day of the feast to aid the family in the following months.[46]

It is probable that the *kenduri* had an anologous function for rural Malays before Independence. McAllister goes on to suggest that "in the not-so-distant past, the actual feasting at the *kenduri* itself probably helped to redistribute calories, and especially protein, as a large animal was often slaughtered and the meat fed to participants."[47] She also points out that *kenduri* reinforce the survival strategy of sharing resources among relatives and neighbors on whom a family's economic survival may well depend. They also affirm solidarity among the people concerned: "the *kenduri* provides an encouragement for close kin and neighbors in similar economic circumstances to periodically pool resources, a strategy which may enhance the life chances of all."[47] There is every reason to believe that this was an effect of *kenduri* in the pre-Independence years as well.

Two forms of charity enjoined by Islam, *zakat* and *fitrah,* may also have spread out resources among village poor, and to some extent redistributed them from those better off. *Fitrah* represents the obligation of every Moslem to give charity at the end of the fasting month of Ramadan; this takes the form of a measure of rice given by each family. Swift related a dispute between the state government and the villagers he studied in the late 1950s arising from the former sending *amil,* religious officials, to the village to collect *fitrah* for the first time. This was resisted by villagers who regarded it "not [as] a Government tax, but a charity to be given with proper ceremonial to whomsoever the donor judged fit to receive it (from amongst those qualified to receive it under Muslim law)." Generally these were to *orang alim,* pious men in the village able to recite the prayers required on ritual occasions, and they included some who may have been poor.[49] For the late 1970s, Scott recounted part of the *fitrah* rice being given to "poor relatives and neighbors" in a Kedah village.[50]

In the same study, Scott observed that *zakat,* a tithe of padi given as charity at harvest time, was "an important supplement to the income of poor, landless families."[51] There is no direct evidence available for the pre-Independence period that the giving of *zakat* and *fitrah* had similar effects at that time, but the studies just cited strongly suggest this.

As can be surmised by the description of these redistributive mechanisms, although the subsistence ethic did encompass, in part, a discourse and etiquette of euphemization, it was also grounded in a far more thoroughgoing ideology of communal sharing and generosity within the *kampong.* This ideology harkened back to what Scott has called the "remembered village,"[52] but in these years it invoked an idealized past, the kin-ordered village community of the prewar period. The values expressed in this ideology were precapitalist or, perhaps more accurately, *anti*-capitalist. Banks writes of such a vision of the ideal past: "the great differences in wealth that informants see today [ca. 1968] in Sik, did not exist in the past to the same degree. The local ethos was egalitarian; even men who grew up in Sik and became civil servants posted in the district would sit and have coffee and cakes in the same shops and at the same tables with poorer peasants."[53]

The redistributive practices I have described above were supported by the sanction of village opinion—the verbal manifestation of the subsistence ethic. Consider the responses of residents of one village in the 1950s to the "meanness" of a man buying land in the village:

Such activity is accompanied by a chorus of direct or indirect comment disparaging the effort. "Do you want to own everything?. . . What is the good of all that wealth if you won't allow your children to taste it?. . . Just look at him, he's the richest man in the village and is still not satisfied. . . . Come now, we are not strangers (are related). Lend me—(although because we are not strangers there isn't much hope that I'll repay you)."[54]

Local opinion affirming sharing and generosity within the village was manifested in a complex variety of behaviors—rumor, gossip, backbiting, subtle recriminations of ungenerous behavior bringing on a sense of *malu,* or "shame"—well understood in rural Malay communities. Thus, for example, "a man who had no children to tap his holdings and who seemed to be getting along adequately would be regarded as a miser if he tapped his own trees, disdaining all of those poorer individuals around him who could use the income from tapping his trees."[55] In the case of a *bagi dua* arrangement, where the landowner is much better off than the sharetapper, "local sentiment applauds the owner who provides free access to mangles and criticizes the owner who does not;"[56] "not to give a loan to a fellow villager is mean, and even to insist on repayment is not well regarded;"[57] or "if *orangorang kaya* [rich persons] interact with other villagers as if they were no wealthier than anyone else, they receive the esteem that they think to be their due. But if there is any conscious effort at exclusiveness or any evidence of not being *halus* ["refined"] in social relations, then *orangorang kaya* may be used in a derogatory sense, as it is when it is applied to the urban wealthy and to members of other *bangsa*—such as Chinese."[58]

So much for the situation of the 1950s, as best it can be reconstructed. To conclude this section, with the "Green Revolution" of the late 1960s and the 1970s, it was the disappearance and weakening of these redistributive practices—and transparent violations of the subsistence ethic—that go far toward explaining the proletarianization or marginalization of substantial numbers of rural Malays, as they were forced to leave their natal *kampong* to seek wage labor in Malaysia's major cities or, a fortunate few, to occupy new land in FELDA resettlement schemes, in the 1960s, 1970s, and 1980s.

Peasant Resistance in an Age of Reaction: Subdued, Not Extinguished

Despite their growing destitution, poorer Malays continued to engage in resistance to exploitation and neglect by the state, their well-to-do covillagers, and, perhaps, to colonial capitalism itself, during these years. Yet actions of peasant resistance came to be increasingly constrained in this period.

Above all, this was due to the measures taken against the rural population by the state as part of the Emergency. Even among rural Malays, though far less of course than among the Chinese suspected of Communist sympathies and "disloyalty," police intelligence about illegal activity improved markedly as a result of government vigilance and surveillance. The civilian bureaucracy also grew greatly in size in the 1950s; administrators and clerks were more dense "on the ground" in the countryside. Because civilian-bureaucratic and military objectives were now intertwined, they were more aware of events and conditions in local areas, compared to the late 1940s.[59] The conversion of tens of thousands of young Malay men into army soldiers and police no doubt instilled discipline in one section of the rural population otherwise most inclined to resistance to state actions. Moreover, episodes of state repression against dissenting Malays at escalating levels of violence were made widely known. These ranged from the banning of organizations and arrests of leaders of the legal left wing of the nationalist movement considered in the previous chapter, to the counter-insurgency annihilation campaigns against the MCP's Tenth Regiment consisting of Malay guerrillas in Pahang.[60] All these factors taken together in the countryside must have had, at certain times and places, a chilling effect on those covert forms of resistance by Malay peasants, such as illegal settling on state land discussed previously. Nonetheless, peasant resistance to state restrictions on land use took the form of illegal squatting and to prohibited planting of rubber, as it had previously. Padi farmers protested vigorously when state policies toward padi pricing threatened their livelihood. Agricultural laborers and sharecroppers engaged in pilferage and sabotage of landowners' crops when they felt the latter abused them.

Anecdotal evidence suggests that widespread illegal squatting by peasants on state land continued to occur during these years. Gibbons, Lim, et al. report in a study conducted in 1975 and 1976 that they found that no less than 9.6 percent of all lots and 7.2 percent of the total area of land in the Muda irrigation scheme in Kedah and Perlis were illegally occupied state land. Apparently, some of these lots were settled in the 1950s for "many of the cultivators of unalienated state land claimed to have been growing padi on the land for at least two decades."[61] Husin Ali reports in a comparative study undertaken in the 1960s of three villages in Kedah, Johore, and Pahang that

> many villagers in the three areas studied have been applying for land but they have failed to obtain any, even after having waited for several years—a quite common situation elsewhere. They try to enlist the help of their elected representatives but to no avail. Therefore, what many of them have done is to organize themselves into small groups, choose their own leaders and then illegally open up the land on their own.[62]

Husin Ali goes on to describe a movement to occupy State forest land in coastal Selangor in the 1960s that involved hundreds of peasants led by a charismatic leader.[63]

Peasants also converted land designated for other uses to rubber smallholdings during these years. In "ricebowl" areas specifically designated for planting padi, where ecological conditions allowed, rural Malays instead planted illegal stands of young rubber trees. This was so widespread in the states of Kedah, Perlis, and Johore, that by 1955 no less than 250,000 acres had been planted illegally out of a total of 1,650,000 acres in smallholdings, though much of this had been planted prior to the occupation.[64]

State policies did not always work to the disadvantage of peasant resistance. The British policy of divide-and-rule during the Emergency, in which officials sought to coopt rural Malays as allies in their assault on the Chinese and Indian labor movement and the MCP insurgency, meant that Malay peasants were in a position of moral strength sufficient at times to publicly resist injurious state actions, if not change them. This was most evident in the extensive protests by Malay padi farmers to the downward manipulation of the wholesale padi price by the government in 1955 described in the previous chapter. The reactions of padi farmers were by no means passive, as this decision directly threatened their subsistence. In the center of the "rice bowl" area of the Kedah Plain, "in a series of emergency gatherings in various rice growing areas, usually docile agriculturalists passed angry resolutions condemning the government's withdrawal of its previously guaranteed price."[65] As a consequence of these protests, state rice policies and the more general problem of poverty among padi farmers became major issues in the 1955 elections.[66]

It is difficult to say much about poorer Malays' resistance to abuses by wealthier covillagers who employed them as sharecroppers or seasonal wage laborers, nevertheless it is certain that it did occur at least occasionally behind the public discourse of *tolong menolong*. Husin Ali reports that

> some peasants express contempt of landlords who are mean and show their anger towards those who take advantage of them through debt-bondage. For instance, in these areas a number of peasants do not hide their feelings towards some landlords and shopkeepers who try to take advantage of them and they go a degree beyond verbal abuse by trying to inflict damage to property belonging to the latter. In Kerdau [Pahang] and Bagan [Johore], some poor peasants practise slaughter-tapping—careless stripping of the bark—so that the rubber trees belonging to some of the landlords are harmed. Although more latex is obtained through the act of slaughter-tapping, this is done at the risk of destroying the trees before long.[67]

Swift mentions sharetappers in a Negri Sembilan village in the 1950s "cheating" landowners by slaughter-tapping and by leaving excess "scrap" rubber in collecting cups, since scrap conventionally belonged to the tapper. But it is unclear from Swift's account whether these actions were real resistance to the abuses of the landowner or merely unprovoked instances of private appropriation.[68]

Another form of peasant resistance may possibly have been directed against rubber estates and other large-scale private or government employers hiring Malays for seasonal or temporary wage labor. Unlike the early twentieth century, Malays by this time began to participate in such employment in large numbers, as mentioned above. However, it may well have been that when reinforced by the "safety net" of redistributive mechanisms described above, the versatile subsistence strategy of poorer Malays allowed them to possess some degree of bargaining power vis-à-vis large-scale capitalist employers. This strategy also included the alternatives of cultivating one's own land, sharetapping or sharecropping the land of others, or finding harvest or miscellaneous wage-labor work within the village. If peasants regarded the wages provided as too low, they could either cease working for capitalist employers, or not be recruited by them to begin with. Certainly another rural Malayan group—Chinese squatters in the 1920s through 1940s—employed a strategy very like the one suggested. When wages in European-owned tin mines and in other industrial work were too low, they would engage instead in commercial vegetable growing on illegally occupied state land, until wages rose to more satisfying levels.[69] But before anything more definitive can be said about how commonly rural Malays tried to use such leverage vis-à-vis large-scale employers, further investigation must clearly be undertaken.

CHAPTER EIGHT

Epilogue and Conclusion

Epilogue: Neocolonialsim and Changes in the Peasantry, 1957-1985

Since Independence in 1957, Malaysia has entered a period of neocolonial capitalist development. This period has been marked by the consolidation of an oligopoly capitalist economy with continued high levels of foreign investment and economic influence. During this period the colonial Malay aristocratic-administrative elite and its descendants have emerged as the members of a new Malay bourgeois class and as the holders of paramount political power. There have been shifts in power within a ruling coalition of political parties and groups representing this new class, Chinese, and Indian national bourgeoisies, and —indirectly — transnational capitalists.[1]

Developments within Malaysian capitalism during this period have included, first, import-substitute and, later, export-oriented industrialization, as well as the rise of American, Japanese, Hong Kong, and Singaporean corporations and their joint-venture subsidiaries to positions of major influence within the economy. There occurred also the loss of dominance by the plantation and mining sectors on which colonial British and other European capital was based, and the emergence, since 1969, of state capital as an important factor within the national economy. The result has been a new concentration of capital within the large-scale corporate sector such that a few hundred corporations — and particularly the largest conglomerates largest them — hold most of the means of production and wealth within that sector.[2] Moreover, it is the owners and directors of these large conglomerates, which consist of a relatively small group of individuals (indigenous Chinese capitalists, the representatives of foreign corporate investors, and members of the Malay governing elite), who can be said to constitute Malaysia's new bourgeois class. Through their interlocking directorates and intermarriages, their holding companies and multisectoral investment combines, the members of this class control the commanding heights of the Malaysian economy.[3]

The arrangements for transition from colonial to postcolonial rule in the 1950s, culminating in Independence in 1957 and the defeat of the communist insurgency, provided the traditional Malay administrative-aristocratic elite with the opportunity to take control of the highest levels of state power.[4] During the 1960s, those several hundred Malays who were prominent members of royal or aristocratic families, or who had played administrative roles under the British, mobilized their lower-level Malay supporters, including wealthier members of the Malay peasantry, through the UMNO party organization. They brought into being the coalition known as the Alliance, with Chinese and Indian capitalists and the leaders of the parties these capitalists financed (the Malaysian Chinese Association, and the Malaysian Indian Congress). Through electoral successes they attained control of the national and (most) state governments. They consolidated their positions of power and influence among Malays by providing government patronage to their supporters within UMNO. They established a congenial investment setting for both indigenous Chinese and Indian capitalists and foreign investors by continuing the policies and practices of the late colonial administration. These included repressing organized labor, providing tax and other incentives to investors and, most critically for the Malay peasantry, promoting increased productivity and output in the padi sector as one means of maintaining industrial harmony and low wages in the corporate sector.

By 1969, however, the tenuous political coalition of the Alliance, grounded in bargaining between the various ethnic segments of the Malaysian upper class, found itself unable to meet the challenge of non-Malay lower-class discontent, manifested in the resounding electoral defeat of Alliance candidates in the urbanized areas where most Chinese and Indians lived. Nor was it able to curb the expressions of dissatisfaction among the Malay petite bourgeoisie which culminated in the May 13, 1969 ethnic riots. The result was a "crisis in legitimacy" for the Malaysian state which has led to a major shift in the balance of power among partners within the national ruling coalition. From a laissez-faire setting which favored indigenous Chinese and Indian capital, the balance within the coalition has shifted to one in which the partnership between the Malay administrative-aristocratic elite and foreign capitalists now dominates. This change in the balance of forces within the ruling coalition, now designated the National Front, has led to three major developments.

First, the New Economic Policy has been implemented with two avowed goals — to "restructure" the Malaysian economy so as to erase the association between "race" and "economic function," and to "eradicate poverty." The New Economic Policy can be viewed as the mythic charter for redistributive policies which have provided urban Malays with real access to employment, particularly within the government civil service and the large-scale industrial sector,[5] and have assisted wealthier segments of rural Malay society to prosper. However, these reallocative policies have generally been at the expense of the non-Malay lower classes and poorer Malays. Moreover, they have been predicated on rapid economic expansion, which only held true —and then unevenly — for certain periods since the early 1970s (e.g., the late 1980s) and not others (e.g., the mid 1980s). Thus the promise of the New Economic Policy to "eradicate poverty" has not yet been realized. Nor has it, therefore, successfully neutralized the challenge to the Malay governing class and its policies posed by the processes of rural marginalization and proletarianization and by popular resistance among Malays, led by PAS and other Islamic reformist and populist groups.

A second development during the post-1969 period has been the reimplementation of coercive and repressive policies toward the non-Malay working class and petite bourgeoisie. Among them are the use of the Internal Security Act to detain without trial labor union leaders and leftist intellectuals, amendments to the Trade Unions Act and Industrial Relations Act to deregister unions, and changes to the Societies Act to curb political participation by Chinese associations in national politics.[6]

A third development has been the accelerated economic aggrandizement of the Malay administrative-aristocratic elite. This has taken two forms: first, through its partnership with foreign capitalists (e.g., through being provided with well-paid directorships in return for political protection), and second, through its use of state capital to acquire and control the majority of wealth within the financial, plantation, and mining sector of the economy.[7]

Rural Transformations in Post-Independence Malaysia

Inevitably, the changes in Malaysian society sketched out above have impinged directly and indirectly on the Malay peasantry. Events in the Malaysian countryside since 1957 have, in one sense, shown a continuity with the processes described in preceding chapters, but, in another, they reflect the qualitatively new conditions of life for the Malay peasantry which have arisen during the postcolonial period. These events cannot be discussed at length here, but only mentioned insofar as they bear on the themes of this book, and then only in the form of generalizations that would require qualification depending on regional and local conditions.[8]

The unstable balance of factors in the 1950s between, on one side, those that promoted the marginalization and proletarianization of poorer Malays, and on the other side, those that allowed them to sustain their economic and social position within the village community, such as their versatile subsistence strategies, the subsistence ethic, and redistributive practices, was tipped decisively in the former direction by the developments of the 1960s, 1970s and 1980s. Where redistributive mechanisms have not disappeared entirely, as has occurred with many seasonal wage-labor opportunities once offered by landowners to poor neighbors, they have been weakened. An example is the increased difficulty for the village poor in obtaining *zakat* charity.[9] De Koninck testifies to a more general phenomenon when he writes that "among the communities studied there is ample evidence of the gradual disappearance of traditional practices for the social redistribution of surplus."[10] This has been particularly true for Malays who cultivated padi as tenants, but also applies to rubber sharetappers and Malays engaged in growing other crops as sharecroppers or tenants.

The class division described for the 1950s between large landowners on one side, and small owner-operators, sharecropper-tenants, and rural wage laborers on the other, has further intensified because of the "Green Revolution" subsidies provided by the Malaysian state to the rural sector.[11] Large landowners who were previously landlord-rentiers have transformed themselves into capitalist farmers capable of earning profits from their far more productive plots (compared to before Independence) due to the application of Green Revolution inputs. In the case of the padi sector,[12] the use of these new technical inputs, which include the mechanization of ploughing and harvesting, doublecropping, and the use of chemical fertilizers and pesticides, has amply rewarded richer peasants and landowners with higher yields, incomes, and the capacity to extract higher rents from tenants. Unlike small-scale farmers elsewhere where the Green Revolution has taken place, smaller landowners and tenants, who *have* adopted these inputs, have thereby faced a crisis of "overinvestment." The sheer cost of these inputs has forced them to seek work as agrarian wage laborers in order to survive economically.[13]

At the same time, the *social organization* through which these inputs have been applied has initiated changes in the use of labor and land which have deprived smaller landowners, tenants, and agricultural laborers of access to land to cultivate and of wage-labor work during planting and harvesting.[14] For instance, comparisons of land tenure in the Muda padi-growing area between 1955 and 1975-76 allow us to infer that large landowners took back land previously rented out to tenants and began to supervise its cultivation themselves.[15] By the late 1970s, the mechanization of harvesting displaced poorer villagers who had previously earned wages by harvesting; women working in transplanting teams found that they could no longer find work when mechanized harvesting allowed broadcast seeding rather than requiring transplanting. With the new surplus in local labor supply, capitalist farmers were able to reduce wages to those relatively few workers they still employed. Tenants unable to rent in land thus found village wage-labor opportunities simultaneously reduced. Ex-tenants and padi wage laborers not able to obtain land from close kin to cultivate appear to have been marginalized. They were either forced to outmigrate from their natal villages or, with their subsistence so severely threatened, required to reduce their expenditures on ritual obligations to the point that they could no longer play the ritual and social roles expected of them in the village (see p. 148 below).

Similarly, provisions for replanting rubber smallholdings with high-yielding stock have generally rewarded wealthier smallholders with incentives to replant, while discouraging the majority of smallholders with very small rubber stands from replanting.[16] Thus the devolutionary trend observed in the colonial period has continued for a majority of *smallholders* if not of the *area* tapped. By 1985, almost one half of the 400,000 hectares held in smallholdings of less than one hectare average area had not been replanted since the 1950s, while of the 400,000 hectares of smallholdings of one to five hectares in average area, almost all had been replanted.[17] This forced peasants owning the smallest and lowest-yielding smallholdings in many instances to sell their land and turn to other forms of employment, such as sharetapping the larger smallholdings of their (relatively) wealthy neighbors. Since being eligible to replant depended first on having title to the smallholding, those who were *already* sharetappers received fewer benefits than owners from the replanting programs. As was true during the colonial period, an export "cess" was exacted from the rubber they earned under *bagi dua* just as it was for the owners of the smallholdings.[18]

Part of Malaysia's recent export-diversification program has involved promoting the cultivation of oil palm in the place of rubber among rural Malays. This is a "rational" state response to the decline in the international market share of natural rubber vis-à-vis synthetics, and to the consequent need to reduce rubber acreage in production in order to avoid a glut in supply. Insofar as Malay landowners have substituted oil palm for rubber,[19] the demand for local labor has decreased,[20] since unlike rubber trees which must be tapped every other day or so, oil palms require harvesting of their kernels only every several weeks, and this has often been done by contract labor. This too has led to a decline in wage-labor opportunities for rural Malays who previously had been sharetappers. There has thus been increased differentiation between those whom Rudner has referred to as "the dominant peasant class of Malaysian rubber producers" and their landless or near landless fellow villagers.[21]

It was precisely the new potentials for commercial profit due to the increased labor productivity provided by Green Revolution inputs that have spurred larger landowners to become capitalist farmers. Thereby they violate the village subsistence ethic by rescinding tenancy, sharecropping, and wage-labor opportunities previously extended to their poorer neighbors as mechanisms of redistribution in the form of *tolong menolong*.

The consequences of increased class division and the new pressures toward marginalization and proletarianization in the Malaysian countryside have been several. One has been the increased economic immiserization of marginalized Malay small landowners, tenants, and agricultural workers, particularly among padi cultivators.[22] Despite the suffering imposed on them with the advent of the Green Revolution, small-scale farmers have resisted leaving the land they cultivate because of the freedom it affords them to control their own labor. Where they have been able to remain by combining their own cultivation with wage labor work, they have done this "simply by overwork and tightening their belts." De Koninck refers to this as "resistance by self-exploitation."[23]

It is also important, however, to note the social de-gradation that many have been forced to endure because of their inability to meet the expenses of ritual and other obligations of everyday village life. As Scott has recently observed:

> poverty is far more than a simple matter of not enough calories or cash. This is particularly the case in Sedaka [in Kedah] where no one is in imminent danger of actually starving. For most of the village poor, poverty represents a far greater threat to their modest standing in the community. It is possible in any peasant community to identify a set of minimal cultural decencies that serve to define what full citizenship in that local society means. These minimal cultural decencies may include certain essential ritual observances for marriages and funerals, the ability to reciprocate certain gifts and favors, minimal obligations to parents, children, relatives, and neighbors, and so on. . . . *All* of these decencies . . . assume a certain level of material resources necessary to underwrite them. To fall below this level is not merely to be that much poorer materially; it is to fall short of what is locally defined as a fully human existence. It is as much a socially devastating loss of standing as it is a loss of income.[24]

However, this was how better-off villagers treated their poorer neighbors, who could not afford to meet the expenses of *kenduri* and other ritual obligations in the village Scott studied on the Kedah Plain.[25] For the first time in rural Malaysian history, the increasing economic superfluity of poorer Malays — from the perspective of village landowners, shopkeepers, and moneylenders — has translated into their social redundancy as well. This is a major change in the character of Malay *kampong* life.

Another consequence has been the flight, particularly by poorer young Malays, both men and women, from the rural *kampong* to the cities and larger towns of the peninsula, particularly to the Klang Valley (Kuala Lumpur, Petaling Jaya, and Klang), to Seremban, and Johore Bahru, to seek wage-labor employment in either government civil service or in the large-scale industrial sector.[26] A recent study by Hirschman supports the rationality of such migration, for it concludes that it is precisely in these larger cities and towns with above-average growth rates that wage labor is to be found and unemployment is lowest.[27] Nonetheless overall unemployment remained high at that time among young urban Malays, with 24.6 and 19.3 percent unemployment indices among, respectively, men and women between the ages of 15 to 24, as of 1970.[28] With the inception of export-oriented industrialization in the 1970s, unemployment among urban Malays decreased; according to government figures, from 1971 to 1980 a total of 1.3 million jobs were created in the secondary and tertiary sectors, while unemployment for all Malays fell from 8.1 percent in 1970 to 5.1 percent in 1980.[29] In the new factories that have been created as a result of Malaysia's export-oriented industrial growth, those Malays who have found work, especially younger women, have been subjected to new forms of industrial discipline and bodily regulation by employers and representatives of the state.[30]

Such migrants have not, however, severed ties with their natal villages. As young Malay adults have migrated to cities and towns for government or industrial employment, their home villages have become remittance-supported "labor reserves" in which grandparents and elder kinfolk rear the migrants' children, whose parents cannot afford to raise them in the cities where they work.[31] This subsidizing of the cost of reproduction of labor, as Meillasoux has pointed out, represents the "over-exploitation" of proletarian families by oligopoly capitalism which has become increasingly prevalent in rural areas of the Third World.[32] (However, Meillasoux's argument that such subsidizing arises because of the functional needs of capitalism is untenable, as are similar functionalist claims elsewhere, for the reasons given in chapter 1.)

Yet a third consequence, and one salient in the recent history of the Malaysian countryside, has been the episodic protests and demonstrations by poorer rural Malays against the neocolonial state and its adverse policies. Notable among them were the 1974 marches in Baling and Sik districts and the rally in Baling district by impoverished rubber cultivators, and the 1980 demonstration by Muda Project padi farmers in Alor Star, the capital of the state of Kedah. Over the course of 1974, as a result of a sharp reduction in international demand, the price of rubber fell sharply. This short-term price fall came after a long period of decline in rubber prices, as auto manufacturers and other large-scale consumers in industrialized countries substituted synthetic for natural rubber in tire manufacturing from the 1960s onward. During the same period, the cost of living, and particularly the cost of food — its largest component for the peasantry — rose sharply. The government took few steps either to protect rubber prices or lower the cost of foodstuffs. Poorer smallholders and rubber tappers were left destitute and threatened with starvation. As the situation worsened in late 1974, thousands of rural Malays marched on the towns of northern Perak and Kedah states to protest. Thirty thousand held a mass march and rally in the town of Baling in northeastern Kedah, while demonstrations also occurred in Sik district and other areas, to show displeasure with government inaction.[33] These protests are described briefly in chapter 2.

In early 1980, the government instituted a new forced-savings scheme for padi cultivators receiving the government-guaranteed price support. The scheme decreased the amount of cash income available to cultivators after sale of their padi to the National Padi Board *(Lembaga Padi Negara)*. In reaction, thousands of Malay padi farmers from the Muda Irrigation Project on the central Kedah Plain converged on the city of Alor Star to demonstrate against the forced-savings scheme and protest vocally and, in some instances, violently to the Chief Minister of the state.[34] This protest is also referred to in chapter 2. Much as during the colonial period, rural Malays made clear their willingness to resist state policies which adversely affected them, although the enfranchisement of Malay peasants from whom UMNO sought electoral support encouraged them to be more overt in their protests than during the colonial period.

As has been true of other manifestations of popular rural discontent since Independence, the 1974 Baling march and rally and the 1980 Alor Star demonstration were met with the repressive power of the contemporary Malaysian state, i.e. with arrests and detentions. The emergence of significant rural discontent, manifested in these events and others (e.g., the protests of FELDA settlers) and of a new militance on the part of first-generation Malay proletarians in the cities and towns,[35] has come to pose a significant challenge to the legitimacy and authority of UMNO.

A major base of UMNO support in rural areas has been the village elites of relatively large-scale landowners, whose transformation from rentiers into capitalist farmers has led them to rescind the tenancy, sharecropping, and wage-labor opportunities they previously offered their poorer covillagers. They have thus weakened this specific redistributive mechanism, and reneged on fulfilling this obligation in their preexisting patron-client ties with poorer Malays. The legitimacy of UMNO in Malay *kampong* has thus been further called into question.

One important "safety valve" for rural Malay discontent has been the Federal Land Development Authority (FELDA) land settlement schemes that have been initiated since the late 1950s.[36] Eligible poor rural Malays with little or no land to cultivate have, almost exclusively, been selected for settlement.[37] Establishment of the schemes has involved the clearing of new agricultural lands (in most cases) in previously remote forest areas; the major crops planted in terms of area on the land cleared have been oil palm and rubber, with cocoa and sugar being crops of lesser importance. By 1981, almost 71,000 families have been settled on 308 schemes occupying 565,000 hectares of land.[38] Typically in recent years, each family has been provided with a plot of fourteen acres in oil palm or of twelve acres in rubber from which it draws income.[39] A comparison of net incomes for families in one scheme found that from an annual pre-settlement income of $3,000, the average income of a settler family has increased to more than $12,000 —well above the government-defined "poverty line."[40] Settlement on these schemes has thus afforded these families at least temporarily what appears to be a rare opportunity to escape the downward spiral of factors pressing them toward marginalization or proletarianization.

However, FELDA schemes have been extremely limited in their effects in ameliorating rural Malay poverty, and furthermore, the increases in income for settler families are often deceptive. Although in the interval from approximately 1960 to 1981 FELDA has settled 71,000 families, during the same years the rural population has grown by more than two and one half million people. According to Peacock, "it is clear that FELDA settlement schemes have not substantially relieved pressures on existing land. For the fortunate few who are selected, it must be similar to winning a lottery. The majority of the rural poor are not touched by the schemes."[41]

Moreover, although the rare chance of being accepted as a FELDA settler family provides hope of sorts for poor rural Malays, those who have actually been settled on FELDA schemes have found conditions there far less enchanting. Despite impressive net incomes, their "take home" incomes have actually been considerably less because they have had to repay FELDA with interest for the cost of land clearance and settlement (for which FELDA uses outside firms with contract labor) during the stipulated fifteen-year repayment period. Large proportions of families are in arrears in their repayment of credits and loans to FELDA, thus delaying beyond the fifteen year period their receipt of the title to their plots. Although their monthly incomes are pegged to the changing prices of palm oil and rubber, FELDA has insisted on deducting their repayments in fixed amounts, making settler incomes subject to uncontrollable fluctuations. As a result of these arrangements, some settler families *still* have disposable incomes below the "poverty line."

Life on FELDA schemes has also entailed new forms of regimentation for rural Malays. Production in the schemes has been organized along plantation lines, imposing on settler families daily systems of bureaucratic regulation and constraint reminiscent of a Foucaultian nightmare:[42]

the visitor cannot fail to be impressed by the efficiency of work organisation on a FELDA oilpalm scheme. In the established estate tradition, the entire working population "musters" at 5:00 to 5:30 a.m., while the mandors and Field Assistants allocate the day's tasks: harvesting on a monthly cycle, weeding, manuring, pruning, pollinating and maintaining access paths. Work ends in the early afternoon when all supervisors report in detail on the day's activities. The work is intensively supervised; for example, a worker who has weeded a row of palms reports the fact to his mandor by putting a slip of paper on a thorn.[43]

The imposition of such discipline is in line with FELDA aspirations to move away from being an agency primarily devoted to providing rural Malays with land toward becoming a profitable large-scale agribusiness seeking to maximize output at lowest cost.[44]

Finally, as the FELDA settler population grows older, there are few employment opportunities for the rapidly growing population of children of settlers. FELDA has made little provision to provide them with land beyond that already allocated to their parents, and, as a result, they face a bleak future of reduced family incomes if they remain on the schemes.[45]

Under these conditions of discipline and denial it is not surprising that settlers have resisted bureaucratic direction in various ways. Scheme administrators have sought to use Islam as both the idiom of and device for intensive regulation, for instance by calling assemblies in mosques in order to stifle dissent. In contrast, "settlers confide that informal prayer groups often serve as important political nuclei in the schemes, providing opportunities for discussion out of the pervasive official earshot."[46] And settlers have on occasions actively protested the imposition of official policies in a way consistent with the long tradition of Malay peasant avoidance protest:

> there have also been disconcerting acts of collective hostility. During the 1970s, price fluctuations and management policies on savings and loan repayments prompted that action peculiar to estate agriculture in Asia, the 'kerau': FLDA officials were confined to their offices by crowds for lengthy periods.[47]

In the face of the growing economic inequality among Malays of different classes,[48] the ideology of ethnic preference articulated in the New Economic Policy, which has provided the charter of legitimacy for UMNO rule, can no longer be sustained without obvious contradictions. Of course, a compelling question is to what extent this economic inequality has general *social salience* in Malay society. Recent evidence suggests that it does. Scott, for instance, has described a peasant community in Kedah where the village poor are extremely aware of their subordination, and view village landlords and other local UMNO supporters as responsible. As Scott's work and that of other writers make clear, the ideology of PAS on the local rural level articulates from the perspective of the rural poor the themes of rural class struggle in religious and ethical terms.[49] Meanwhile, non-Malays from the working class and petite bourgeoisie have grown increasingly discontent with the ethnically discriminatory policies and programs of the New Economic Policy which have been adverse to their own economic interests and have threatened their cultural autonomy.

As class polarization among Malays continues, driven in large part by the processes of marginalization and incipient proletarianization whose origins have been reconstructed in this study, and as the mechanisms by which the Malaysian neocolonial state supports capitalist domination become increasingly transparent, a pivotal crisis of authority for those who control the Malaysian state becomes both more probable and less avoidable.

An Aside: Alternative Explanations of Rural Poverty

It is appropriate to conclude this epilogue with a brief review of the explanations of rural Malay poverty alternative to that provided in this book. As was discussed in chapter 1, if we leave aside the "world systems" approach, which was the object of extensive critique there and to which I return in the Conclusion, these explanations fall into "cultural," demographic, and "structural" accounts.

Among the various cultural explanations invoked, many have been refuted *en passant* in these pages. For instance, the view of Malay predisposition to "leisure" rather than industriousness has been repudiated as being inaccurate. To the extent that such a predisposition did exist, it could be seen as signalling a form of resistance to onerous wage-labor work in colonial capitalist enterprise. An egalitarianism militating against capital accumulation can be seen as based in the peasant subsistence ethic and mechanisms of redistribution. One cultural practice, Islamic inheritance law, has also been invoked as a major impediment to progress. It is best considered below in relation to the demographic account.

This latter explanation states that rural population growth in the 1950s and 1960s drove up rents, led to fragmentation of holdings (in combination with Islamic law emphasizing partible inheritance) and inhibited technological progress. In fact, Malay population growth during these years was exceedingly rapid — about 2.5 percent per year in the intercensal decade 1947 to 1957. Nevertheless, this study has traced the origins of rural Malay poverty and immiseration in these years to the preexisting "working out" of a complex dual dialectic — a dialectic of interaction between rural Malay communities and the colonial state, and a related long-term dialectic of internal class differentiation within these communities.

Only for the postwar period, when capitalist relations of production based on sharecropping and wage labor became common within rural Malay communities, does "population pressure" become at all relevant to the explanation of rural Malay poverty. And this is, as Engels pointed out, only because under capitalism "the pressure of population is not upon the means of subsistence but upon the means of *employment,*" contrary to the naturalized depiction of human society put forth by Malthus and his followers.[50]

For our purposes here, there are two major shortcomings of the demographic account of rural Malay poverty. First, its overly schematic and formalized abstractions — "birth rate," "net reproductive rate," "exponential growth," etc. — turn attention toward the dynamics of biological reproduction of a group and away from the social, economic, and political constraints on its livelihood and use of productive resources. The demographic account assumes these resources, such as land, to be fixed or stable in size and condition as elements of "nature." In fact, however, both their state of development and their appropriation by human beings are technologically *and* socially determined, *within historically changing constraints.* The power of these statistical abstractions to explain rural resource distribution is thereby reified, and given unjustifiable importance. Second, the demographic account assumes that human beings consume resources, but neglects the fact that their labor power — in all its aspects of energy, skill, and technique — also develops these resources to a determinate state of production over time. Taken together, these two objections underlie Engels' critique that, in capitalism as an historically specific mode of production, resources are first and foremost means of employment, and only secondarily means of subsistence. The force of the argument of this study is to take account of both the development of resources available to a growing rural Malay population over a period of more than one hundred years, *and* of the changing constraints on their appropriation arising from state policies and internal class divisions. To do so is to emphasize that Malay peasants have actively transformed "nature" and affected the structure of the colonial economy, rather than being the passive victims of both as well as of their own biological fertility.

This is not, however, to dismiss the problems associated with rural Malay population growth, but rather to balance accounts. The political and economic constraints placed on livelihoods of rural Malays by the colonial state in earlier periods set limits to the level of productive output, to the productivity, and to the distribution of what was produced by rural Malays for their subsistence. That is, the active transformative capacity of their labor power was held within these increasingly constricted limits. But during the postwar decade, rapid population growth among rural Malays exacerbated the effects of these political and economic constraints. The causes of this growth are unclear, but I suspect they represent a strategy on the part of poorer rural Malays responding to new economic aspirations by asserting control over family labor through having children. In this sense, and only in this sense, did increased population contribute to rural Malay poverty.

A similar argument applies to Islamic inheritance law and to *adat* inheritance prescriptions. Like population growth, once enacted in practice, these cultural codes distributed resources more widely across the rural population, but only within a set of imposed political and economic constraints on livelihood that changed over time but had long had inimical effects. And, given that rural Malays had *already* been made poor by these constraints, inheritance practices of equipartibility became an element of a primary redistributive mechanism to *alleviate* rural poverty. That mechanism was the passing down of land and other tangible productive assets from an elder generation to their children and other close kin. In effect Gibbons, Lim et al. make the more general point when they conclude for the Muda irrigation area that, "these social institutions [of Islamic inheritance] rather than causing rural Malay poverty, can be said to have alleviated its impact to some extent by distributing ownership of padi land widely in the community and thus providing a means of making a living to persons and households whose employment prospects otherwise would have been very bleak."[51]

The most prominent "structural" account of the causes of rural Malay poverty is that of Ungku Abdul Aziz.[52] He proposes four forms of "exploitation" as the causes of poverty. Two forms are the high rents charged on land with insecurity of tenure, and the exploitation of rural Malays working as wage laborers. The findings of this study support Ungku Aziz's claim that these two forms of exploitation are indeed causes of rural poverty. This book has sought to reconstruct the origins and sources of variation in these mechanisms of surplus appropriation.

His other two proposed forms of exploitation are more debatable. One consists of the excessive margins charged by merchants in the countryside for the services they provide; the other is the high rates of interest charged by moneylenders and shopkeepers for their loans and credit extended to farmers. Thus, middlemen, shopkeepers, rice millers, and moneylenders have been seen as taking advantage of rural Malay peasants by charging exorbitant interest on loans, or by buying peasant products cheap and selling to them imported or processed commodities dear.[53] Historically, most of these countryside merchants have been either Chinese or Chettiars from India, although, as I mentioned in chapter 6, the presence of Malay shopkeepers in some numbers has been observed in the postwar period.

In particular, officials of the Malaysian state believe that the notorious *padi kuncha* arrangement of Chinese shopkeepers has been responsible for driving padi farmers into destitution, landlessness and overall immiseration. Shopkeepers would purchase padi "futures" at a depressed price from padi farmers and, in return, provide them with small loans and credit through the long months before padi harvest. Similarly, it has been asserted that Chinese rubber dealers engage in regional price-setting cartels that would deny a fair price to Malay rubber smallholders for their rubber.[54]

Snodgrass and others have summarized the conclusions of empirical case studies that have tested Ungku Aziz's claims that shopkeepers' and dealers' margins are excessive, and that high rates of interest are extracted on loans and credit extended to rural Malays.[55] Snodgrass finds that the evidence, although scattered and episodic, does not support these claims. Profit margins appear relatively low, given various overhead costs, and "it does seem safe at this point to say that 'exploitation' of rural Malays is much less widespread than has been averred in some structuralist commentaries and that private markets have provided the peasant farmer with ancillary services far more competitively and efficiently than has been assumed by policy-makers."[56] Therefore, the latter two claims of the structural account must be rejected.

Although levels of "reasonable" profit-taking can always be disputed, Snodgrass does hint at the extremely important additional point that compared to the monopsonist (and monopoly) characteristics of the higher levels of the distribution system, the market conditions prevailing among local, lower-level dealers with whom Malay farmers come into daily contact appear to be far more competitive.[57] This is consistent with the organization of a distribution system associated with an oligopoly large-scale capitalist sector, such as Malaysia's.

Restraint of trade and the taking of excess profits from oligopoly and oligopsony were, in general, privileges reserved during the colonial period to the British operators of "agency houses." Since Independence, these have belonged to members of Malaysia's new bourgeoisie, who own and control the large-scale importing, exporting, and distributing firms, and not to the petty shopkeepers and dealers who maintain the termini of the wholesaling and retail hierarchies. Rural Malay farmers have been exploited by excessively high prices for the manufactured goods they buy, and by excessively low prices for the primary commodities they produce and sell. The causes of such excess profit-taking are found at the tops of these hierarchies, and not at their bottoms; in air-conditioned skyscrapers in Kuala Lumpur and Singapore, and not in the modest establishments of shopkeepers in the countryside. This profit-taking has long exacerbated the other factors described in this study which have inhibited rural Malay well-being from the early twentieth century to the present.

Conclusion: The Malaysian Paradox Reconsidered

The foregoing chapters have been an attempt to reconstruct the resistance of the Malay peasantry to British colonial rule over a period of approximately one hundred years from the end of the precolonial period until Independence in 1957. Indeed, one principal point of this study is that the history of the Malay peasantry under British colonial rule is without question one of active *resistance*. It is not a history of passive incorporation into some capitalist master plan implemented by an omniscient colonial state for the exploitation of non-European peoples in Malaya, as appears to be assumed by advocates of the functionalist "world systems" approach described in chapter 1.

A second major point is that the history of Malay peasant resistance has not, for the most part, been one of high drama, rebellions or uprisings, guerrilla warfare, or labor strikes against either capitalist enterprise or the colonial state. In contrast such was the resistance of immigrant Chinese and Indian proletarians who engaged in the most overt and violent forms of class struggle against both institutions, before and during the Emergency period. Instead, Malay peasant resistance has been in a low key, played largely pianissimo: covert, popular, and extensive but rarely organized; continuous and quotidian rather than episodic and spectacular; and manifested in evasion and noncooperation masked as compliance, rather than in confrontation. Moreover, as previous chapters attest, there has been an essential continuity in forms of peasant avoidance protest from the precolonial era to the present. That is, the relationship of rural Malays to the colonial state and to colonial capitalism over this period can only be described, as James C. Scott has put it, as one of "everyday forms of peasant resistance" and the deployment of the "weapons of the weak" against the strong.[58] Scott has observed:

> The history of Malay peasant resistance to the state . . . has yet to be written. When, and if, it is written, however, it will not be a history in which open rebellion or formal organizations play a significant role. . . . Resistance to colonial rule was marked far less by open confrontations than by willful and massive noncompliance with its most threatening aspects, for example, the persistent underreporting of landholdings and crop yields to minimize taxes, the relentless disregard for all regulations designed to restrict smallholders' rubber planting and marketing, the unabated pioneer settlement of new land despite a host of laws forbidding it.[59]

Thus, for instance, as described in the preceding chapters, rural Malays in great numbers illegally occupied State lands. They planted prohibited rubber on forest and swamp lands newly alienated for padi and on lands previously under padi cultivation. They did so despite the regulations and practices of the colonial administration designed to curb the competitive threat they posed to plantation capitalism. During most of the colonial period, rural Malays persisted in planting and tapping rubber smallholdings, despite official opposition and discouragement.

Of course, the forms that resistance and evasion by the Malay peasantry to the state took were not uniform. They varied depending on their location within regional economies and the constraints that location imposed on them. The inducements and pressures by the administration directed toward rural Malays to grow padi for the market in the years immediately after World War I, in the 1930s, and in the late 1940s and early 1950s were episodic because they were cued to the world capitalist business cycle as it impinged on the colonial economy. But they were effective only against those peasants who lived in "rice bowl" semicore areas, and who had little or no other choice. Yet, once implicated in commercial padi production by the administration's manipulation of padi price incentives and the promises of government development programs, Malay peasants in semicore areas were prompt to resist en masse the government's actions when these caused peasant incomes to drop and jeopardized peasant livelihoods. This was evident from the 1955 and 1980 protests by padi planters described above. Malays in core areas of the west coast continued to plant —

when they could — and tap rubber smallholdings instead of cultivating padi, while even in semicore areas after the Japanese occupation, peasants planted rubber when they were able to get away with doing so. By the 1950s, rural Malays in both core and semicore areas began to flee padi farming in massive numbers. As road networks and trading system expanded after World War II, Malays in peripheral areas turned to rubber planting and tapping, not to commercial padi cultivation. Alternatively they migrated to more populous areas to find wage labor. When the livelihoods of rubber smallholders were threatened by the measures of the state, they protested vocally and at times violently. Example include their response to the imposition of the Stevenson scheme in 1922 and their marches and demonstrations in Baling and elsewhere when rubber prices fell precipitously in 1974, more than fifty years later.

If massive but unspoken circumvention of laws and regulations, footdragging in compliance, occasionally vocal (but rarely violent) protest, and flight are not the features of high historical drama, they are nonetheless the elements out of which a history of Malay resistance to and evasion of the domination of the colonial state and Malayan capitalism must be written. Most important, and necessary to resolve the paradox about the primitive accumulation process set forth in chapter 1, peasant resistance and evasion were partly successful in retarding rural Malay marginalization and proletarianization and in challenging the dominant position of colonial capitalism. However, since Independence the outcome of the struggle has not been in doubt, and poorer Malay peasants have clearly been the losers in it, while their wealthier fellow villagers have prospered.

The general paradox discussed in chapter 1 is that, although the primitive accumulation process for colonial capitalism in the Third World was by no means predetermined, it has nevertheless occurred with tragic regularity. As such, the paradox poses profound issues of historical causation, of the relative force and balance of chance and necessity, and of subjective praxis and objective conditions in the historical process. It may not prove possible to resolve the paradox in its general form, but certainly the findings of the present study are relevant to its deconstruction and, thus transformed, to its eventual resolution. Restated for the instance of Malaysia, the paradox is that, despite the fact that the primitive accumulation process in colonial Malaya was not inevitable — events could have happened differently at many turns — there was active peasant resistance to it; and despite the fact that the colonial state faced serious internal contradictions in its own development, nonetheless, the marginalization and proletarianization of the Malay peasantry began to occur, and still continue to do so. In this sense, colonial and neocolonial capitalism have triumphed.

Marx observed that

men make their own history, but they do not make it just as they please; they do not make it under circumstances chosen by themselves, but under circumstances directly encountered, given and transmitted from the past.[60]

Central to the present work is the assumption that *both* parts of Marx's principle are crucial and, moreover, apply to men and women — to the officials of the colonial state, to the colonial capitalists they supported, *and* to the Malay peasants whom the first sought to control and regulate, the second to exploit and hold back. That is, the history of the conflict was a dialectical one: those on either side sought to "make their own history" in struggles with those on the other, but neither was "able to make it just as they please" but had to confront and attempt to overcome "circumstances directly encountered, given and transmitted from the past," including the presence and subjective praxis of those on the other side.

Within this dialectical struggle, the principal actors on whom this study has focused have been the Malay peasantry and the administrators of the British colonial state, while colonial capitalists have generally been accessories. By themselves, European plantation and mining capitalists did not exercise coercive or ideological power directly over the peasantry, but rather only indirectly through the colonial administration and its Malay elite clients. Thus within this struggle, the character of the relationship between European capitalists —both in England and in the colony itself — and colonial officials became crucial to the primitive accumulation process. At present too little is known about this relationship and its consequences for the history of the Malaysian peasantry.

I have suggested above (see pp. 94-96) reasons why the goals and perspectives of colonial capitalists and officials were generally compatible — they shared material interests (e.g., the investments of high officials in planting and mining enterprise) and most core cultural values. Nevertheless, it can never be assumed that they were identical. If in some sense the colonial state "represented" the interests of the European, especially the British bourgeoisie, its administrators at no time represented the interests of *all* European capitalists in Malaya, much less immigrant Chinese or Indian capitalists. Ties of patronage between individual capitalists and officials no doubt existed (though little has been written about them). Officials acted to police colonial capitalism against individual capitalists who violated class interests, as when they implemented rubber restriction schemes which were aimed not only at Malay smallholders but at the plantations as well. Colonial officials did have material interests and ideological commitments distinct from those of capitalists. These included, among other, advancing up the bureaucratic hierarchies of the colony and even of the empire, ensuring the longevity of their employment, implementing a vision of "progress" and stability, and meeting standards of administrative "service" to King and Empire.[61] Moreover, British policies in Malaysia were at all times constrained by more encompassing imperial strategic concerns in the Colonial

Office; Malayan officials were responsible first to their superiors in London and only then (and derivatively) to local capitalists. To state it plainly, Malaya was, in relative terms, a very small possession in a very large empire, with comparatively little economic or strategic significance during most of the colonial period. The British Malayan Civil Service, its interests, and commitments to Malayan capitalism were matters of relatively small moment within the larger imperial scheme of things.[62] This was true until the end of World War II, when Malaya's role as principal dollar-earner in the Sterling area became of overriding importance to Great Britain. Perhaps all of these considerations explain why, as in times of prosperity such as the early 1900s, "the commercial interest in the East chafed under what they saw as a civil service dictatorship, a closed corporation in which they had no direct voice, especially in the vital area of finance."[63]

The interests and commitments of officials from the middle to late colonial period (from 1900 onward) were, moreover, different from those of officials of earlier periods. Not only can gross contrasts be made with officials in the eighteenth century, exemplified by military adventurers like Raffles and Light; rather, changes occurred in the course of bureaucratic succession within the Malayan Civil Service (MCS) itself, as Allen has shown. Allen refers to the fateful transition, dating from approximately 1890, from a generation of colonial officials who were "freebooters and eccentrics" to a succeeding generation whose "values and prejudices" were those of "a very small sector of British society which we may most readily identify if we label it the Public School-Oxbridge Class."[64] He goes on to state that "this 'takeover' of the M.C.S. by Public School-Oxbridge graduates, which was not carried out altogether without bitterness, I would regard as one of the watersheds in the history of British Malaya."[65] At least two other partial successions leading to changes within British officialdom appear to have occurred. One came after World War I, when new men with battle-field promotions followed many of the "Public School-Oxbridge graduates" who were war casualties.[66] A similar one occurred after World War II, when a cohort of men with administrative specialist training but little Malayan experience came to occupy positions previously held by MCS officers interned in Changi who had died or retired early because of medical disability.[67] However, little is known in detail about either.

A set of issues deserving much further research concerns the ways in which the class backgrounds and professional socialization of colonial civil servants were conditioned by political and ideological developments of the middle and late colonial periods within Britain itself (e.g., liberal reform movements, trends toward professionalization within the colonial services), and how they reflected class, ethnic, regional, and other differences within the home country.[68] Surely, changes in the composition of the administrative corps affected by these developments ha l important consequences for the specific policies and practices adopted by officials toward the Malay peasantry, although we have little knowledge of these consequences in detail.

My claim then is that the colonial state may "reflect" capitalist interests, but for all that cannot be reduced to a reflection of these interests, for those controlling and operating it had other, ancillary aims as well. Thus some autonomy from the needs of capitalist accumulation existed for the colonial state and its officials. And, therefore, the struggle between the Malay peasantry and the colonial state has to some extent, a dynamic *not* reducible to the primitive accumulation process, although this process was *central* to it. A realm of "free play" existed.

As an example, the *Malay Reservations Enactment* of 1913 was clearly implemented in ways compatible with and favorable to the land needs of colonial plantation enterprise, but it was by no means predictable from the requirements for accelerated capital accumulation among British and other European rubber companies at the time. Rather, this *Enactment* followed from the aims and efforts of colonial administrators to stabilize Malay peasants on the land, and to bend their independent wills to the task of becoming the "yeoman peasantry" which official nostalgia for an ideal feudal past required them to be.[69] The design by officials to exploit rural Malay cultivators by transforming them into suppliers of cheap rice to plantation and mining proletariats came after and not before the Enactment. However, the impulse of officials to dominate rural workers by reducing them to ciphers within their nostalgic vision did, however, precede the *Enactment,* was crucial to its origin, and predisposed officials later toward exploiting padi farmers in order to maintain low rice prices and industrial harmony within the colonial economy.

Not only was the conflict between the Malay peasantry and the colonial state constrained by official aims and interests at times oblique to the requirements of capitalist accumulation; even when official policies and strategies were congruent with these requirements, it was by no means the case that the power of the state to execute these policies and strategies was assured. Thus, for instance, in chapter 4 I discussed the limits on the econor ic, coercive, and ideological power of the colonial state to restrain rural Malays from planting rubber in the early 1900s: the administration was undermanned; official opinion was at first divided; the attention of officials was directed elsewhere to developments within the tin mining industry (and the threats these posed to British dominance of it); there were conflicts between different bureaucratic levels of the colonial service; and financial resources were being directed toward road and rail construction and the building of other infrastructure, and not toward regulating the production of rural Malays. In general, then, it can never be assumed that the colonial state possessed the power necessary to promote successful capitalist accumulation by curbing competition from indigenous producers.

As the foregoing chapters have demonstrated, in many ways the policies and strategies of the colonial administration directed against rural Malays were reactions to events beyond its control. They were not elements of some colonialist master plan geared toward exploitation of the peasantry and initiated from a position of near omnipotence. For instance, as described above, periodic attempts by administrators to stimulate padi production by Malays arose on one side from pressures on the state to curb the outflow of foreign exchange reserves during periods of depression or of scarcity of rice imported from elsewhere in the British empire. On the other side, there were realistic fears that domestic rice scarcities would both drive up the cost of wages and lead to labor "unrest" among the immigrant proletariat. After the early 1930s, it is true, officials came to view rural Malays as constituting a reserve of food suppliers for the non-Malay proletariat at times of rice scarcity. But this was an opportunistic reaction to events and not — at least until the postwar period — the basis for a long-term policy.

Interests and commitments on the part of colonial officials tangential to the requirements of colonial capitalism, limits on the forms of power exercised by the colonial state, its necessarily reactive rather than initiatory character — all represent systemic limits on the capacity of the colonial state to affect the outcomes of events in which the Malay peasantry was implicated in ways that consistently favored capitalist accumulation. Moreover, earlier solutions to problems, later when conditions had changed, posed new problems in themselves. For instance, official encouragement of rural Malays to settle new land from the turn of the century onward as part of the process of "opening up" the peninsula provided Malays with the opportunity to plant rubber, and, thus, eventually to pose a competitive challenge to the European rubber estates. Decisions once made were played out irreversibly, and later became those preexisting conditions that constrained the subsequent choices that could be made. To consider but one aspect: an early commitment by the state toward the closing years of the nineteenth century to a plantation-based agrarian economy (rather than, for instance, to the settler colonialism found in Australia, Kenya, or elsewhere) brought on later problems whose dimensions could not be at all apparent at the time. These included the necessity to secure an immigrant proletariat, discipline it, and prevent "unrest," find food for it, protect its health, limit indigenous competition, etc. — all in the interest of capitalist accumulation. These later problems had to be dealt with both in terms of exogenous developments (e.g., variations in rice harvests in Burma or Thailand, changes in the international prices of rubber or tin, fluctuations in overseas migration of workers from China or India) *and* resistance by both Malays and non-Malays to playing their respective roles in the colonial economy envisioned for them by officials and capitalists. It is factors such as these that represented those "circumstances directly encountered, given and transmitted from the past" with which colonial officials at any one time had to contend.

If, heretofore, functionalist accounts of the primitive accumulation process within the setting of the "world system" have argued, in effect, that colonial capitalists and administrators "make history" while non-European peoples —peasants and others—do not, then the main purpose of the present study has been to demonstrate that these accounts are seriously one-sided and inadequate. That is, first, as I have been asserting, neither colonial administrators nor capitalists made history "under circumstances of their own choosing." Second, indigenous peoples—in this instance Malay peasants—even though "they [did] not make it just as they please," *did* "make history."

From the late nineteenth century onward, rural Malays sought to participate in and accomodate to the colonial economy, and often did so successfully. In the foregoing chapters, there is little evidence to support the assertion of one observer that "colonialism and all that it entailed opened the indigenous Malaysian peasant society to the ravages of world market forces, especially after the introduction of the cash crop, rubber."[70] Instead, Malay peasants on their own showed a remarkable capacity to engage in cash crop production and to be capable indeed at it, to the point that they came to challenge the dominant position of the European rubber industry. Moreover, they were generally disinclined throughout most of the colonial period to cultivate cash crops which were economically unrewarding, particularly padi, except when they had little or no alternative, as among Malays in semicore areas.

As long as noncapitalist relations of production prevailed within Malay society, that is, while labor and land were not treated as commodities, and as long as the colonial state did not interfere with the conditions under which peasant production took place, Malay engagement with the commercialized colonial economy proved to be enviable indeed. Even after the administration succeeded in transforming indigenous labor and land into commodities within the colonial economy as a whole, Malay rural social organization provided a buffer against the most deleterious effects of this. As was shown in the previous chapter, for instance, it was the existence of extensive redistributive mechanisms grounded in the peasant subsistence ethic within Malay *kampong* during the postwar period that allowed poorer rural Malays to maintain a precarious subsistence and remain largely outside the permanent wage-labor market. Further, as I have argued, it was peasants' resistance to official efforts to regulate their livelihood, particularly their cultivation of rubber, that allowed many of them to prosper, and delayed substantially their marginalization or proletarianization.

Malay peasants, then, in their everyday livelihood established an undeniable presence within the colonial economy, one which came to threaten the core process of capital accumulation in the European plantation sector. As I have demonstrated in chapter 5, it was this challenge to colonial capitalism itself that called forth a systematic repressive response on the part of colonial officials in tandem with plantation capitalists. It was in this period of crisis during the interwar period first of stagnation and then of depression, that one of the two master-strokes of the primitive accumulation process was delivered against the Malay peasantry. This was the implementation of the rubber restriction schemes which prevented Malay smallholders from planting new rubber trees, while encouraging plantations to replant. By its rigorous imposition of these schemes on the peasantry, the colonial state initiated a long-term devolutionary process that made it impossible for large numbers of Malay peasants to reproduce their means of livelihood until after Independence and — for many —not even then.

This process was reinforced by the other master-stroke. This one was struck from the early 1930s onward, but most strongly after the Japanese occupation, by which rural Malays were enjoined through persuasion, economic inducement, and compulsion to persist in cultivating padi, even though padi growing for small farmers was probably the least remunerative agricultural occupation open to them. By the 1950s, flight out of padi production was the understandable response of many Malay peasants. However, at that time, for most this left only two options: outmigrating to work as sharetappers within the deteriorating rubber smallholding sector and facing eventual destitution, or working as wage laborers on rubber estates and similar enterprises, or in government service. Hit hard by both strokes, rural Malay communities had begun by the 1950s to undergo an intensified process of internal class differentiation. A relatively few Malays with large landholdings prospered as rentiers, shopkeepers, and moneylenders, while the vast majority stagnated, surviving by combining cultivation on their own extremely small plots with tenancy-sharecropping and seasonal or temporary wage labor.

Neither master-stroke was, in any sense, historically inevitable. However, having been delivered, together they set a series of events into train whose outcome was a peasantry most of whom were poised precariously between destitution and immiserization on one hand, and marginalization and proletarianization on the other, and only protected from the latter by residual redistributive mechanisms within the village. But with the development of the Green Revolution in the 1960s and 1970s and the spur to profit-taking it provided to rentiers-turned-capitalist-farmers, this balance was tipped in the direction of the marginalization of poorer Malays from *kampong* social life and their flight to the cities to seek permanent wage-labor employment, with the exception of a fortunate few who were able to become FELDA settlers.

If there is a resolution of the Malaysian paradox which has been central to the present study, it is to be found in the ways in which the British colonial state "represented" and "reflected" the material interests of colonial capitalists at times of deep crisis for the world capitalist system — for example during the world depression of the 1930s, and again during the immediate postwar period when the domination of colonial capitalism was being challenged in Malaya, as elsewhere throughout the Third World, by new forces for independence and liberation. In contrast, the relationship between colonial capitalism and the colonial state in periods of prosperity was both more complex and problematic. However, the policies and strategies initiated by the state in times of crisis and subsequently sustained, altered irreversibly the prospects for rural Malay livelihood and social integrity. At such times, the relationship between the British administration and colonial capitalism was not so much rendered transparent as simplified and reordered toward the central priority of reproducing those conditions that ensured capitalist accumulation when it was most threatened. At these times Malay peasant resistance and evasion, the militance of the non-Malay proletariat, and the systemic constraints on the power of the colonial state discussed above were overcome by the massed power of the state and Malaysian capitalism organized in tandem.

Nonetheless, the conflict has not been without great cost to Malaysian capitalism and the larger world order of which it was and remains a part. Although Malaysian capitalism and the neocolonial state are presently triumphant over the Malay peasantry and both the Malay and non-Malay proletariats, in the future they must face their transformed opponents in new struggles. The outcomes of these struggles are by no means predetermined or certain, and revolutionary changes may yet emerge from them.

Notes

PREFACE

1. Malcolm Caldwell, "War, Boom, and Depression," in *Malaya: The Making of Neo-Colony,* edited by Mohamed Amin and M. Caldwell, Nottingham: Spokesman Books, 1977, p. 63 note 33.
2. Peter J. Rimmer and Lisa M. Allen, *The Underside of Malaysian History: Pullers, Prostitutes, Plantation Workers...,* Singapore: Singapore University Press, 1990.
3. Ibid., p. 3.
4. Jomo K.S., *Growth and Structural Change in the Malaysian Economy,* London: McMillan, 1990; idem, *Beyond 1990: Considerations for a New National Development Strategy,* Kuala Lumpur: Institut Pengajian Tinggi/Institute of Advanced Studies, Universiti Malaya, 1989.
5. Shamsul, A.B., *From British to Bumiputera Rule: Local Politics and Rural Development in Peninsular Malaysia,* Singapore: Institute of Southeast Asia Studies, 1986.
6. Patrick Sullivan, *Social Relations of Dependence in a Malay State: Nineteenth Century Perak,* Kuala Lumpur: Malaysian Branch of the Royal Asiatic Society Monographs, 10, 1982.

CHAPTER ONE

1. The terms "peasant" and "peasantry," which I use frequently in this study have, in general, become unrespectable, often for sound theoretical reasons, given the imprecision and tendency toward essentialization with which they were employed in many early studies. Instead, "simple commodity producers" or "petty commodity producers" and the "forms of production" associated with them have come to be the preferred concepts. The concepts "peasants" and "peasantry" appear to have come under a theoretical cloud for the first time with the Marxist-structuralist critique by Judith Ennew, Paul Hirst, and Keith Tribe, " 'Peasantry' as an Economic Category." They proposed that "simple commodity production" was a more theoretically productive concept. Subsequent discussion and controversy over the theoretical value of "simple commodity production" or "petty commodity production" can be found *inter alia* in Joel Kahn, "From Peasants to Petty Commodity Production in Southeast Asia"; Harriet Friedmann,

"Simple Commodity Production and Wage Labour on the American Plains";
idem, "Household Production and the National Economy: Concepts for the
Analysis of Agrarian Formations"; Carol A. Smith, "Labor and International
Capital in the Making of a Peripheral Social Formation"; idem, "Forms of
Production in Practice: Fresh Approaches to Simple Commodity Production";
Michel-Rolph Trouillot, "Caribbean Peasantries and World Capitalism: An
Approach to Micro-level Studies."

I defend my use of these terms, in part on the grounds that some portmanteau
concept such as "peasant" is needed in the present instance of an historical
analysis where the changing meanings of "commodity" and "commodity
production" in Malaysia are being traced over time. At no point in what follows
do I refer to a "peasant economy" or "peasant mode of production," or engage in
similar reifications. Furthermore, the use of "peasant" and "peasantry" instead
has two other advantages. First, unlike "simple/petty commodity producer," it
avoids an implicit economism by recognizing the existence of social and
political processes as well as economic ones in everyday rural life. Second, like
other terms I use (e.g., "cultivator," "farmer") both terms are intrinsically
relational. Therefore, of necessity they dynamically implicate "the state,"
"agrarian capitalism" etc. in ways that the following analysis sets out to clarify
rather than presuppose. Here I invoke Wittgenstein's dictum in *The
Philosophical Investigations* that the meaning of concepts is found in their use,
to suggest that this entire book sets out to define what "peasants" and
"peasantries" in Malaysia were and are.

2. Michael Stenson, *Class, Race and Colonialism in West Malaysia;* Robert L.
   Bach, "Historical Patterns of Capitalist Penetration in Malaysia"; W. Richards,
   "The Underdevelopment of West Malaysia," Shamsul Amri Baharuddin, "The
   Development of the Underdevelopment of the Malaysian Peasantry"; Jomo
   Kwame Sundaram, *A Question of Class.*

3. Stenson, *Class, Race and Colonialism,* p. xi.

4. Ibid., p. 4.

5. Bach, "Historical Patterns," p. 469.

6. Ibid., p. 472.

7. Ibid., p. 473.

8. See, e.g., Richards, "Underdevelopment," and Shamsul, "Development of the
   Underdevelopment."

9. I state "so-called 'cultural' explanations" because all such explanations
   presuppose an overly idealist conceptualization of culture, and the definition of
   culture is itself as much at issue as the specific use of this conceptualization to
   account for the condition of the contemporary Malay peasantry. For a good
   discussion of "cultural" accounts, see Donald R. Snodgrass, *Inequality and
   Economic Development in Malaysia,* pp. 112–24, and for a specific village study
   emphasizing "cultural" and demographic factors, see M.G. Swift, "Economic
   Concentration and Malay Peasant Society."

10. Robert Ho, "The Evolution of Agriculture and Land Ownership in Saiong
    Mukim"; idem, "Land Ownership and Economic Prospects of Malayan

Peasants"; M.G. Swift, *Malay Peasant Society in Jelebu;* idem, "Economic Concentration"; Rosemary Barnard, "The Role of Capital and Credit in a Malay Rice-producting Village," pp. 116, 122–23, 125, 135; Brien K. Parkinson, "Non-economic Factors in the Economic Retardation of the Rural Malays." For a critique of Parkinson's argument, see William Wilder, "Islam, Other Factors and Malay Backwardness."

11. Lim Chong-Yah, *Economic Development of Modern Malaya,* pp. 173–74; Swift, "Economic Concentration," pp. 244 ff.

12. For a relevant critique of neomalthusian models, see Donald M. Nonini, "Varieties of Materialism," pp. 33–49.

13. Ho, "Land Ownership," p. 92.

14. Swift, "Economic Concentration," p. 244.

15. The foremost proponent of this view has been Ungku Abdul Aziz: Ungku Abdul Aziz, "Facts and Fallacies on the Malay Economy"; idem, "Facts and Fallacies About the Malay Economy, in Retrospect with New Footnotes"; idem, "Poverty and Rural Development in Malaysia." See the discussion of this approach in Snodgrass, *Inequality,* pp. 124–31. For a theoretical analysis of the issues involved, see C.R. Wharton, "Marketing, Merchandizing, and Money-lending."

16. Stanley Diamond, "Rethinking the Primitive" (personal communication).

17. For a good review of "dependency theory," a set of theoretical propositions closely aligned to "world systems" theory, and of their shortcomings, see Fernando Henrique Cardoso, "The Consumption of Dependency Theory in the United States."

18. For relevant critiques of functionalist theory in anthropology, see Paul Diener and Eugene E. Robkin, "Ecology, Evolution, and the Search for Cultural Origins"; Nonini, "Varieties."

19. Peter Worsley, "One World or Three," p. 306.

20. Diener and Robkin, "Ecology, Evolution."

21. What can be viewed as domains of "free play" and indeterminacy at the international or "world systems" level can, of course, be characterized as dialectical processes of struggle with their regularities at the national, regional, and local levels of these societies.

22. Joel S. Kahn, "The Social Context of Technological Change in Four Malaysian Villages," p. 559.

23. Worsley, "One World," p. 307.

24. Terence Hopkins, "The Study of the Capitalist World-Economy," p. 34. Nor has there been much new interest on the part of world-systems theorists, since Hopkins wrote in 1979, in theoretically understanding the cultural and ideological dimensions of colonial and neocolonial social orders. One possibly relevant recent focus was on "antisystemic movements" vis-à-vis the world capitalist system, including peasant movements. (see, e.g., Samir Amin et al., *Transforming the Revolution: Social Movements and the World-System.*) Although in other respects some of this work represents an important theoretical contribution, there is no sustained attempt to examine the relationship between the cultural and ideological features of domination *and* resistance to it in these

social orders, on one hand, and the processes of class differentiation and deployment of state power, on the other. Instead, spatial consociation (between the emergence of certain movements and "core" and "periphery") substitutes for contextualization and causal explanation. Functionalist accounts of their existence are still put forward; for instance, that social movements "are themselves products of the system, one way of its adjusting to its contradictions." Ibid., p. 181.

25. Specific interest in Malay peasant resistance reflects recent theoretical developments among social historians, anthropologists, and political scientists studying agrarian transformations and "everyday forms of peasant resistance" across rural Southeast Asia. See "Special Issue *(Journal of Peasant Studies):* Everyday Forms of Peasant Resistance in South-East Asia," edited by James C. Scott and Benedict J. Tria Kerkvliet, 1986.

26. Lim Teck Ghee, *Peasants and Their Agricultural Economy in Colonial Malaya, 1874–1941;* Hua Wu Yin, *Class and Communalism in Malaysia;* Mohamed Amin, "Appendix: British 'Intervention' and Malay Resistance"; Malcolm Caldwell, "War, Boom and Depression"; Cheah Boon Kheng, "Hobsbawm's Social Banditry, Myth, and Historical Reality"; Shaharil Talib, *After Its Own Image,* esp. chapters 5–6, pp. 114–75; idem, "A Revolt in Malaysian Historiography"; James de Vere Allen, "The Kelantan Uprising of 1915"; Ibrahim Nik Mahmood, "The To' Janggut Rebellion of 1915."

27. Clive S. Kessler, "Islam, Society and Political Behaviour"; idem, *Islam and Politics in a Malay State;* Shamsul Amri Baharuddin, "A Revival in the Study of Islam in Malaysia"; Mohamed, "Appendix."

28. James C. Scott, *Weapons of the Weak.*

29. Zawawi Ibrahim, "Malay Peasants and Proletarian Consciousness"; Fatimah Halim, "Rural Labour Force and Industrial Conflict in West Malaysia."

30. Fatimah, "Rural Labour Force"; for the Alor Star "riots", see *New Straits Times* of January 27, 1980; on the FELDA scheme conflicts, see *New Straits Times,* July 3, 1978 and July 1, 1979.

31. Shaharil Talib, "Voices from the Kelantan Desa." See also the references to Malay society given in Khoo Kay Kim, "Recent Malaysian Historiography."

32. Cheah Boon Kheng, "Social Banditry and Rural Crime in North Kedah, 1909–1929"; idem, "Hobsbawm's Social Banditry."

33. Shaharil Talib, *After Its Own Image,* pp. 134–75.

34. Zawawi Ibrahim, "Malay Peasants and Proletarian Consciousness"; idem, "Perspectives Towards Investigating Malay Peasant Ideology and the Bases of its Production in Contemporary Malaysia"; idem, "Investigating Peasant Consciousness in Contemporary Malaysia."

35. The comparative literature on state formation is voluminous and crosses several disciplines. For an excellent overview of the issue of state formation within anthropology, see the introduction by Christine W. Gailey and Thomas C. Patterson, "Power Relations and State Formation," and other essays in *Power Relations and State Formation.* See also Christine W. Gailey, "The State of the State in Anthropology." For a classic study of the changing relationship between

a non-European state and kin-ordered communities, see Stanley Diamond, "Dahomey: A Proto-state in West Africa." The spatial dimensions of precapitalist state administrative power have been most thoughtfully analyzed by G. William Skinner, "Cities and the Hierarchy of Local Systems," esp. pp. 301–44.

36. Karl Marx, *Capital.*

37. Giovanni Arrighi, "Labor Supplies in Historical Perspective." p. 214.

38. Anthony Short, *The Communist Insurrection in Malaya, 1948–1960.*

39. E.K. Fisk, "Rural Development Problems in Malaya," p. 254.

40. Syed Husin Ali, *Social Stratification in Kampong Bagan,* p. 40.

41. See Fatimah Halim, "The Major Mode of Surplus Labour Appropriation in the West Malaysian Countryside," on sharecropping as the major mode of surplus labor appropriation in rural Malaysia.

42. Peter J. Wilson, *A Malay Village and Malaysia,* pp. 74–77.

43. Swift, *Malay Peasant Society,* pp. 53, 168.

44. Mokhzani Abdul Rahim, "Comments in the Colloquium, 'The Dynamics of Social Change and Economic Development in the Rural Sector of Malaysia,'" p. 39.

45. Cited in D.S. Gibbons, Lim Teck Ghee, G.R. Elliston, and Shukur bin Kassim, *Land Tenure in the Muda Irrigation Area,* p. 158, Table 77; *relong* have been converted to acres as the area unit.

46. Ibid., p. 165.

47. The percentage of landless tenants among all households was as follows: 44.1 percent in 1964–65, in M. Kuchiba and Y. Tsubouchi, "Paddy Farming and Social Structure in a Malay Village," p. 468; 44.4 percent in 1975 in a village in Perlis, and 44.6 percent in 1967 in a village in Yan, Kedah, both reported in Kenzo Horii, *Rice Economy and Land Tenure in West Malaysia,* p. 93 (Table 7–1); and 56.1 percent in 1967 in Rosemary Barnard, "The Modernization of Agriculture in a Kedah Village, 1967–1978."

48. Gibbons, Lim, et al., *Land Tenure,* p. 166; Rice Production Committee, *Report of the Rice Production Committee, Volume I,* pp. 81–82.

49. Gibbons, Lim, et al., *Land Tenure,* p. 166.

50. Ibid., p. 157.

51. Cited in ibid., p. 173.

52. Kuchiba and Tsubouchi, "Paddy Farming," p. 466 (Table 1), found 16.5 percent of all households dependent on wage labor; Barnard, "Role of Capital and Credit," p. 114, found 26.5 percent so dependent. Both villages studied were less than ten miles from Alor Star.

53. Syed Husin Ali, *Malay Peasant Society and Leadership,* p. 84.

54. Mokhtar Tamin, "Comments in the Colloquium, 'The Dynamics of Social Change and Economic Development in the Rural Sector of Malaysia,'" p. 57.

55. Horii, *Rice Economy,* pp. 93, 80, 119, resp.; the study year was 1968–1969.

56. Ibid., pp. 118–28. It should be stated that it is unfortunate, in the study cited and in many others, that insufficient attention is paid to the division of labor between genders and between generations within families whose members included, along with nonmembers, the persons constituting the "household" unit. An exclusive focus on "households" as units of analysis and on the work of "heads of household" not only directs attention away from family strategies for upward mobility, but also glosses over conflicts between men and women and parents and children—both features central to a domestic political economy among the Malay peasantry. This is a shortcoming of many of the studies cited here but, sad to say, there are no alternatives for the period under discussion.

57. Manning Nash, *Peasant Citizens: Politics, Religion and Modernization in Kelantan, Malaysia,* pp. 20, 26.

58. Ibid., p. 22.

59. Sharifah Zaleha Hassan, "Institution Vs. Technology in the Fishing Industry"; Yap Chan Ling, "Fishery Policies and Development with Special Reference to the West Coast of Peninsular Malaysia from the Early 1900's"; Horii, *Land Tenure,* pp. 126–28; Raymond Firth, *Malay Fishermen: Their Peasant Economy.*

60. Firth, *Malay Fishermen,* p. 342.

61. Husin Ali, *Malay Peasant Society,* p. 83.

62. Fisk, "Rural Development Problems."

63. Calculated from Lim Chong-Yah, *Economic Development,* pp. 31–32, and from M.V. Del Tufo, *Malaya: A Report of the 1947 Census of Population,* p. 104.

64. Fisk, "Rural Development Problems."

65. Lim, *Economic Development;* Fisk, "Rural Development Problems."

66. Del Tufo, *Malaya,* Tables 103 and 104; Department of Statistics, Federation of Malaya, *1957 Population Census of the Federation of Malaya,* Vols. 2–13, Table 16. The "economically active population" of Malays included "wage laborers," "self-employed" (including both "own account" workers and "employers"), and "unpaid family labor." The statistics of the 1957 census considered all "Malays," "Indonesians" and aborigines together under the misleading label of "Malaysians"; the 1947 statistics for these groups had to be so aggregated for comparability.

67. Commissioner of Labour, Malayan Union, *Annual Report of the Labor Department for the Year 1947,* p. 14. Such "encouragement" had long before been provided in a disguised form, as subsequent chapters of this study demonstrate.

68. Appendix 4.8 in Lim, *Economic Development,* p. 334, from the *Rubber Statistics Handbook,* 1947, 1957 and 1962. These include immigrant Javanese under "Malays." According to Del Tufo, *Malaya,* p. 114, indigenous Malays in 1947 made up about two thirds of all "Malaysians" resident on estates, while immigrant Indonesians, about one third. The distinction between indigenous Malays and immigrants from Java, Sumatra, and elsewhere in Indonesia is an important one to make for the postwar period, because of the unique sociocultural characteristics and relative poverty of the latter. This is particularly true for the three states where immigrant Indonesians form substantial minorities

of all "Malays"—Selangor, Johore, and Perak (44.8, 31.8 and 19.5 percent, respectively, in 1947). Unfortunately, this distinction is not always preserved in census and other records. For the historical analysis that follows, except where explicit otherwise, indigenous Malays and the immigrant Javanese, Boyanese, Menangkebau, etc. assimilating to them are treated in the same way because of their juridical identity as far as the British colonial administration was concerned; more locally-oriented studies in the future may improve on the present work by differentiating among immigrant "Malay" subethnic groups and their culturally-informed actions vis-à-vis the British.

69. Commissioner of Labour, Federation of Malaya, *Annual Report of the Labor Department for the Year 1948*, p. 7.

70. Lim, *Economic Development*, p. 122.

CHAPTER TWO

1. Michael Adas, "From Avoidance to Confrontation."

2. Patrick Sullivan, *Social Relations of Dependence in a Malay State: Nineteenth Century Perak*, pp. 20–22.

3. Such overland trade occurred most commonly in the south, where relative lack of topographic barriers allowed earlier hinterland integration, e.g., Malacca with Negri Sembilan or Negri Sembilan with Pahang. See J.N. Anderson and W.T. Vorster, "Diversity and Interdependence in the Trade Hinterlands of Melaka"; William D. Wilder, *Communication, Social Structure and Development in Rural Malaysia. A Study of Kampong Kuala Bera*. Sullivan does note the existence of inland paths that connected lower Perak to central Selangor and to Pahang, and upper Perak to Kedah and Patani. Sullivan, *Social Relations of Dependence*, p. 22.

4. Zaharah binti Haji Mahmud, "The Period and Nature of 'Traditional' Settlement in the Malay Peninsula"; James C. Jackson, "Rice Cultivation in West Malaysia."

5. J.H. Gullick, *Indigenous Political Systems of Western Malaya*, pp. 25–26.

6. Ibid., p. 21.

7. For Perak, see Gullick, *Indigenous Political Systems*, p. 105; for Pahang, calculated from Jomo, *A Question of Class*, p. 8; for Negri Sembilan, Gullick, *Indigenous Political Systems*, p. 105; for Kedah, calculated from Jomo, *A Question of Class*, p. 8, and from Sharom Ahmat, "The Structure of the Economy of Kedah, 1879–1905," p. 2, using as a base population the total Malay agricultural population found in the 1911 census.

8. Wong Lin Ken, *The Malayan Tin Industry to 1914*, pp. 17–21.

9. Sharom, "Structure of the Economy of Kedah," pp. 7–9, 20.

10. Carl Trocki, *Prince of Pirates*. Gambier was a yellowish gum extracted from a Malayan vine *(Uncaria gambir)*, and exported for tanning and dyeing during this period.

11. Zaharah, "Period and the Nature of 'Traditional' Settlement," pp. 87–91.

12. Gullick, *Indigenous Political Systems, pp. 29–30*.

13. Zaharah, "Period and the Nature of 'Traditional' Settlement," p. 104.

14. Jomo, *A Question of Class*, p. 7; Sharom, "Structure of the Economy of Kedah," p. 2.
15. Jomo, *A Question of Class*, p. 19.
16. The argument that it has been population pressure on land that has caused labor intensification in padi growing in Malaya is one which, for the most part, is unsustainable. There are, in general, serious theoretical objections to the argument by Boserup and others (Ester Boserup, *The Conditions of Agricultural Growth*) that population pressure brings on intensification. See Donald M. Nonini, "Comment on 'Quantum Adjustment, Macroevolution and the Social Field"; and idem, "Varieties of Materialism." These objections appear to apply to the Malayan case.
17. Louis Golomb, personal communication.
18. Gullick, *Indigenous Political Systems*, p. 20.
19. Gullick, *Indigenous Political Systems*, p. 30; Jomo, *A Question of Class*, p. 5; David Banks, *Malay Kinship*, p. 31.
20. David S.Y. Wong, *Tenure and Land Dealings in the Malay States*, p. 10.
21. Banks, *Malay Kinship*, p. 3.
22. Roger Keesing, *Kin Groups and Social Structure*, p. 99.
23. Gullick, *Indigenous Political Systems*, p. 33.
24. Ibid., p. 32.
25. Ibid., p. 33.
26. Ibid., p. 30; emphasis added.
27. J.M. Gullick, "The Negri Sembilan Economy of the 1890's," p. 45.
28. Shamsul A.B., *From British to Bumiputera Rule: Local Politics and Rural Development in Peninsular Malaysia*, pp. 17–18.
29. On the precapitalist nature of *kenduri* in Malay villages, see Carol Lynn McAllister, "Women and Feasting." Bailey observes what many others have also noted: "In the past, traditional redistributive obligations modified local economic inequalities and offered social prestige and respect to wealthy villagers who provided loans, gave large feasts, and were otherwise generous with their wealth." Conner Bailey, *The Sociology of Production in Rural Malay Society*, p. 13.
30. Jomo, *A Question of Class, p. 5*.
31. Gullick, *Indigenous Political Systems, p. 6*.
32. Trocki, *Prince of Pirates;* James C. Jackson, *Planters and Speculators: Chinese and European Agricultural Enterprise in Malaya, 1896–1921*.
33. Trocki, *Prince of Pirates*, p. 155.
34. Ibid., p. 208.
35. Ibid., p. 211.
36. Sharom, "Structure of the Economy of Kedah," p. 10.
37. Ibid., pp. 10–11, 18–20.
38. R. Bonney, *Kedah 1771–1821*, p. 6.
39. Gullick, *Indigenous Political Systems*, p. 126.
40. W.E. Maxwell, "The Law and Customs of the Malays with Reference to the Tenure of Land", p. 108.

41. Ibid., p. 110.
42. Gullick, *Indigenous Political Systems*, pp. 34–36.
43. Maxwell, "Law and Customs of the Malays," p. 92.
44. Wong, *Tenure and Land Dealings*, p. 17.
45. Quoted in Wong, *Tenure and Land Dealings*, p. 18.
46. Descriptions of debt-bondage and slavery are given in Gullick, *Indigenous Political Systems*, pp. 101–3; Jomo, *A Question of Class*, pp. 7–9; Sullivan, *Social Relations of Dependence*, pp. 45–69.
47. Sharom Ahmat, quoted in Jomo, *A Question of Class*, p. 24, footnote 11.
48. Wong, *Tenure and Land Dealings*, p. 20, writes that "Kedah, situated between Penang and Perak, saw in 1883 the promulgation of two proclamations by its Sultan which purported, *inter alia,* to impose land-tax *(hasil tanah)* on all land-holdings, to require the obtaining of a permit for clearing forest land, and to provide for the issue of documents of title for occupied land." See also Shaharil Talib, *After Its Own Image.*
49. Wong, *Tenure and Land Dealings*, p. 10.
50. Ibid., p. 16.
51. Paul Kratoska, "The Peripatetic Peasant and Land Tenure in British Malaya," p. 20.
52. Wong, *Tenure and Land Dealings*, p. 10.
53. Maxwell, "Law and Customs of the Malays," p. 80.
54. Wong, *Tenure and Land Dealings*, pp. 11–12.
55. Ibid.
56. Maxwell, "Law and Customs of the Malays," p. 92.
57. Wong, *Tenure and Land Dealings*, p. 14.
58. See Sharom, "Structure of the Economy of Kedah," pp. 4–5.
59. Adas, "From Avoidance to Confrontation."
60. Ibid., p. 218.
61. Ibid., pp. 220–25.
62. Ibid., p. 225.
63. Ibid., p. 217.
64. Ibid., pp. 232–38.
65. Gullick, *Indigenous Political Systems*, p. 73.
66. Ibid., p. 127.
67. Sharom Ahmat, "The Political Structure of the State of Kedah 1879–1905," p. 121.
68. Gullick, *Indigenous Political Systems*, p. 113.
69. Ibid., p. 119.
70. Maxwell, "Law and Customs of the Malays," p. 113.
71. Quoted in Maxwell, "Law and Customs of the Malays," p. 108.
72. Khoo Kay Kim, *The Western Malay States 1850–1873: The Effects of Commercial Development on Malay Politics*, pp. 22–28.
73. Adas, "From Avoidance to Confrontation," p. 229.
74. *Far Eastern Economic Review*, December 13, 1974, p. 13.

75. James C. Scott, *Weapons of the Weak,* pp. 275–76.

CHAPTER THREE

1. Dun J. Li, *British Malaya: An Economic Analysis:* pp. 50, 62.

2. "The rapid increase of revenue in British Malaya was one of the best illustrations of how fast that country was developing economically.... If we were to choose a single year as the dividing line after which a stable stage [of revenues] was reached, that year would be 1916." Li, *British Malaya,* p. 26.

3. The use by the Andayas of the landmark year 1919, by which time all of the states which were to compose the Unfederated Malay States had come under direct British control, supports the periodization offered here. See the history of political expansion by the British into the Malayan peninsula from 1874 to 1919, in Barbara Watson Andaya and Leonard Y. Andaya, "The Making of British Malaya, 1874–1919," in *A History of Malaysia,* pp. 157–204.

4. J.W.W. Birch, appointed the Resident to Perak, attempted in 1875 to centralize revenue collection in Perak under his control, rather than leaving this to the district chiefs. He sought also to intervene against elite slaveholding. Moreover, his actions, carried out in an insulting manner that violated etiquette among the Perak nobility, were provocative and seriously transgressed noble prerogatives; in November 1875 he was assassinated. Mounting a punitive expedition, the British summoned troops from India and Hong Kong, hung three Malays whom they regarded as directly responsible for Birch's killing, and exiled Sultan Abdullah and several major chiefs. The demonstration effects of the British response to the Birch assassination persisted for decades after, discouraging overt anti-British activity among the Malay elites. See Barbara W. Andaya and Leonard Y. Andaya, *A History of Malaysia,* pp. 157–63. On the British use of military force against Malay popular uprisings—notably, the Perak and Negri Sembilan wars of the 1870s, the To' Janggut uprising in Kelantan in 1915, and the Trengganu Rebellion in 1928—see Mohamed Amin, "British 'Intervention' and Malay Resistance." See also the article by Allen, one of the earliest in the literature to raise the importance of Malay resistance: J. de V. Allen, "The Kelantan Uprising of 1915."

5. These developments are covered in Emily Sadka, *The Protected Malay States 1874–1895;* and Eunice Thio, *British Policy in the Malay Peninsula, 1880–1910.*

6. Higher officials in the Colonial Office in London sought to act as a brake on the territorial acquisitions and administrative innovations initiated by their subordinates, the "men-on-the-spot," the Colonial Governors. Nonetheless, during these years governors and Residents exercised great latitude and initiative in deciding to expand and exercise British rule, particularly when their campaigns could be justified by imperial strategic concerns (e.g., rivalries with France and Germany). They were rarely contradicted in practice by the Secretary of State or other officials in London. On the Victorian Colonial Office and its organization, see W. David McIntyre, *The Imperial Frontier in the Tropics 1865–75,* pp. 17–74.

7. Sadka, *Protected Malay States,* pp. 296–97.

8. Ibid., p. 297.

9. Ibid., pp. 298–99.

10. See below, pp. 51–53, 63–65.

11. Sadka, *Protected Malay States,* p. 354, notes for instance that "the sale of fruit, especially durians, was an important supplement to income; in the 1890s, the land rent for the Kuala Kangsar district was paid for out of the sale of durians."

12. Sadka, *Protected Malay States,* p. 287.

13. Cheah Boon Kheng, "Social Banditry and Rural Crime in North Kedah, 1909–1929," p. 110. It is true that the *ra'ayat* had previously been required by the Sultan's proclamation of 1883 to pay land tax *(hasil tanah);* this lasted until 1887, when a new proclamation abolished the land tax for most *ra'ayat* by commuting it to a *kerah* obligation, while the land tax was eliminated altogether for any *Raja, Syed,* "person of good birth," *Haji,* or *Lebai. (Syed* is a title for a male descendant of the Prophet Muhammed; *Haji* refers to any Muslim male who has undertaken the pilgrimage to Mecca; *Lebai* is a title specifically for a mosque official attending to the order of the service, or, in general, to any pious male elder.) This was the situation in Kedah until 1909. See ibid., footnotes 37 and 39.

14. Conner Bailey, *Broker, Mediator, Patron, and Kinsman,* pp. 30–31.

15. According to Jackson, *Planters and Speculators* pp. 18, 26, gambier and pepper remained the most important commercial crops in Johore until about 1910; the *kangchu* system of revenue-generation was abolished only in 1917.

16. Thio, *British Policy in the Malay Peninsula,* pp. 244–45.

17. Paul H. Kratoska, "Penghulus in Perak and Selangor."

18. Kenelm O.L.Burridge, "Rural Administration in Johore," p. 30.

19. Bailey, *Broker, Mediator, Patron and Kinsman,* pp. 30–37. This point is reinforced by Cheah, "Social Banditry and Rural Crime," pp. 102–3, who found that many *penghulus* in rural *mukims* connived with gangs of bandits to protect them from discovery or capture. After the appointment of District Officers in 1905 to replace district chiefs, District Officers for several years complained in their reports that the work of *penghulus* was poor, presumably referring to their lack of cooperation in what the British considered vital areas of administration. See ibid., p. 102.

20. It appears that the British were able only in the 1920s and 1930s to achieve a subordination of *penghulus* to District Officers in Kedah and Perlis comparable to what had been achieved in the other states by 1920.

21. This is not to argue, however, that there was *no* participation by rural Malays in wage labor, but rather that they undertook such wage labor, usually contract labor, intermittently as part of a broad-based strategy of economic survival, which also included rubber and padi sharecropping, cultivating one's own lands, migrating to areas of new settlement, etc. This strategy was associated most closely with areas in which rubber shallholding was concentrated to which I refer in chapter 5 below as "core" areas. Shamsul, *From British to Bumiputera Rule,* provides an important example of just such rural Malay involvement in

contract labor from the early 1900s onward, which deserves more discussion than I can give it here.

22. Sadka, *Protected Malay States,* pp. 324–25.

23. For the years between 1898 and 1906, see Victor Purcell, *The Chinese in Malaya,* p. 188; for the years between 1905 and 1920, see Li, *British Malaya,* pp. 28–29.

24. These are summarized in Li, *British Malaya,* pp. 28–32; also see Syed Hussein Alatas, *The Myth of the Lazy Native,* pp. 91–93.

25. Li, *British Malaya,* p. 29.

26. Ibid.

27. Adoption of a further mechanism for coopting the Malay elite came in 1910 with the founding of the Malay Administrative Service (MAS). For this and other developments, see Jagjit Singh Sidhu, *Administration in the Federated Malay States 1896–1920,* pp. 109–34; Khasnor Johan, *The Emergence of the Modern Malay Administrative Elite;* William R. Roff, *The Origins of Malay Nationalism,* pp. 11–31, 100–1, 105; Yeo Kim Wah, "Grooming of an Elite"; idem, *The Politics of Decentralization: Colonial Controversy in Malaya 1920–1929,* pp. 160–204.

28. Sadka, *Protected Malay States,* pp. 324–63; Chai Hon-Chan, *The Development of British Malaya 1896–1909.* In the 1890s and early 1900s, the administration of the Federated Malay States (F.M.S.) spent large proportions of its revenues on road and railway construction and other public works; according to Li, *British Malaya,* p. 32, the F.M.S. spent almost half of its total revenue in 1896 on this category, and in 1898, it spent 57 per cent of all revenues on railways alone. After the British came into formal control of Kedah and Johore in later years, expenditures on public works were comparable. It should be added that other than provision of capital, the British role in the construction of public works—in line with Orientalist ideology—was envisioned as one of design and oversight, or, as Sir Frank Swettenham put it, "to direct and control a plentiful and efficient supply of native labour," and that the actual work was performed by poorly paid Chinese and Indian coolies (*British Malaya,* 2nd ed., quoted by Colin E.R. Abraham, "Racial and Ethnic Manipulation in Colonial Malaya," p. 21).

29. On the organization of the Chinese tin-mining industry and the encouragement provided it by British officials in the two decades between 1874 and 1895, see Wong Lin Ken, *The Malayan Tin Industry to 1914—With Special Reference to the States of Perak, Selangor, Negri Sembilan, and Pahang.*

30. See Charles Kingsley Meek, *Land, Law and Custom in the Colonies,* pp. 32–56.

31. Wong, *Tenure and Land Dealings,* p. 78.

32. James C. Jackson, *Planters and Speculators,* pp. 252–53.

33. Ibid.; Wong, *Tenure and Land Dealings,* 1975.

34. Gullick, "Negri Sembilan Economy of the 1890s," p. 41.

35. Wong, *Tenure and Land Dealings,* pp. 72–73.

36. "Law and Customs of the Malays," Maxwell's long essay referred to in the previous chapter, is a masterpiece of conscientious Orientalism that deserves further critical scrutiny for its imbrication of the ideological justification for the

new land regulations with a historical vision of political rule in imagined "petty Asiatic States."

37. Sadka, *Protected Malay States*, p. 329.

38. Ibid., p. 328.

39. R. D. Hill, *Agriculture in the Malaysian Region*, p. 142. Eunice Thio, *British Policy in the Malay Peninsula 1886–1901*, p. 115, reports that by 1890 the Padang district of western Johore had an estimated population of 10,000 Javanese, most of whom grew betelnuts.

40. Tunku Shamsul Bahrin, "The Pattern of Indonesian Migration and Settlement in Malaya," pp. 233–36, 244.

41. Ibid., pp. 244, 249–53.

42. James C. Jackson, "Rice Cultivation in West Malaysia," p. 90.

43. Sadka, *Protected Malay States*, p. 328.

44. Hill, *Agriculture in the Malaysian Region*, p. 142.

45. Sadka, *Protected Malay States*, p. 328; Tunku Shamsul, "Pattern of Indonesian Migration and Settlement," p. 247; Jackson, "Rice Cultivation in West Malaysia," p. 86.

44. Ooi Jin-Bee, *Peninsular Malaysia*, p. 124.

45. Tunku Shamsul, "Pattern of Indonesian Migration and Settlement," p. 253.

46. "[The settler's] return to his original village usually aroused a great deal of excitement and curiosity. His fellow-villagers were normally impressed by the manner of his dress and the presents he brought home. Answers to inquiries about opportunities in Malaya were often so glowing and exaggerated, that his return to Malaya was accompanied not only by his family but also by other relatives and friends." Ibid., p. 243.

49. Tunku Shamsul writes that the leader "had to command the respect and loyalty of all the members of the group," in order to gain their compliance in communal land clearance. Ibid., p. 253. Thus his position was structurally similar to that of *penghulu* in the Malay village community of the precolonial period.

50. Ibid., pp. 252–54.

51. See Roff, *Origins of Malay Nationalism*. On pp. 154–55, 172–73, and *passim*, he makes clear the influence of Indonesian publications and Indonesian nationalism on Malay ethnicity during the colonial period.

52. Jackson, *Planters and Speculators*.

53. Ibid., pp. 187–88. See for instance, the problems European planters experienced in securing immigrant laborers in Johore in the 1880s in Trocki, *Prince of Pirates*, pp. 195–98.

54. Virginia Thompson, "Notes on Labor Problems in Malaya," p. 14.

55. Lim, *Peasants and Their Agricultural Economy*, pp. 72–73.

56. See chapter 2, above.

57. Tunku Shamsul, "Pattern of Indonesian Migration and Settlement," p. 253.

58. Ibid., p. 239.

59. Gullick, "Negri Sembilan Economy of the 1890s."

60. As to the existence of communal sharing within the village community, Gullick found "interesting" the statement "in the Annual Report for 1888 that when the Rembau Malays sell padi among themselves they do so at a fixed, conventional price as though it were not an ordinary article of commerce." Ibid., p. 46.
61. Ibid., p. 41.
62. Ibid., p. 42.
63. Ibid., pp. 42–43.
64. Maxwell, "Law and Customs of the Malays," p. 124.
65. Gullick, "Negri Sembilan Economy of the 1890's," pp. 43–44.
66. Bailey, *Broker, Mediator, Patron and Kinsman*, pp. 3–35.
67. Ibid., pp. 35–36.
68. Ibid., p.36.
69. A topic well worth investigating in terms of these new dyadic relationships between the *ra'ayat* and the state is the new Islamic administration affecting *kampong* life which was established by the British from the 1880s onward (the officially organized and recognized *ulama, imams,* and *kathis*) and their codification of a synthesis of Islamic law and *adat* as these came to be applied to inheritance, marriage and divorce, and the imposition of *zakat* and *fitrah*. See Moshe Yegar, *Islam and Islamic Institutions in British Malaya: Policies and Implementation.* My hunch would be that this codification, when combined with the new surveillance of daily life under the British administration, reinforced the new individualization of landholding, the commoditization of land, and the emergence of the nuclear family as a focal social unit in the village.
70. Hill, *Agriculture in the Malaysian Region,* pp. 97–98.

CHAPTER FOUR

1. On the considerable technical and scientific assistance the British government provided European plantation capitalists, see Lucile H. Brockway, *Science and Colonial Expansion,* pp. 141–66.
2. David S.Y. Wong, *Tenure and Land Dealings in the Malay States,* pp. 71–72.
3. Tunku Shamsul, "Pattern of Indonesian Migration and Settlement," p. 239. This was a strategy later adopted by impoverished Chinese farmers during the depression of the 1930s and after the Japanese occupation, although with generally far less felicitous outcomes (such as forced removal), given the anti-Chinese biases of British officials.
4. Ibid., p. 239, footnote 9.
5. W.E. Maxwell, "The Law and Customs of the Malays with Reference to the Tenure of Land," p. 122.
6 Ibid.
7. Wong, *Tenure and Land Dealings,* p. 72.
8. Syed Hussein Alatas, *The Myth of the Lazy Native,* p. 126.
9. I have no evidence to support this suggestion, but submit that to assume that the *ra'ayat* were universally ignorant of what British officials, planters, and others

thought of them, or were unable to "game" the situation when they did know how they were regarded, is a patronizing assumption that would not be empirically sustained upon investigation. More research here is clearly indicated.

10. Cheah Boon Kheng, "Social Banditry and Rural Crime in North Kedah, 1909–1929."

11. Ibid., pp. 110–11.

12. Ibid.

13. Ibid., pp. 107–8.

14. Ibid., p. 108.

15. Ibid., p. 105.

16. Ibid., p. 113.

17. Ibid.

18. Ibid., p. 114.

19. See James C. Scott, *The Moral Economy of the Peasant.*

20. Cheah remarks that during the early years of the twentieth century in Kedah, in the rural areas, "police outposts were few, isolated, and mostly non-existent. Large rural districts like Kubang Pasu, Padang Terap, Kota Star, and Kuala Muda were covered by only a few area police posts each manned by a small force of six or seven men under a corporal." Cheah, "Social Banditry and Crime," p. 101.

21. "Kapitan" was the term used to designate the paramount leader of a local Chinese community up to this time. A man of wealth and high social standing, he was selected by local Chinese as their representative to British colonial authority, was recognized formally by the British in this position, and given various privileges, such as revenue farms. As such, he played a unique role as broker between local Chinese and British officials. See G. William Skinner, "Overseas Chinese Leadership: Paradigm for a Paradox."

22. On official efforts in the 1890s and subsequently against Chinese secret societies, see Victor Purcell, *The Chinese in Malaya;* on the government's assistance to European tin mining enterprise against Chinese tin mining capitalists ("advancers") in the years after 1900, and on the connection between the operation of revenue farms and the profitability of mining by Chinese labor-intensive methods, see Wong Lin-Ken, *The Malayan Tin Industry to 1914,* pp. 216–27. Of the cessation of revenue farming, Butcher writes: "up to about 1900 the farm system was of central importance to the whole economic and administrative structure of these states, whereas after that time officials came to regard the system as increasingly less important to the government and even as an impediment to smooth administration and the achievement of the government's economic objectives." J.G. Butcher, "The Demise of the Revenue Farm System in the Federated Malay States," p. 388. In another article Butcher notes the importance of eliminating the discharge ticket system and curbing the power of the Kapitan China: Idem, "Towards the History of Malayan Society: Kuala Lumpur District, 1885–1912."

23. Butcher, "Towards the History of Malayan Society," p. 111.

24. Li, *British Malaya*, p. 38.

25. See John G. Butcher, *The British in Malaya, 1880–1941*.

26. Syed Hussein, *Myth of the Lazy Native*, Ch. 5, pp. 70–79.

27. J.H. Drabble, *Rubber in Malaya, 1896–1922: The Genesis of the Industry*, pp. 1–47; Brockway, *Science and Colonial Expansion*.

28. According to Baran and Sweezy, it was the great "epoch-making innovation," the automobile, that allowed early twentieth-century monopoly capitalism to absorb its capital surplus and utilize its productive capacity, rather than deteriorate into stagnation and depression. If they are correct, the spread effects of "automobilization" were indeed critical to the viability not only of American industrial capitalism, but also of capitalist enterprise in the European colonies linked to it. Paul Baran and Paul Sweezy, *Monopoly Capital*, pp. 216, 231–32. Malaya's dependence on international markets for rubber and tin must be seen in this context.

29. See Ooi Jin-Bee, *Peninsular Malaysia*, p. 240, on the importance of this locational "free lunch" for the development of Malaya's plantation industry.

30. Lim Teck Ghee, *Peasants and Their Agricultural Economy in Colonial Malaya, 1874–1941*, p. 91.

31. Calculated from Appendix III, J. H. Drabble, *Rubber in Malaya*, p. 215.

32. Lim, *Peasants and Their Agricultural Economy*, p. 90.

33. Drabble, *Rubber in Malaya*, p. 72.

34. Lim, *Peasants and Their Agricultural Economy*, pp. 91–92.

35. Ibid., p. 92.

36. The politics of lobbying by British planters, the newly-formed Rubber Growers Association, and the Planters Association of Malaya in the creation of the Immigration Fund are described in J. Norman Parmer, *Colonial Labor Policy and Administration: A History of Labor in the Rubber Plantation Industry, c. 1910–1941*, pp. 38–78. See also R.N. Jackson, *Immigrant Labour and the Development of Malaya 1786–1920*, pp. 109–26.

37. Parmer, *Colonial Labor Policy and Administration*, Table 4, p. 273.

38. Calculated from ibid., p. 278.

39. The connection between maintaining low rice prices and low wages was one explicitly made by planters and officials; see, for instance, the deliberations of the General Labour Committee of British Malaya reported by ibid., pp. 175–79.

40. Lim, *Peasants and Their Agricultural Economy*, p. 120.

41. Li Dun Jen, *British Malaya: An Economic Analysis*, p. 40.

42. Calculated from Ooi Jin-Bee, "Rural Development in Tropical Areas, with Special Reference to Malaya", p. 131, Fig. 26.

43. Paul H. Kratoska, "Rice Cultivation and the Ethnic Division of Labor in British Malaya", p. 313; idem, "'Ends that We Cannot Foresee,'" pp. 159, 160.

44. Kratoska, "Rice Cultivation," p. 303.

45. Paul H. Kratoska, *The Chettiar and the Yeoman*, pp. 9–11. I thank Paul Kratoska for emphasizing to me in a personal communication the importance of the rapid

increase in land prices in these years for peasant indebtedness and loss of land. Chettiars were members of a caste in India who came to occupy positions as moneylenders both in India itself and in the British colonial possessions to which they migrated.

46. The words of the District Officer are cited by Drabble, *Rubber in Malaya,* p. 73; the characterization of the Malay peasant as "thriftless" is that of Governor Sir John Anderson of the Federated Malay States in 1908, cited by Kratoska, *Chettiar and the Yeoman,* p. 17. In the passage cited, Anderson is referring to the practice of Malays of charging land as collateral for loans used for *kenduri* or "feasts" on major ritual occasions such as marriages and circumcisions. The *kenduri,* viewed as an "extravagance" by colonial officials thoroughly embued with the capitalist ethos about the use of money, was (and is) a major means by which membership in a Malay peasant village is validated and reaffirmed. See David Banks, *Malay Kinship,* pp. 158–61; Carol Lynn McAllister, "Women and Feasting"; James C. Scott, *Weapons of the Weak,* pp. 169–78, 238–39.

47. Lim, *Peasants and Their Agricultural Economy,* p. 75; see also William R. Roff, *Origins of Malay Nationalism,* pp. 123–24.

48. P.T. Bauer, *The Rubber Industry: A Study in Competition and Monopoly,* pp. 60–63, 361–62; idem, "Some Aspects of the Malayan Rubber Slump 1929–1933"; Lim, *Peasants and Their Agricultural Economy,* Appendix 7.1.

49. Lim, *Peasants and Their Agricultural Economy,* p. 143. In official parlance, "smallholdings" were parcels of rubber land of less than 100 acres, while parcels greater than 100 acres were designated "estates."

50. Lennox A. Mills, *British Rule in Eastern Asia,* p. 192.

51. Lim, *Peasants and Their Agricultural Economy,* p. 116.

52. Ibid., p. 119.

53. Lim, *Peasants and Their Agricultural Economy,* p. 76.

54. On both the growing influence of planters with Malayan and Colonial Office officials, and on the wartime rubber situation, see J.H. Drabble, *Rubber in Malaya,* pp. 123–55.

55. Rubber Growers Association Memorandum, p. 9, cited in Drabble, *Rubber in Malaya,* p. 140, footnote 4.

56. Mills, *British Rule in Eastern Asia,* p. 252.

57. See James de Vere Allen, "Malayan Civil Service, 1874–1941: Colonial Bureaucracy/Malayan Elite," pp. 152, 160.

58. Lim, *Peasants and Their Agricultural Economy,* p. 82.

CHAPTER FIVE

1. On Guillemard's "decentralization" scheme and reactions to it, see Yeo Kim Wah, *The Politics of Decentralization: Colonial Controversy in Malay 1920–1929;* on Clementi's scheme a decade later and the response by Europeans and Chinese, see Rupert Emerson, *Malaysia,* pp. 312–57.

2. Emerson, *Malaysia: A Study in Direct and Indirect Rule,* pp. 348–49.

3. Yeo, *Politics of Decentralization,* p. 47.

4. W.G.A. Ormsby-Gore, *Report by the Right Honourable W.G.A. Ormsby-Gore, M.P. (Parliamentary Under-Secretary of State for the Colonies) on His Visit to Malaya, Ceylon, and Java During the Year 1928*, p. 141.

5. Ooi Jin Bee, "Rural Development in Tropical Areas, With Special Reference to Malaya," pp. 142–55.

6. Ibid.

7. P.T. Bauer, "The Economics of Planting Density in Rubber Growing," 1961c, p. 240.

8. Lim Teck Ghee, "Malayan Peasant Smallholders and the Stevenson Restriction Scheme 1922-28," p. 115. Lim Teck Ghee, *Peasants and Their Agricultural Economy*, p. 146, provides examples suggesting that Malay peasant smallholding production was even higher. J.H. Drabble, "Malayan Rubber Smallholdings in the Inter-War Period: Some Preliminary Findings," pp. 61-72, has recently challenged these figures, but there are problems with his analysis (see Note 30 below).

9. Clifford Geertz, *Agricultural Involution,* Chapter 1. In light of the foregoing, Drabble's comment that "any purely physical comparison with estates would inevitably be unfavourable to smaller owners," (J.H. Drabble, *Rubber in Malaya 1876-1922,* p. 204), and his remarks elsewhere about the "poor physical appearance of the [small] holdings" (J.H. Drabble, "Malayan Rubber Smallholdings in the Inter-war Period," p. 67) and the "better physical appearance" of Chinese than Malay smallholdings (ibid., p. 71), uncritically recapitulate the views of British officials, planters, and other European observers of the time. Thus, for instance, B.J. Eaton wrote in 1923 that the Malay peasant owns a few acres "on which fruit trees, coconuts and rubber *grow in confusion, generally untended.*" B.J. Eaton, "Agriculture," p. 199, cited in Syed Hussein Alatas, *The Myth of the Lazy Native,* pp. 78-79; emphasis added.

10. That is, direct variation of supply produced with price.

11. Lim, *Peasants and Their Agricultural Economy,* pp. 143–44; Ooi, "Rural Development." For a specific village example, albeit from a later period, see M.G. Swift, *Malay Peasant Society in Jelebu,* p. 27.

12. James C. Scott, personal communication. Scott observes that this exceptional behavior is consistent with Chaianov's theory of the peasant household economy. For examples of ways in which peasant production under specific conditions defies the norms of capitalist rationality, see A.V. Chaianov, *The Theory of Peasant Economy,* pp. 39–40. One prevailing belief among British officials was that whenever Malay smallholders faced falling prices, they would proceed to "slaughter tap" their trees, that is, tap their trees so frequently that the bark would not renew, and the trees would become diseased and give low yields or none at all (See William R. Roff, *Origins of Malay Nationalism,* p. 205). If so, it would be an example of the supposed "short-run economic orientation" of the Malay peasant so decried by certain anthropologists (e.g., Swift, "Economic Concentration and Malay Peasant Society," p. 246). But the facts do not bear out this belief; in fact, it is belied by an important government survey by the Department of Agriculture, *Bark Consumption and Bark Reserves on Small Rubber Holdings* in 1934, which officials chose to ignore. This study showed

that in the unrestricted period from 1929 to 1931, peasants did not overtap their trees, for bark reserves were quite adequate. For further evidence, see P.T. Bauer, "Some Aspects of the Malayan Rubber Slump 1929-1933," 1961a, p. 194.

13. For confirmation of this claim, see the extensive argument given in P.T. Bauer, *The Rubber Industry.*

14. Malcolm Caldwell, "War, Boom and Depression," pp. 39–40.

15. The regional analysis that follows is inspired by the approach of G. William Skinner. See G. William Skinner, "Regional Urbanization in Nineteenth Century China," pp. 211-52, and idem, "Marketing Systems and Regional Economies: Their Structure and Development." The principal materials used in the analysis here are district-level data for the period from 1911 to 1941 on population densities, physiography, transport networks, and on the economic activity of rural Malays on the west coast. In some ways district-level data are too crude or aggregated for analysis, and local-level data on population and economic activity would have been preferable. Moreover, it is necessary to be cautious because administrative districts and spatially-organized economic systems are not congruent in most instances, but overlap. Nonetheless, as an approximation, and because district-level data are the most detailed available, they must and can serve for the purpose of the discussion here.

Basically, after a review of sources and study of the physiography of the peninsula and district-level population densities, I determined that all districts with a density below 75 persons per square mile in 1931 could be regarded as "peripheral." All districts above that density in 1931 in which (based on data available) the majority of Malays appeared to be exclusively padi cultivators I called "semicore"; and all other districts in 1931 above that density (in which rural Malays showed mixed livelihoods in rubber, coconuts, padi, fishing etc.) "core" districts. The thresholds I set dividing "core," "semicore," and "periphery" districts are arbitrary, but they are not without justification. They are justified by recourse to mutually reinforcing criteria from population density distributions; the distributions of industrial, infrastructural, and agrarian resources which allow local populations of specific sizes to be supported; and variations in topography. Thus, for example, major infrastructural facilities (e.g., harbors, paved roads, railway termini) were concentrated in core districts which included or were close to large urban centers (such as Kuala Lumpur, Ipoh, Penang), and located in lowland areas accessible to the coast; in contrast, peripheral districts were characterized not only by low population densities, but also by highland or swampland topography, and by remoteness from both urban centers and infrastructural facilities. The following sources were used: M.V. Del Tufo, *Malaya: A Report of the 1947 Census of Population,* Table 4, "Areas, Populations and Density of Districts Compared with 1931"; C.A. Vlieland, *A Report on the 1931 Census,* Map 1 and Tables 1–7; Ooi Jin-Bee, *Peninsular Malaysia* ; Lim Chong-yah, *Economic Development of Modern Malaya,* pp. 72–96, 158–62, 272–82; Norton Ginsberg and Chester F. Roberts, Jr., *Malaya* ; Lim Heng Kow, The Evolution of the Urban System in Malaya ; R.D. Hill, *Rice in Malaya: A Study in Historical Geography;* Donald M. Nonini, "The Chinese

Community of a West Malaysian Market Town: A Study in Political Economy," pp. 14–72.

16. For 1931, these "core" areas are defined in terms of the following districts: for the northern region centered on Georgetown and, secondarily, Ipoh—Penang Northeast, Balik Pulau, Bukit Mertajam, Nibong Tebal, Kuala Muda, Kulim, Bandar Bahru, Larut and Matang, Kuala Kangsar, Kinta, and Dindings districts; for the central region focused on Kuala Lumpur— Lower Perak, Ulu Selangor, Kuala Lumpur, Klang, Ulu Langat, Kuala Langat, Seremban, Tampin, Port Dickson, Alor Gajah, Jasin and Muar districts; for the southern region centered on Singapore — Batu Pahat and Kukup (Pontian) districts (Johore Bharu district was itself peripheral). The average population density of these twenty-five core districts was 351 persons per square mile in 1931.

17. In 1931, the "semicore" areas would be defined in terms of these districts: Perlis, Kubang Pasu, Kota Star, Yen, Butterworth, Krian and Malacca Central; by the late 1930s, due to new government irrigation projects, Sabak Bernam and Kuala Selangor districts would also be included. The average population density of these nine semicore districts was 299 persons per square mile in 1931.

18. E.H.G. Dobby, "The North Kedah Plain: A Study in the Environment of Pioneering for Rice Cultivation," p. 314.

19. Drabble, *Rubber in Malaya,* p. 161.

20. See the section "The Capitalist Business Cycle, Colonial Rice Policy and the Peasantry" below.

21. Department of Agriculture, *Annual Report for the Year 1936,* p. 736.

22. In 1931, the following districts defined peripheral areas within the regions of the west coast: in the northern region — Padang Terap, Baling/Sik, Langkawi (peripheralized as an island), Upper Perak, Cameron Highlands, and Batang Padang districts; in the central region — Kuala Pilah and Jelebu districts; in the southern region — Segamat and Johore Bharu districts. The average population density of these ten peripheral districts was 43 persons per square mile. Of course, the eastern verges of some "core" districts, e.g., Kuala Kangsar and Ulu Selangor, were extremely mountainous and sparsely populated, and the coastal swamplands in other "core" districts, e.g., Dinding and Lower Perak, precluded dense settlements or extensive road networks. In a more fine-grained analysis than is possible here, both physiographic forms would definitely be considered to indicate "peripheral" status. It should be added that if this study were to deal with the history of the regional systems that arguably constituted British Malaya's *national periphery* —the regions in Kelantan and Trengganu delineated by the drainage areas of rivers flowing to the northeast, and to the east in Pahang and eastern Johore, the major locational contrast would, of course, be between these systems and Malaya's western coastal "core."

23. David Banks, *Malay Kinship,* p. 31. Note that on Map 1, what is now Sik District was (circa 1931) included in Baling District.

24. Hill, *Rice in Malaya,* pp. 62–63.

25. Banks, *Malay Kinship,* p. 36, for example, observes of Malays from the upland margins of eastern Kedah that after the introduction of rubber, they "were

willing to leave their fields behind and travel great distances into faraway districts and neighboring states for a chance to plant or even to tap rubber smallholdings." As another example, from the interwar period up to the advent of extensive double-cropping in the 1970s, a large proportion of peasants in the Kedah Plain migrated to other areas in search of seasonal employment during the off season for padi. James C. Scott, personal communication.

26. The politics of lobbying the Colonial Office on the part of the Rubber Growers Association from 1919 to 1922 for the compulsory restriction of rubber production in Malaya, which eventually took the form of the Stevenson Scheme, are described by Drabble, *Rubber in Malaya,* pp. 156-204. Drabble's observations there (pp. 165, 167) also make it clear that one of the primary objectives of the scheme being made compulsory by law rather than voluntary was to force the peasant smallholding sector to curb output in tandem with the plantations.

27. Lennox Mills, *British Rule in Eastern Asia,* pp. 191–92; see Present Rubber Situation in British Colonies and Protectorates Committee (Stevenson Committee), *Report and Supplementary Report of the Committee,* for details of the scheme.

28. Lim, *Peasants and Their Agricultural Economy,* p. 145.

29. P.T. Bauer, "The Working of Rubber Regulation," 1961b.

30. Ibid., p. 243. A recent study, Drabble, "Malayan Rubber Smallholdings," has sought to challenge this claim. However, Drabble's criticisms of Bauer's *Rubber Industry* and Lim's "Malayan Peasant Smallholders" are unconvincing. A major shortcoming of Drabble's study is his conclusion that (against Bauer's claim that smallholders had higher yields than estates because of their denser holdings) the data he arrays demonstrates that "in this period of the industry's operation a given tree density cannot be taken as an *a priori* indication of any particular level of yield per acre." ("Malayan Rubber Smallholdings," p. 70.) This is a fallacious conclusion because, first, Bauer's claim was based on empirical research, not on *a priori* convictions (Bauer, *Rubber Industry,* pp. 33–39, 96–97) and, second and more seriously, because the data that Drabble cites in support of his conclusion (from his Fig. 1 and Tables 1 and 3) concern variations in yield and density for trees in smallholdings *only,* and therefore have no bearing on *comparisons* between estates and smallholdings, which was Bauer's concern. Most scholars who have investigated the question have accepted Bauer's 1948 work as authoritative. Until more thorough analysis demonstrates the contrary, I shall do likewise.

31. Lim, Peasants and Their Agricultural Economy, pp. 149–50.

32. Ibid., pp. 145–46.

33. Ibid., pp. 146–47.

34. Ibid., p. 150.

35. Ibid., p. 151.

36. Ibid., pp. 148–49; Drabble, "Malayan Rubber Smallholdings," p. 68.

37. Lim, *Peasants and Their Agricultural Economy,* p. 148.

38. See Bauer, *Rubber Industry,* pp. 36–41, 56–59; Ooi, "Rural Development"; Dept. of Agriculture, *Bark Consumption.*
39. Lim, *Peasants and Their Agricultural Economy,* p. 154.
40. Ibid.
41. Calculated from Bauer, "Working of Rubber Regulation," 1961b, pp. 246–47.
42. Li, *British Malaya,* p. 32.
43. Quoted by Lim, *Peasants and Their Agricultural Economy,* p. 193; emphasis added.
44. Mills, *British Rule in Eastern Asia,* p. 204.
45. Lim, *Peasants and Their Agricultural Economy,* p. 194.
46. Ibid.; *Mills, British Rule in Eastern Asia,* pp. 204–5.
47. Bauer, *Rubber Industry;* idem, "Malayan Rubber Slump 1929-1933; idem, "Working of Rubber Regulation."
48. Bauer, *Rubber Industry,* pp. 88–100; see also Lim, *Peasants and Their Agricultural Economy,* pp. 193–94.
49. Bauer, *Rubber Industry,* p. 60.
50. Ibid., pp. 61-62, 361–62.
51. Calculated from Lim, *Peasants and Their Agricultural Economy,* Appendix 7.1, p. 258.
52. See James C. Scott, *The Moral Economy of the Peasant,* pp. 13–34.
53. Bauer, *Rubber Industry* p. 64.
54. Department of Agriculture, *Annual Report for the Year 1937,* pp. 407–8. For the trade in coupons among Chinese smallholders, see Lee Suat Beng, "The Effect of Rubber Price Fluctuations on Rubber Smallholders," pp. 178–92, and see "Editor's Note," ibid., p. 192.
55. Li, *British Malaya,* p. 71.
56. Lim, *Peasants and Their Agricultural Economy,* pp. 143–44; also see Swift, *Malay Peasant Society,* pp. 27–37, who observed this strategy in fieldwork in 1955: "The variable which determines the amount of subsistence production is the price of rubber. When this is buoyant the peasant abandons the plots for domestic consumption he made during a period of depressed prices" (p. 27).
57. Paul H. Kratoska, "The Chettiar and The Yeoman"; idem, "Rice Cultivation and the Ethnic Division of Labor in British Malaya"; idem, "'Ends That We Cannot Foresee.'"
58. Kratoska, "'Ends,'" p. 149.
59. Ibid., p. 150.
60. Ibid., p. 168.
61. Ibid., p. 150.
62. Ibid.
63. Kratoska, "Rice Cultivation," p. 314.
64. John G. Butcher, *The British in Malaya, 1880–1941,* pp. 23-49, 76-96; see also James de Vere Allen, "Malayan Civil Service, 1874–1941," pp. 167–71.

188   British Colonial Rule

65. See Butcher, *British in Malaya*, pp. 147–66.
66. Yeo, *Politics of Decentralization*, pp. 339–340; emphasis added.
67. Allen, "Malayan Civil Service," p. 171; Butcher, *British in Malaya*, pp. 81–82.
68. Allen, "Malayan Civil Service," p. 171.
69. Butcher, *British in Malaya*, pp. 81–82. Allen, "Malayan Civil Service," p. 165; Yeo Kim Wah, "The Grooming of an Elite," p. 291.
70. The five mechanisms just mentioned recur repeatedly at times of confrontation between the colonial administration and subordinate, non-British classes and ethnic groups within colonial society. For an excellent case study of conflict between the colonial state and Indian plantation laborers which illustrates the operation of these mechanisms, see H.E. Wilson, "The Klang Strikes of 1941: Labour and Capital in Colonial Malaya."
71. Ooi, "Rural Development," pp. 149–50.
72. Lim, *Economic Development*, pp. 122–23.
73. Bauer, "Working of Rubber Regulation," 1961b, p. 192.
74. From 1931 onward during the depression, estate production did continue, along with replanting. Drabble writes, "Relatively few companies put their properties on a care-and-maintenance basis during the worst of the slump in 1931–32. Most kept up production and were able to effect major cuts in costs." John Drabble, "Politics of Survival: European Reaction in Malaya to Rubber Smallholders in the Inter-war Years," p. 70.
75. Federal Legislative Council, Federation of Malaya, "Final Report of Rubber Small-Holdings Enquiry Committee," pp. 680–87.
76. Lim, *Peasants and Their Agricultural Economy*, p. 195.
77. Colonial policies toward rice imports have to be considered in terms of more inclusive *imperial* concerns about the balance of trade between Great Britain and the other industrial powers, particularly the United States. By the 1930s, Malaya had become *the* principal earner of American dollars within the British empire to pay for the war debts of Great Britain to the United States, and to finance Great Britain's international trade. Thus, a recession or depression not only disturbed the fragile balance of *local* (i.e., Malayan) colonial finance, but that of British imperialism taken as a whole. (Caldwell, "War, Boom and Depression," p. 42.)
8. For an example of official thinking on this matter from a slightly later period, see Martin Rudner, "Agricultural Policy and Peasant Social Transformation in Late Colonial Malaya," pp. 44-45.
79. Chester Roberts, *The Area Handbook on Malaya*, pp. 377–78.
80. Cheng Siok Hwa, "The Rice Industry of Malaya: A Historical Survey," p. 135.
81. Ibid., p. 143.
82. Lim, *Peasants and Their Agricultural Economy*, pp. 122–23.
83. Ibid., pp. 123–24, 136 notes, 81–85.
84. This response by the government shows the *systematic* nature of the primitive accumulation process. British officials' overriding goal was to provide sufficient rice *from whatever source* necessary to maintain low wages and curb labor discontent. However, this does not mean that individual officials, from

departments with specific constituencies, did not at times urge wage increases when rice was not sufficient, as did the Controller of Labour in 1920 to the Planters' Association of Malaya. (J. Norman Parmer, *Colonial Labor Policy and Administration*, p. 176.) However, such opinions were decidedly in the minority. With the recession of 1920, this and other reform proposals were quietly put aside. The culture of imperialism uniting British officials and colonial capitalists was perhaps most transparent in its silences.

85. Lim, *Peasants and Their Agricultural Economy*, Appendix 6.2, p. 256.

86. Kratoska, "'Ends,'" pp. 163–66.

87. Mills, *British Rule in Eastern Asia,* p. 263; Lim, *Peasants and Their Agricultural Economy*, p. 196.

88. Calculated from Department of Agriculture figures, 1922-1938, provided in Lim, *Peasants and Their Agricultural Economy,* Appendix 6.2, p. 256, for the Federated Malay States; for the Unfederated Malay States, see Lim, *Economic Development*, Appendix 6.2, p. 341.

89. See Lim, *Economic Development*, pp. 341–42: Appendices 6.2 and 6.3 on wet padi production and acreage from 1932 onward; see Lim, *Peasants and Their Agricultural Economy*, 1977, pp. 181–90. Also see Dobby, "North Kedah Plain," pp. 306–7, and Fig. 29 on p. 311 on increases in padi acreage for these years; he notes in the Kedah Plain, "new padilands were carved out from the swamp by peasants at the rate of 5000 acres a year." (p. 307)

CHAPTER SIX

1. The forcible resettlement of Chinese "squatters" not only cut off MCP guerrillas from their rural support base (the Min Yuen or "masses' movement") and thus from their lines of supply, which was its ostensible purpose, but also drove a substantial proportion of resettled Chinese back into urban and rural wage labor by destroying their productive property and by separating them from the land they had previously farmed. Malcolm Caldwell, "From 'Emergency' to 'Independence,' 1948-57," pp. 233–38, emphasizes the industrial discipline thesis. Francis Loh Kok-Wah, "Beyond the Tin Mines: The Political Economy of Chinese Squatter Farms in the Kinta New Villages, Malaysia," demonstrates that "squatting," when combined with vegetable gardening, provided rural Chinese with an alternative livelihood that allowed them to resist wage-labor exploitation by mines, estates, and industrial enterprise.

2. Cheah Boon Kheng, *Red Star Over Malaya,* pp. 27-34, 41-42.

3. Jaafar bin Hamzah, "The Malays in Tasek Gelugor During the Japanese Occupation," p. 61.

4. Cheah, *Red Star*, pp. 32, 36-38.

5. For a local-level study of Malay peasant experiences during the Occupation, see Jaafar, "Malays in Tasek Gelugor."

6. Ibid., p. 60.

7. Ibid., p. 60.

8. Cheah, *Red Star*, pp. 33-36, 45, 70; Victor Purcell, *The Chinese in Southeast Asia*, (2nd Edition) p. 311.

9. Cheah, *Red Star*, p. 45.

10. Ibid., pp. 195-240.

11. For the important events of the interregnum year, see ibid., pp. 127-293.

12. Ibid., pp. 12, 101-23.

13. William R. Roff, *The Origins of Malay Nationalism, p. 222. On the KMM* in general, see Roff, pp. 230-35.

14. On Sultan Idris Training College as, in a sense, the birthplace of radical Malay nationalism, see ibid., pp. 142-157.

15. Cheah, *Red Star*, pp. 101-23.

16. Ibid., pp. 34-35, 108-12.

17. Ibid., pp. 113-16.

18. These events are described in detail in ibid., pp. 115-23.

19. Ibid., p. 101.

20. In 1946, the Pan-Malayan and Singapore General Labour Unions were succeeded by the Pan-Malayan Federation of Trade Unions and the Singapore Federation of Trade Unions, respectively.

21. M.R. Stenson, *Industrial Conflict in Malaya: Prelude to the Communist Revolt of 1948;* Charles Gamba, *The Origins of Trade Unionism in Malaya: A Study in Colonial Labour Unrest;* Michael Morgan, "The Rise and Fall of Malayan Trade Unionism, 1945-50"; Virginia Thompson, *Labor Problems in Southeast Asia*.

22. What can be observed for both the prewar period of labor militance from 1937 to 1941 and the postwar period from 1945 to 1948 are repeated transgressions by plantation, mining, industrial, and government employers of a "moral economy" held to by Chinese, and probably Indian, wage laborers. One element of this moral economy was the expectation that workers were entitled to a wage (and to rice that was their staple food and represented a large proportion of their budgets) sufficient for their survival. For the prewar period, see Donald M. Nonini, "Popular Sources of Chinese Labor Militance in Colonial Malaya, 1920-1941." The notion of "moral economy," of course, comes from E.P. Thompson, "The Moral Economy of the English Crowd in the Eighteenth Century."

23. Stenson, *Industrial Conflict*, pp. 108, 114.

24. On the history, organization, and aims of the Malayan Communist Party during the interwar and immediate postwar years, see, from contrasting points of view, Gene Z. Hanrahan, *The Communist Struggle in Malaya;* Stenson, *Industrial Conflict;* Stephen M.Y. Leong, "Sources, Agencies and Manifestations of Overseas Chinese Nationalism in Malaya, 1937-1941"; Morgan, "Rise and Fall"; Malcolm Caldwell, "From 'Emergency' to 'Independence,' 1948-57."

25. Stenson, *Industrial Conflict,* argues that, although by 1948 the MCP was *preparing* for armed revolt, it did not actually commence this on its own initiative, much less on that of the Communist International. Its actions were rather in response to the British administration's repression of the Party and the labor unions it influenced or controlled in mid-1948.

26. On the comprehensive scope of these Regulations and measures, see Caldwell, "From 'Emergency' to 'Independence'," pp. 221-22.

27. N.J. Funston, *Malay Politics in Malaysia: A Study of UMNO and PAS,* pp. 40-41.

28. On the military importance of such a buffer zone, see M.R. Stenson, "The Ethnic and Urban Bases of Communist Revolt in Malaya."

29. Ibid., pp. 137, 332-33 (endnote 18).

30. Ibid., p. 137.

31. Commissioner of Labour, *Annual Report of the Department of Labor for the Year 1948,* p. 7; M.G. Swift, *Malay Peasant Society in Jelebu,* p. 161.

32. For an example of the recognition of the relationship between padi prices and wages by employers during the interwar years, see chapter 4, footnote 39.

33. S.S. Awbery and F.W. Dalley, *Labour and Trade Union Organization in the Federation of Malaya and Singapore,* p. 6.

34. Ibid., p. 19.

35. Morgan, "Rise and Fall," pp. 156-58; see A.J. Stockwell, "British Imperial Policy and Decolonization," p. 78, for specific balance of payment figures for these years; see also Caldwell, "From 'Emergency' to 'Independence'," pp. 242-49, for a discussion of the links between Britain's balance of payment concerns in the postwar years and strategic competition with the United States over spheres of influence in Southeast Asia.

36. Martin Rudner, "Agricultural Policy and Peasant Social Transformation in Late Colonial Malaya," p. 10.

37. Benedict Anderson, *Imagined Communities: Reflections on the Origin and Spread of Nationalism.* Anderson's analysis of the sources of nationalism in Latin America appears to be applicable also to Malay nationalism. The "pilgrim creole functionaries" from various administrative units of the Spanish empire on their "pilgrimages" to Spain came to meet one another and found that they had the "shared fatality" of being born in the New World but of being unable, despite their accomplishments, to rise to the top of the imperial bureaucracy because of being barred by Spanish *peninsulares.* In the cases of the two groups described below who came to contest control over the postwar nationalist movement, the radical vernacular-educated Malay intelligentsia and the English-educated administrative-aristocratic elite, members of each group came to meet one another in a pan-Malayan setting — the Sultan Idris Training College in one case, the Malay College at Kuala Kangsar in the other — and to acquire a sense of "shared fatality" despite their regional and subethnic loyalties, and to experience a common frustration with the limits to which they were allowed to rise in the bureaucracy imposed by the British-instituted color bar. Similarly, Anderson's "provincial creole printmen" have parallels in the Malay journalists of the vernacular press of the 1920s and 1930s discussed by Roff in *Origins,* pp. 157-77. See Anderson, *Imagined Communities,* pp. 50-65.

38. It is necessary to point out that at local and regional levels, these identities and the social schisms they marked did not disappear, but persisted and provided the source for factional divisions within UMNO and other Malay parties during the last years of colonial rule and after Independence.

39. On the Malayan Union scheme and the widespread Malay opposition to it, see J. de Vere Allen, *The Malayan Union;* A.J. Stockwell, *British Policy and Malay Politics During the Malayan Union Experiment, 1942-1948;* and Mohamed Noordin Sopiee, *From Malayan Union to Singapore Separation: Political Unification in the Malaysian Region.*

40. Funston, *Malay Politics,* p. 78.

41. William R. Roff, *The Origins of Malay Nationalism;* Radin Soenarno, "Malay Nationalism, 1900-1945"; Funston, *Malay Politics in Malaysia,* pp. 24-38; Khoo Kay Kim, "Sino-Malaya Relations in Peninsular Malaysia Before 1942."

42. Roff, *Origins,* p. 211.

43. Ibid., pp. 212-21.

44. See Ibid., pp. 142-57, 221-35; Funston, *Malay Politics,* p. 31.

45. Roff, *Origins,* p. 143.

46. Funston, *Malay Politics,* pp. 39-40; Cheah, *Red Star,* pp. 278-80.

47. Ahmad Boestamam, *Carving the Path to The Summit,* pp. 22-27.

48. Funston, *Malay Politics* p. 40.

49. Ibid., p. 39.

50. Ibid., p. 40.

51. William R. Roff, "Translator's Introduction," p. xxi.

52. Funston, Malay Politics, p. 40.

53. Roff, *Origins,* pp. 235-47; Khasnor Johan, *The Emergence of the Modern Malay Administrative Elite;* Yeo Kim Wah, "Grooming of an Elite: Malay Administrators in the Federated Malay States, 1903-1941."

54. Mavis Puthucheary, *The Politics of Administration,* pp. 4-17: see esp. Table 2.4 on p. 16; Yeo Kim Wah, "Grooming of An Elite."

55. Yeo, "Grooming," p. 293.

56. For biographical data on Onn bin Ja'afar, see Roff, *Origins,* p. 168.

57. Ibid., pp. 235-47.

58. Funston, *Malay Politics,* pp. 75-79.

59. Allen, *The Malayan Union,* pp. 57-71.

60. On the Federation of Malaya agreement, see R.S. Milne and Diane K. Mauzy, *Politics and Government in Malaysia,* pp. 29-30.

61. Funston, *Malay Politics,* pp. 40-41. See also Roff, "Translator's Introduction," pp. xvii-xxiii.

62. Ahmad Boestamam, *Carving the Path,* p. 65.

63. The outcome of an episode that arguably is the closest to radical intervention by the Malaysian state in rural relations of production is instructive — the attempt by the Minister of Agriculture, Aziz bin Ishak, to convert privately-owned rice mills in Perak and Province Wellesley into farmers' cooperatives in the early 1960s. This led to a conflict between the Malayan Chinese Association — which numbered among its prominent supporters Chinese rice millers — and UMNO leaders. The upshot was that the Prime Minister nullified Aziz's

program, and soon thereafter dismissed him from his ministerial post. See Gayl D. Ness, *Bureaucracy and Rural Development in Malaysia*, p. 225.

64. Clive S. Kessler, "Islam, Society and Political Behaviour: Some Comparative Implications of the Malay Case," pp. 43-45.

65. Roff, "Translator's Introduction," pp. xxv-xxviii; R.K. Vasil, *Politics in a Plural Society: A Study of Non-Communal Political Parties in West Malaysia*, pp. 167-82.

66. Ness, *Bureaucracy and Rural Development*, pp. 89-90.

67. Quoted from Robert Heussler, *Completing a Stewardship: The Malayan Civil Service, 1942-1957*, p. 115; see also pp. 115-20.

68. A.F. Robertson, *People and the State: An Anthropology of Planned Development*, p. 239.

69. Ness, *Bureaucracy and Rural Development*, pp. 219-20.

70. Husin Ali, *Malay Peasant Society and Leadership*, p. 139; Wan Hashim, *A Malay Peasant Community in Upper Perak: Integration and Transformations*, pp. 85-86.

71. Lim Chong-Yah, *Economic Development of Modern Malaya*, pp. 31-32.

72. Rudner, "Agricultural Policy," pp. 42-47. This was a continuation of the guaranteed minimum price first offered by the state in the late 1930s. On padi price policies during the postwar period, see R.D. Hill, *Agriculture in the Malaysian Region*, pp. 15, 117-18; and C.P. Brown, "Rice Price Stabilization and Support in Malaysia."

73. Rudner, "Agricultural Policy," pp. 18-22; see also Lim Chong-Yah, *Economic Development*, pp. 162-67, 177-78. Kratoska notes that by this period, government attempts to stimulate padi production were explicitly directed toward what I have called "semicore" areas: there was "an important feature of post-war rice policy, a distinction made by the government between 'rice bowl' areas, which were the focus of efforts to stimulate commercial rice production, and other locations where rice was a subsistence crop and there was little scope for expansion." Paul H. Kratoska, "Review of *Issues in Malaysian Development*," p. 402.

74. Rudner, "Agricultural Policy ," p. 42.

75. Ibid., p. 18.

76. Ibid., p. 13.

77. Calculated from Lim, *Economic Development*, Appendices 6.2 and 6.3, pp. 341-42.

78. Rudner, "Agricultural Policy," p. 18.

79. Ibid.

80. Ibid., p. 21.

81. Ibid., pp. 45-47.

82. Ibid., p. 45.

83. Hill, *Agriculture*, p. 15.

84. Lim, *Economic Development*, pp. 31-32.

85. Cited from 1947 and 1957 census figures by Rudner, "Agricultural Policy," footnote on p. 56.
86. Colin Barlow, *The Natural Rubber Industry: Its Development, Technology, and Economy in Malaysia,* p. 81.
87. On the smallholding sector in the postwar years and state policies toward it, see ibid., pp. 76-92, and Martin Rudner, "Malayan Rubber Policy: Development and Anti-Development during the 1950s," pp. 235-41.
88. Rudner, "Malayan Rubber Policy," pp. 241-53.
89. Barlow, *Natural Rubber Industry,* p. 81.
90. Rudner, "Malayan Rubber Policy," pp. 243-44; see also W. M. Corden, "Prospects for Malayan Exports", p. 94.
91. M.G. Swift, "The Accumulation of Capital in a Peasant Economy," p. 29, in a study of a Negri Sembilan village in the 1950s writes: "the result is that most of the replanting takes place on the land of those who are more interested in the accumulation of property than the enjoyment of current income. While this group includes some of the wealthier villagers, it is mainly members of the clerical class who are able to take advantage of the [replanting] grant, since they accumulate property in the village while they are working elsewhere."
92. Rudner, "Malayan Rubber Policy," p. 243.
93. Ibid., p. 252.
94. David S. Gibbons, *RISDA, Its Farmers' Associations and Reduction of Poverty among Rubber Smallholders in Peninsular Malaysia (Final Report),* pp. 13-14.
95. Ibid., p. 43.
96. Ibid., pp. 49-51.
97. See Rudner, "Malayan Rubber Policy," p. 243.
98. Barlow, *Natural Rubber Industry,* p. 86.
99. Ibid., pp. 95-96.

CHAPTER SEVEN

1. T.H. Silcock and Ungku Abdul Aziz, "Nationalism in Malaya," p. 270.
2. Rudner, "Agricultural Policy and Peasant Social Transformation in Late Colonial Malaya," pp. 15, 31-36; Syed Husin Ali, *Social Stratification in Kampong Bagan;* idem, *Malay Peasant Society and Leadership,* pp. 77-80, 87; M.G. Swift, *Malay Peasant Society in Jelebu,* pp. 168-69; idem, "Economic Concentration and Malay Peasant Society"; Lim Chong-Yah, *Economic Development of Modern Malaya,* pp. 168-70.
3. Husin Ali, *Malay Peasant Society and Leadership,* pp. 78-79.
4. Sinnappah Arasaratnam, *Indians in Malaysia and Singapore.* Revised Edition, p. 103.
5. James Puthucheary, *Ownership and Control in the Malayan Economy,* pp. 10-12; Husin Ali, *Malay Peasant Society and Leadership,* pp. 78-80, 90; James C. Scott, *Weapons of the Weak,* pp. 15-17; M.G. Swift, "The Accumulation of Capital in A Peasant Economy," p. 33.

6. Husin Ali, *Malay Peasant Society and Leadership*, pp. 132-40.
7. Rudner, "Agricultural Policy," p. 15.
8. Rice Production Committee, *Report of the Rice Production Committee, Volume I*, pp. 81-82, 93-94. For Kedah, the Committee observed on pp. 81-82 that "rent is steadily increasing. Whereas until the war, it was delivered in kind (clean padi) at the landlord's door, it was alleged that today only 10% of landlords accepted such payment. It was stated that in 1949 rent was 80 gantangs, or 25% on a yield of 2 kunchas, plus $45/- per relong; in 1950 it had generally increased to 6 naleh (1 naleh=16 gantangs) per relong, plus $60/- to $65/-; in 1951 it had increased to 7 naleh and $80–90 relong; and it was alleged that owners were now [1952–53] asking for rent in cash of $120–130 per relong."
9. Swift, "Economic Concentration," pp. 248-49.
10. See Chapter 2, p. 35.
11. Scott, *Weapons*, pp. 16-17, provides an interesting example of a wealthy villager, Haji Broom, "sweeping" up the lands of others through the practice of "promised sale," *jual janji*, in which he loaned villagers money in return for which, if they did not repay within a certain time, he was entitled to take possession of their land.
12. Husin Ali, *Malay Peasant Society and Leadership*, p. 87.
13. Puthucheary, *Ownership and Control*, p. 11.
14. Swift, "Economic Concentration," p. 254.
15. Ibid., pp. 263-64.
16. Rudner, "Agricultural Policy," p. 57.
17. See chapter 8, pp. 153 ff.
18. Husin Ali, *Malay Peasant Society and Leadership*, pp. 84-85.
19. Pierre Bourdieu, *Outline of a Theory of Practice*, p. 191.
20. David Banks, "Changing Kinship in North Malaya," p. 1260.
21. Banks, "Changing Kinship," pp. 1260-61.
22. B. Stein, "The Malays in Malaya," pp. 439-42; M.G. Swift, *Malay Peasant Society*. The inheritance status of rubber lands under *adat perpatih* has been the object of dispute; see Stein, "Malays in Malaya," pp. 441-42.
23. D.S. Gibbons, Lim Teck Ghee et al., *Land Tenure in the Muda Irrigation Area: Final Report, Part 2: Findings*, pp. xvii, xxi, 148-52. Note that there were two measures of land concentration used: (a) the change in the number of landowners as a proportion of all padi farmers; and (b) changes in the proportion of land owned by certain percentages of owners. On *both* measures, land concentration decreased over this period (p. 49).
24. Calculated from Gibbons, Lim et al., *Land Tenure*, Tables 20 and 21, pp. 52-53.
25. Ibid., Table 21, p. 53.
26. Swift, *Malay Peasant Society*, p. 38.
27. Gibbons, Lim et al., *Land Tenure*, p. 50.
28. For one example, see Peter J. Wilson, *A Malay Village and Malaysia*, p. 75.

29. See Wan Hashim, *A Malay Peasant Community in Upper Perak: Integration and Transformations,* p. 53.

30. Ibid., pp. 52-53.

31. Wilson, *A Malay Village,* p. 96.

32. Ibid.

33. Swift, *Malay Peasant Society,* p. 48.

34. Wilson, *A Malay Village,* pp. 74-76.

35. Banks, "Changing Kinship," p. 1267.

36. Swift, *Malay Peasant Society,* pp. 53-54.

37. Rice Production Committee, *Report of the Rice Production Committee,* pp. 81-82.

38. Cited in Gibbons, Lim et al., *Land Tenure,* Table 80, p. 174.

39. Swift, *Malay Peasant Society,* pp. 49-50.

40. Ibid., p. 68.

41. Ibid., p. 70.

42. Ibid., p. 152.

43. Ibid., p. 39; for a similar phenomenon on the east coast, see Conner Bailey, *The Sociology of Production in Rural Malay Society,* p. 39.

44. Swift, *Malay Peasant Society,* pp. 74-75, 153.

45. Husin Ali, *Malay Peasant Society and Leadership,* pp.53-54; Wan Hashim, *A Malay Peasant Community,* pp. 41-42; Swift, *Malay Peasant Society,* pp. 48-49; for the east coast, see Bailey, *Sociology of Production,* pp. 64, 210.

46. Carol McAllister, "Women and Feasting: The Impact of Capitalism and Islamic Revival on Ritual Exchange in Negeri Sembilan, Malaysia," pp. 13-14.

47. Ibid., pp. 14-15.

48. Ibid., p. 14.

49. Swift, *Malay Peasant Society,* pp. 93-94.

50. Scott, *Weapons,* p. 10.

51. Ibid.

52. Ibid., pp. 178ff.

53. Banks, "Changing Kinship," pp. 1264-65.

54. Swift, "Economic Concentration," p. 252.

55. Banks, "Changing Kinship," p. 1267.

56. Bailey, *Sociology of Production,* p. 157.

57. Swift, *Malay Peasant Society,* p. 74.

58. Wilson, *A Malay Peasant Village,* p. 135.

59. From 1947 to 1957, the number of male civilian government employees grew by 39 percent; Gayl D. Ness, *Bureaucracy and Rural Development,* p. 65. Milton Esman, *Administration and Development in Malaysia: Institution Building and Reform in a Plural Society,* p. 70, estimates that by 1965 there were 310,000 civilian public employees out of a total labor force of about 3.2 million persons.

This means that about one out of every ten economically active persons was employed by the government; he notes that "by international standards this is a high figure, comparable to such countries as the United Kingdom and Denmark."

60. Malcolm Caldwell, "From 'Emergency' to 'Independence'," pp. 225-26.
61. Gibbons, Lim, et al., *Land Tenure*, p. 141.
62. Husin Ali, *Malay Peasant Society and Leadership*, p. 157.
63. Ibid., pp. 158-60.
64. Rudner, "Agricultural Policy," p. 21.
65. Ibid., p. 47.
66. Ibid., pp. 47-49.
67. Husin Ali, *Malay Peasant Society and Leadership*, pp. 97-98.
68. Swift, "Economic Concentration," p. 257.
69. Francis Loh Kok-Wah, "Beyond the Tin Mines: The Political Economy of Chinese Squatter Farmers in the Kinta New Villages, Malaysia," pp. 55-63.

CHAPTER EIGHT

1. The analysis of the post-Independence political economy of Malaysia which follows draw on: Michael Stenson, "Class and Race in West Malaysia"; idem, *Class, Race and Colonialism in West Malaysia;* Ozay Mehmet, *Development in Malaysia: Poverty, Wealth and Trusteeship;* Lim Mah Hui, *Ownership and Control of the One Hundred Largest Corporations in Malaysia:* idem, "Ethnic and class Relations in Malaysia"; idem, "The Ownership and Control of Large Corporations in Malaysia"; idem, "Contradictions in the Development of Malay Capital"; Lim Mah Hui and William Canek, "The Political Economy of State Policies in Malaysia"; James J. Puthucheary, *Ownership and Control in the Malayan Economy;* E.L. Wheelwright, "The Political Economy of Industrialization in Malaysia"; R.S. Milne and Diane K. Mauzy, *Politics and Government in Malaysia;* Hing Ai Yun, "Capitalist Development, Class and Race"; Fatimah Halim, "Rural Labour Force and Industrial Conflict in West Malaysia"; idem, "Capital, Labour and the State"; idem, "Workers' Resistance and Management Control"; Basuki Gunawan and Rabeendran Raghaven, et al., *The Emergence of the Malay Business Class in West Malaysia.*
2. Lim, *Ownership and Control.*
3. Lim, *Ownership and Control;* idem, "Ownership and Control of Large Corporations"; Gunawan and Raghavan et al., *Emergence of the Malay Business Class,* pp. 38–54; Mehmet, *Development in Malaysia,* pp. 132–54. Of these, Mehmet's study is the most current.
4. Stenson, "Class and Race," p. 45; Milne and Mauzy, *Politics and Government,* pp. 29–43.
5. See Ozay Mehmet, "Malaysian Employment Restructuring Policies," pp. 980–81.
6. See Amnesty International, *Report of an Amnesty International Mission to the Federation of Malaysia, 18 November–30 November 1978;* Far Eastern

Economic Review, "Malaysia," in *Asia 1980 Yearbook;* idem, "Malaysia," in *Asia 1981 Yearbook;* Simon Barraclough, "Political Participation and its Regulation in Malaysia;" Malayan Law Journal, Excerpts from Government *Gazette;* Fatimah Halim, "Rural Labour Force and Industrial Conflict in West Malaysia," pp. 281, 295 footnote 61.

7. The first trend is described in Lim, *Ownership and Control,* and idem, "Contradictions;" the second in Mehmet, *Development in Malaysia,* pp. 135–47, and in Lim, "Contradictions."

8. For instance, the condition of rural Malays in the Northeastern coastal region of the states of Kelantan, Trengganu, and Pahang would require separate treatment from that of Malays living in the western coastal agricultural regions who have been the focus of this study.

9. For a study of one village in the Kedah Plain that treats these changes in detail, see James C. Scott, *Weapons of the Weak.*

10. Rudolphe De Koninck, "Getting Them to Work Profitably: How the Small Peasants Help the Large Ones, the State and Capital," p. 41.

11. See Stenson, "Class and Race," pp. 49–51; Scott, *Weapons,* pp. 76–85, 124–25, 181–82; Fatimah Halim, "Differentiation of the Peasantry"; idem, "Rural Labour Force"; Ramli Mohamed, "The Role of the State in Economic Development."

12. On the changes in the padi sector summarized in the following sentences, see D.S. Gibbons, Lim Teck Ghee, et al. *Land Tenure in the Muda Irrigation Area;* and Scott, *Weapons;* Rudolphe De Koninck, "The Integration of the Peasantry: Examples from Malaysia and Indonesia"; idem, "Getting Them to Work Profitably"; David S. Gibbons, Rodolphe De Koninck et al., *Agricultural Modernization, Poverty and Inequality,* pp. 21–22, 135–37, 203–9.

13. De Koninck, "Getting Them to Work profitably," pp. 38–39.

14. Scott, *Weapons,* pp. 49–85, 100–25, 155–69. Scott describes a curvilinear change in the demand for padi wage labor. At first, with the Green Revolution inputs of double-cropping, fertilizer use, and improved irrigation and drainage, the demand for labor rose; but at a later state (by the late 1970s) the appearance of the combine harvester caused the demand for labor to fall steeply.

15. Gibbons, Lim et al., *Land Tenure,* pp. xviii, 152, 169–77.

16. According to Fatimah, "Rural Labour Force," p. 276, larger smallholders can afford to replant because they are able to replant only part of their holding, and thus do not suffer a total loss of income for six years from replanting; they can hire men and rent tractors to clear forest land; they have the political connections needed to obtain state subsidies and "cut red tape." All these stratagems are unavailable to owners of smaller smallholdings.

17. *New Straits Times,* "Consolidating Future of the Smallholders."

18. Fatimah, "Rural Labour Force," p. 276.

19. In 1973, there were 161,000 hectares of oil palm smallholdings in West Malaysia compared to 1,105,000 hectares of rubber smallholdings; a large share of the oil palm smallholding area was held by non-Malays. Colin Barlow, *The Natural Rubber Industry,* Table 1.4, p. 439.

20. Barlow in ibid, p. 396, shows that the costs of labor for oil palm are considerably lower per unit area cultivated than for rubber. This is consistent with what I found from my own conversations with oil palm smallholders and rubber smallholders in Malaysia.

21. Martin Rudner, "Development Policies and Patterns of Agrarian Dominance in the Malaysian Rubber Export Economy," p. 86.

22. Gibbons, Lim et al., *Land Tenure*, p. 178, conclude that "As of 1975/76 the 50.1% of padi farmers in the MADA area who operated small farms accounted for only 19.5% of all the padi land and had an average farm size of 2.2 relong, well below what was required for an average-sized household primarily dependent on padi to live above the poverty line." An "average-sized family of 5.6 persons" would have required 4 relong of padi land to earn an annual income of $2,400, in order to be placed above the "poverty line" (p. 152).

23. De Koninck, "Getting Them to Work Profitably," p. 39.

24. Scott, *Weapons*, pp. 236–37.

25. Ibid, pp. 237–38.

26. Peter J. Rimmer and George C.H. Cho, "Urbanization of the Malays Since Independence." Maila Stivens, "Women and Development in South-East Asia II," pp. 26–27, writes of three villages in Negri Sembilan in the 1980s that "the situation has generally been one of static or declining productivity and backwardness, leading to a readiness on the part of villagers to become wage workers in the expanding industrial capitalist sector."

27. Charles Hirschman, "Unemployment among Urban Youth in Peninsular Malaysia, 1970," pp. 406, 410–12.

28. Ibid., p. 401, Table 1. Hirschman's "unemployment index" combines the official unemployment rate with an estimate of the rate of "discouraged" workers no longer actively seeking employment, and he correctly considers this index to be a more accurate measure of persons not employed who would be employed if they could find work: see pp. 396–98. For Hirschman's purposes, he defined "urban" for the sample he studies as referring to towns of at least 5,000 population (p. 401).

29. Government of Malaysia, *Fourth Malaysia Plan 1981–1985,* pp. 42, 57.

30. Aihwa Ong, *Spirits of Resistance and Capitalist Discipline: Factory Women in Malaysia.*

31. Maila Stivens, "The Political Economy of Kinship in Rembau, Negeri Sembilan, Malaysia"; idem, "Workshop Paper: Women and Their Land."

32. Claude Meillasoux, *Maidens, Meal and Money.*

33. *Far Eastern Economic Review,* December 13, 1974, p. 13; *Far Eastern Economic Review,* January 10, 1975, p. 29; Richard Stubbs, "Malaysia's Rubber Smallholding Industry," pp. 86–90; Wan Hashim, *A Malay Peasant Community in Upper Perak,* pp. 90–91, 185–88; Conner Bailey, *The Sociology of Production in Rural Malay Society,* pp. 163–64.

34. See *The Star,* January 27, 1980; *New Straits Times,* January 27, 1980; *The Star,* "The Kedah Farmers' Demo"; *The Star,* January 18, 1980.

35. Such militance was evident in the 1979 strike by the Airline Employees Union, partly under Malay leadership, against the government-owned airline, MAS. Several union leaders were detained under the Internal Security Act, and the Union was deregistered. See Amnesty International, *Report*, pp. 12–13.

36. On the FELDA schemes, see Mehmet, *Development in Malaysia*, pp. 62–70; A.F. Robertson, *People and the State: An Anthropology of Planned Development*, pp. 232–92.

37. Robertson, *People and the State*, p. 263, observes that most settlers have been chosen because they own two acres or less land. According to Mehmet, *Development in Malaysia*, p. 65, "over 95 per cent of the settlers are Malay, with a strong preference given to padi farmers, rubber tappers, fishermen and ex-servicemen."

38. Mehmet, *Development in Malaysia*, p. 63.

39. Robertson, *People and the State*, p. 263.

40. Mehmet, *Development in Malaysia*, pp. 67–68.

41. Frank Peacock, "The Failure of Rural Development in Peninsular Malaysia," p. 385.

42. See, for instance, Michel Foucault, *Discipline and Punish*.

43. Robertson, *People and the State*, p. 266.

44. Ibid., p. 269; Mehmet, *Development in Malaysia*, p. 70.

45. Robertson, *People and the State*, p. 268.

46. Ibid, p. 279.

47. Ibid, p. 286.

48. A 1981 study by Jomo and Ishak suggests not only that income inequality among Malaysians has grown since Independence, but that inequality has increased most *among* Malays over the period from 1957 and 1976. See Jomo Kwame Sundaram and Ishak Shari, "Income Inequalities in Post-Colonial Peninsular Malaysia," pp. 73–74.

49. See Scott, *Weapons;* Kessler, *Islam and Politics in a Malay State: Kelantan 1838–1969;* Shamsul Amri Baharuddin, "A Revival of the Study of Islam in Malaysia."

50. Frederick Engels, *Marx and Engels on the Population Bomb*, p. 86.

51. Gibbons, Lim et al., *Land Tenure*, p. 146.

52. Ungku Abdul Aziz, "Facts and Fallacies on the Malay Economy."

53. A lay version of this account is of long standing. It first appeared among British officials in the early 1900s and was used to justify the *Malay Reservations Enactment* of 1913. The idea was that, since both Chettiar moneylenders and Chinese shopkeepers had been dispossessing rural Malays of their land through loans and *padi kuncha,* land reservations in which only Malays could buy and sell land were necessary to prevent poor farmers from becoming "vagabonds." See Paul Kratoska, "The Chettiar and the Yeoman."

54. Mehmet, *Development in Malaysia*, p. 46.

55. Donald Snodgrass, *Inequality and Development in Malaysia*, pp. 124–31.

56. Ibid., pp. 128–29.
57. Ibid., p. 128.
58. Scott, *Weapons.*
59. Ibid., p. 298.
60. Karl Marx, *The Eighteenth Brumaire of Louis Bonaparte,* p. 15.
61. Although the issue cannot be further explored here, the findings of this study support the more recent work of Ralph Miliband that in states in capitalist social formations, there exist relatively independent "impulses of executive power." Therefore the state cannot be reduced to merely the expression of interests of the capitalist class, and instead there must be said to exist a congenial "partnership between two different, separate forces." See Miliband, "State Power and Class Interests," pp. 69–72.
62. Paul Kratoska, personal communication. I thank Dr. Kratoska for providing this insight.
63. Robert Heussler, *British Rule in Malaya,* p. 231.
64. James de Vere Allen, "Malayan Civil Service, 1874–1941," p. 159.
65. Ibid.
66. James C. Scott, personal communication.
67. Robert Heussler, *Completing a Stewardship,* pp. 115–20.
68. As a point of departure, see R. Heussler, *Yesterday's Rulers,* and references given by Allen, "Malayan Civil Service." In this regard, Heussler, *British Rule,* raises far more questions than it provides answers to, and gives little attention to the attitudes and perspectives of colonial officials toward the Malay peasantry.
69. See Paul H. Kratoska, "Chettiar and Yeoman"; idem, " 'Ends that We Cannot Foresee.' "
70. Shamsul Amri Baharuddin, "The Development of the Underdevelopment of the Malaysian Peasantry," p. 434.

Bibliography

Abdul Aziz, Ungku. "Facts and Fallacies on the Malay Economy." *The Straits Times,* February 28- March 5, 1957.
————. "Facts and Fallacies About the Malay Economy, in Retrospect with New Footnotes." *Ekonomi* 3(1962): 6-30.
————. "Poverty and Rural Development." *Kajian Ekonomi Malaysia* 1,1(1964): 70-105.
Abraham, C.E.R. "Racial and Ethnic Manipulation in Colonial Malaya." *Ethnic and Racial Studies* 6,1(1983): 18-32.
Adas, Michael. "From Avoidance to Confrontation: Peasant Protest in Precolonial and Colonial Southeast Asia." *Comparative Studies in Society and History* 23,2(1981): 217-47.
Ahmad Boestamam. *Carving the Path to the Summit,* translated with an Introduction by William R. Roff. Athens, Ohio: Ohio University Press, 1979.
Akashi, Yoji. "The Japanese Occupation of Malaya: Interruption or Transformation?" In *Southeast Asia Under Japanese Occupation,* edited by Alfred W. McCoy, pp. 65-90. New Haven, CT: Yale University Southeast Asia Studies, 1980.
Allen, James De Vere *The Malayan Union.* New Haven: Yale Southeast Asia Monograph Series, 1967.
————. "The *Ancien Regime* in Trengganu, 1909-1919." *Journal of the Malaysian Branch, Royal Asiatic Society* 41(1968a): 23-53.
————. "The Elephant and the Mousedeer — A New Version: Anglo-Kedah Relations 1905-1915." *Journal of the Malaysian Branch, Royal Asiatic Society* 41,1(1968b): 54-94.
————. "The Kelantan Uprising of 1915: Some Thoughts on the Concept of Resistance in British Malayan History." *Journal of Southeast Asian History* 9,2(1968c): 241-57.
————. "Malayan Civil Service, 1874-1941: Colonial Bureaucracy/Malayan Elite." *Comparative Studies in Society and History* 12(1970): 149-78.

————. "Johore 1901-1914: The Railway Concession: The Johore Advisory Board: Swettenham's Resignation and the First General Advisor." *Journal of the Malaysian Branch, Royal Asiatic Society* 45,2(1972): 1-28.

Amin, Samir, et al. *Transforming the Revolution: Social Movements and the World-System.* New York: Monthly Review Press, 1990.

Amnesty International. *Report of an Amnesty International Mission to the Federation of Malaysia, 18 November-30 November 1978.* London: Amnesty International, 1979.

Anand, Sudhir. *Inequality and Poverty in Malaysia: Measurement and Decomposition.* New York: Oxford University Press, 1983.

Andaya, Barbara Watson, and Leonard Y. Andaya. *A History of Malaysia.* London: Macmillan, 1982.

Anderson, Benedict. *Imagined Communities: Reflections on the Origin and Spread of Nationalism.* London: Verso, 1983.

Anderson, Eugene N., Jr. "A Mosaic of Two Food Systems on Penang Island, Malaysia." In *Food Energy in Tropical Ecosystems,* edited by Dorothy J. Cattle and Karl H. Schwerin, pp. 83-104. New York: Gordon and Breach Science Publishers, 1985.

Anderson, J.N., and W.T. Vorster. "Diversity and Interdependence in the Trade Hinterlands of Melaka." In *Melaka,* (Vol. I), edited by K.S. Sandhu and P. Wheatley, pp. 439-57. Kuala Lumpur: Oxford University Press, 1983.

Arasaratnam, Sinnappah. *Indians in Malaysia and Singapore.* Revised Edition. Kuala Lumpur: Oxford University Press, 1979.

Arrighi, Giovanni. "Labor Supplies in Historical Perspective: A Study of the Proletarianization of the African Peasantry in Rhodesia." In *Essays on the Political Economy of Africa,* edited by J. Saul and J. Woods, pp. 180-234. New York: Monthly Review Press, 1973.

Asad, Talal."Two European Images of Non-European Rule." In Anthropology and The Colonial Encounter, edited by T. Asad, pp. 103-18. London: Ithaca Press, 1973.

Awbery, S.S., and F.W. Dalley. *Labour and Trade Union Organization in the Federation of Malaya and Singapore.* Kuala Lumpur: Government Press, 1948.

A. Azmi Abdul Khalid. "The Federated Malay States: Direction of Trade 1900-1940." *Malaysia in History* 25(1982): 65-73.

Bach, Robert L. "Historical Patterns of Capitalist Penetration in Malaysia." *Journal of Contemporary Asia* 6,4(1978): 458-76.

Bailey, Conner. *Broker, Mediator, Patron and Kinsman: An Historical Analysis of Key Leadership Roles in a Rural Malaysian District.* (Papers in International Studies Southeast Asia Series, 38). Athens, Ohio: Center for International Studies, Ohio University, 1976.

———. *The Sociology of Production in Rural Malay Society*. Kuala Lumpur: Oxford University Press, 1983.

———. "Subsistence Rights and Commercialization in Rural Malay Society." Paper presented at the Annual Meeting, Association for Asian Studies, Boston, Mass., April 9-12, 1987.

Banks, David. "Changing Kinship in North Malaya." *American Anthropologist* 74,5(1972): 1254-75.

———. *Malay Kinship*. Philadelphia: ISHI, 1983.

Baran, Paul, and Paul Sweezy. *Monopoly Capital*. Harmondsworth, England: Penguin Books, 1966.

Barlow, Colin. *The Natural Rubber Industry: Its Development, Technology and Economy in Malaysia*. Kuala Lumpur: Oxford University Press, 1978.

Barnard, Rosemary. "The Role of Capital and Credit in a Malay Rice-producing Village." *Pacific Viewpoint* 14,2(1973): 113-36.

———. "The Modernization of Agriculture in a Kedah Village 1967-1978." *Review of Indonesian and Malayan Affairs* 13(1979): 4-89.

———. "Recent Developments in Agricultural Employment in a Kedah Rice-growing Village." *Developing Economies* 19,3(1981): 207-28.

Barraclough, Simon. "Managing the Challenges of Islamic Revival in Malaysia: A Regime Perspective." *Asian Survey* 23,8(1983): 958-75.

———. "Political Participation and its Regulation in Malaysia: Opposition to the Societies (Amendment) Act 1981." *Pacific Affairs* 57(1984): 450-61.

Bauer, P.T. "The Economics of Planting Density in Rubber Growing." *Economica* (n.s.) 13,50(1946): 131-35.

———. "Malayan Rubber Policies." *Economica* (n.s.) 14,54(1947): 81-107.

———. *The Rubber Industry: A Study in Competition and Monopoly*. London: Longmans, Green and Co., 1948.

———. "Some Aspects of the Malayan Rubber Slump 1929-1933." In *Readings in Malayan Economics,* edited by T.H. Silcock, pp. 185-200. Singapore: Eastern Universities Press, 1961a.

———. "The Working of Rubber Regulation." In *Readings in Malayan Economics,* edited by T.H. Silcock, pp. 242-67. Singapore: Eastern Universities Press, 1961b.

———. "The Economics of Planting Density in Rubber Growing." In *Readings in Malayan Economics,* edited by T.H. Silcock, pp. 236-41. Singapore: Eastern Universities Press, 1961c.

Bender, Barbara. "Emergent Tribal Formations in the American Midcontinent." *American Antiquity* 50,1(1985): 52-62.

Bentley, G. Carter. "Indigenous States of Southeast Asia." *Annual Review of Anthropology* 15(1986): 275-305.

Berwick, E.J.H. *Census of Padi Planters in Kedah, 1955*. Alor Star: Dept. of Agriculture, Federation of Malaya, 1956.

Bonney, R. *Kedah 1771-1821*. Kuala Lumpur: Oxford University Press, 1971.

Boserup, Ester. *The Conditions of Agricultural Growth*. Chicago: Aldine, 1965.

Bourdieu, Pierre. *Outline of a Theory of Practice*. Cambridge: Cambridge University Press, 1977.

Brockway, Lucile, H. *Science and Colonial Expansion: The Role of the British Royal Botanic Gardens*. New York: Academic Press, 1979.

Brown, C.P. "Rice Price Stabilization and Support in Malaysia." *The Developing Economies* 11,3(1973): 164-83.

Burridge, K.O.L. "Rural Administration in Johore." *Journal of African Administration* 9,1(1957): 29-36.

Butcher, John G. *The British in Malaya, 1880-1941: The Social History of a European Community in Colonial South-East Asia*. Kuala Lumpur: Oxford University Press, 1979a.

———. "Towards the History of Malayan Society: Kuala Lumpur District, 1885-1912." *Journal of Southeast Asian Studies* 10,1(1979b): 104-18.

———. "The Demise of the Revenue Farm System in the Federated Malay States." *Modern Asian Studies* 17,3(1983): 387-412.

Caldwell, Malcolm. "War, Boom and Depression." In *Malaya: The Making of a Neo-Colony,* edited by Mohamed Amin and Malcolm Caldwell, pp. 38-63. Nottingham, England: Spokesman Books, 1977a.

———. "From 'Emergency' to 'Independence,' 1948-57." In *Malaya: The Making of a Neo-Colony,* edited by Mohamed Amin and Malcolm Caldwell, pp. 216-65. Nottingham, England: Spokesman Books, 1977b.

Cardoso, Fernando Henrique. "The Consumption of Dependency Theory in the United States." *Latin American Research Review* 12,3(1977): 7-24.

Chai Hon-Chan. *The Development of British Malaya 1896-1909*. (2nd Edition). Kuala Lumpur: Oxford University Press, 1967.

Chaianov, A.V. *The Theory of Peasant Economy*. Manchester: Manchester University Press, 1986.

Cheah Boon Kheng. "Social Banditry and Rural Crime in North Kedah, 1909-1929." *Journal of the Malaysian Branch of the Royal Asiatic Society* 54,2(1981): 98-130.

———. *Red Star Over Malaya: Resistance and Social Conflict During and After the Japanese Occupation, 1941-1946*. Singapore: Singapore University Press, 1983.

———. "Hobsbawm's Social Banditry, Myth, and Historical Reality: A Case in the Malaysian State of Kedah, 1915-1920." *Bulletin of Concerned Asian Scholars* 17,4(1985): 34-51.

Cheng Siok Hwa. "The Rice Industry of Malaya: A Historical Survey." *Journal*

of the Malaysian Branch, Royal Asiatic Society 42,2(1972): 130-44.
Commissioner of Labor, Malayan Union. *Annual Report of the Labor Department for the Year 1947.* Kuala Lumpur: Government Press, 1948.
Commissioner of Labor, Federation of Malaya. *Annual Report of the Labor Department for the Year 1948.* Kuala Lumpur: Government Press, 1949.
Corden, W.M. "Prospects for Malayan Exports." In *The Political Economy of Independent Malaya,* edited by T.H. Silcock and E.K. Fisk, pp. 112–30. Berkeley: University of California Press, 1961.
Courtenay, P.P. "The Plantation in Malaysian Economic Development." *Journal of Southeast Asian Studies* 12(1981): 329-48.
Cowan, C.D. *Nineteenth Century Malaya: The Origins of British Political Control.* (London Oriental Series, 11.) London: Oxford University Press, 1961.
Daud Latiff. "The British Military Administration, September 1945 to April 1946." In *Malaya: The Making of a Neo-Colony,* edited by Mohamed Amin and Malcolm Caldwell, pp. 120-49. Nottingham, England: Spokesman Books, 1977.
De Koninck, Rodolphe. "The Integration of the Peasantry: Examples from Malaysia and Indonesia." *Pacific Affairs* 52,3(1979): 265-93.
―――. "Getting Them to Work Profitably: How the Small Peasants Help the Large Ones, the State and Capital." *Bulletin of Concerned Asian Scholars* 15,2(1983): 32-41.
Del Tufo, M.V. *Malaya: A Report of the 1947 Census of Population.* London: Crown Agent for the Colonies, 1949.
Dennis, Usha Diane. "Rice Cultivation: The Situation in 1930." *Malaysia in History* 25(1982): 105-20.
Department of Agriculture, Federated Malay States. *Annual Reports.* Kuala Lumpur: Government Printers, 1932-38.
Department of Agriculture, Straits Settlements and Federated Malay States. *Bark Consumption and Bark Reserves on Small Rubber Holdings.* Kuala Lumpur: Dept. of Agriculture (Economic Series, 4), 1934.
Department of Statistics, Malaysia. *Population Census of the Federation of Malaya, Reports 1-14.* Kuala Lumpur: Federation of Malaya Department of Statistics, 1958.
―――. *1970 Population and Housing Census of Malaysia: Community Groups.* Kuala Lumpur: Department of Statistics, 1972.
Diamond, Stanley. "Dahomey: A Proto-State in West Africa." Ph.D. diss., Columbia University. Ann Arbor, Mich.: University Microfilms, 1951.
Diener, Paul, and Eugene E. Robkin. "Ecology, Evolution, and the Search for Cultural Origins: The Question of Islamic Pig Prohibition." *Current Anthropology* 19(1978): 493-540.

Dobby, E.H.G. "The North Kedah Plain: A Study in the Environment of Pioneering for Rice Cultivation." *Economic Geography* 27(1951): 294-304.

Dobby, E.H.G. et al. "Part II: Mukim Four, Province Wellesley." *Journal of Tropical Geography* 6,1(1955): 9-35.

Drabble, J.H. "The Plantation Rubber Industry in Malaya Up to 1922." *Journal of the Malaysian Branch, Royal Asiatic Society* 40,1(1967): 52-77.

————. *Rubber in Malaya 1876-1922: The Genesis of the Industry.* Kuala Lumpur: Oxford University Press, 1973.

————. "Malayan Rubber Smallholdings in the Inter-War Period: Some Preliminary Findings." *Malayan Economic Review* 23,2(1978): 61-72.

————. "Peasant Smallholders in the Malayan Economy: An Historical Study with Special Reference to the Rubber Industry." In *Issues in Malaysian Development,* edited by James C. Jackson and Martin Rudner, pp. 69-100. Singapore: Heinemann Educational Books (Asia) Ltd., 1979.

Drabble, J.H., and P.J. Drake. "The British Agency Houses in Malaysia: Survival in a Changing World." *Journal of Southeast Asian Studies* 12,2(1981): 297-328.

Ennew, Judith, Paul Hirst, and Keith Tribe. " 'Peasantry' as an Economic Category." *Journal of Peasant Studies* 4,4 (July 1977): 295-322.

Emerson, Rupert. *Malaysia: A Study in Direct and Indirect Rule.* Kuala Lumpur: University of Malaya Press (1937), 1964.

Esman, Milton. *Administration and Development in Malaysia: Institution Building and Reform in A Plural Society.* Ithaca: Cornell University Press, 1972.

Fatimah Halim. "Differentiation of the Peasantry: A Study of the Rural Communities in West Malaysia." *Journal of Contemporary Asia* 10,4(1980): 400-22.

————. "Rural Labour Force and Industrial Conflict in West Malaysia." *Journal of Contemporary Asia* 11,3(1981): 271-96.

————. "Capital, Labour and the State: The West Malaysian Case." *Journal of Contemporary Asia* 12,3(1982): 259-80.

————. "The Major Mode of Surplus Labour Appropriation in the West Malaysian Countryside: The Sharecropping System." *Journal of Peasant Studies* 10,2-3(1983a): 256-78.

————. "Workers' Resistance and Management Control: A Comparative Case Study of Male and Female Workers in West Malaysia." *Journal of Contemporary Asia* 13,2(1983b): 131-50.

Federal Legislative Council, Federation of Malaya. "Final Report of Rubber Small-Holdings Enquiry Committee." In *Federal Legislative Council, Minutes and Council Papers of the Federal Legislative Council (Fourth*

Session), February 1951 to February 1952. Kuala Lumpur: Government
      Printing Office, 1952, pp. 680-87.
Far Eastern Economic Review. December 13, 1974, p. 13.
————. January 10, 1975, pp. 29-31.
————. *Asia 1980 Yearbook.* Hong Kong: Far Eastern Economic Review, 1980.
————. *Asia 1981 Yearbook.* Hong Kong: Far Eastern Economic Review, 1981.
Firth, Raymond. *Malay Fishermen: Their Peasant Economy.* 2nd Edition. New
      York: W.W. Norton, 1966.
Fisher, C.A. "Malayan Unity in Its Geographical Setting." In *Geographical
      Essays on British Tropical Lands,* edited by R.W. Steele and C.A. Fisher,
      pp. 269-344. London: George Philip and Son, 1956.
Fisk, E.K. "Rural Development Problems in Malaya." *Australian Outlook*
      16(1962): 246-59.
Foucault, Michel. *Discipline and Punish: The Birth of the Prison.* New York:
      Vintage Books, 1977.
Friedmann, Harriet. "Simple Commodity Production and Wage-Labour in the
      American Plains." *Journal of Peasant Studies* 6,1 (1978).
————. "Household Production and the National Economy: Concepts for the
      Analysis of Agrarian Formations." *Journal of Peasant Studies* 7,2
      (1980).
Funston, John. *Malay Politics in Malaysia: A Study of the United Malay
      National Organization and Party Islam.* Kuala Lumpur: Heinemann
      Education Books (Asia), 1980.
Gailey, Christine W. "The State of the State in Anthropology." *Dialectical
      Anthropology* 9,1-4(1985): 65-90.
Gailey, Christine W., and Thomas C. Patterson. "Power Relations and State
      Formation." In *Power Relations and State Formation: Essays From a
      Marxist Perspective,* edited by Thomas C. Patterson and Christine W.
      Gailey. (Archaeology Unit Special Publications, 1.) Washington, D.C.:
      American Anthropological Association, 1987.
Gamba, Charles. *The Origins of Trade Unionism in Malaya: A Study in
      Colonial Labour Unrest.* Singapore: Eastern Universities Press, 1962.
Geertz, Clifford. *Agricultural Involution: The Process of Ecological Change in
      Indonesia.* Berkeley: University of California Press, 1970.
Gibbons, David S., ed. *Daftaran Pekebun Kechil Getah Semenanjung Malaysia,
      1977; Laporan Sementara.* Kuala Lumpur: Rubber Industry
      Smallholders Development Authority, 1983.
————. *Paddy Poverty and Public Policy: A Preliminary Report on Poverty in
      the Muda Area, 1972-1982.* (Center for Policy Research Monographs,
      7.) Penang: Center for Policy Research, Universiti Sains Malaysia, 1984.

————. *RISDA, Its Farmers' Organizations and Reduction of Poverty among Rubber Smallholders in Peninsular Malaysia (Final Report).* Pulau Pinang: Centre for Policy Research, Universiti Sains Malaysia.

Gibbons, David S., Rodolphe De Koninck, et al. *Agricultural Modernization, Poverty and Inequality: The Distributional Impact of the Green Revolution in Regions of Malaysia and Indonesia.* Westmead, England: Teakfield Ltd., 1980.

Gibbons, David S., Lim Teck Ghee, G.R. Elliston, and Shukur bin Kassim. *Land Tenure in the Muda Irrigation Area: Final Report, Part 2: Findings. (Hak Milik Tanah di Kawasan Perairan Muda Laporan Akhir. Bahagian 2: Hasil-hasil Penyelidikan).* (Centre for Policy Research Monographs, 5.) Pulau Pinang: Centre for Policy Research, Universiti Sains Malaysia, 1981.

Ginsburg, Norton, and Chester F. Roberts Jr. *Malaya.* Seattle: University of Washington Press, 1958.

Gopinath, Aruna. "Pahang Under the Resident System (1888-95): The Initial Impact." *Malaysia in History* 23(1980): 31-46.

Gosling, L.A. Peter. "Chinese Crop Dealers in Malaysia and Thailand: The Myth of the Merciless Monopsonistic Middleman." In *The Chinese in Southeast Asia: Volume 1, Ethnicity and Economic Activity,* edited by Linda Y.C. Lim and L.A. Peter Gosling, pp. 131-70. Singapore: Maruzen Asia, 1983.

Gould, Stephen Jay. *The Mismeasure of Man.* New York: W.W. Norton, 1981.

Gowan, Peter. "The Origins of the Administrative Elite." *New Left Review* 162(1987): 4-34.

Gullick, J.M. "The Negri Sembilan Economy of the 1890s." *Journal of the Malayan Branch, Royal Asiatic Society* 24,1(1951): 38-55.

————. *Indigenous Political Systems of Western Malaya.* London: Athlone Press, 1958.

————. *Malay Society in the Late Nineteenth Century: The Beginnings of Change.* Singapore: Oxford University Press, 1987.

Gunawan, Basuki, Rabeendran Raghavan, and Dalf Valenbreder. *The Emergence of the Malay Business Class in West Malaysia.* (Center for the Study of Anthropology and Sociology Publications, 29.) Amsterdam: Center for the Study of Anthropology and Sociology, Dept. of South and Southeast Asian Studies, University of Amsterdam, 1980.

Guyot, Dorothy. "The Politics of Land: Comparative Development in Two States of Malaysia." *Pacific Affairs* 44,3(1971): 368-89.

Hanrahan, Gene Z. *The Communist Struggle in Malaya.* New York: International Secretariat, Institute of Pacific Relations, 1954.

Hawley, Amos, Dorothy Fernandez, and Harbans Singh. "Migration and

Employment in Peninsular Malaysia, 1970." *Economic Development and Cultural Change* 27(1979): 491-504.

Heussler, Robert. *Yesterday's Rulers; The Making of the British Colonial Service.* Syracuse, N.Y.: Syracuse University Press, 1963.

———. *British Rule in Malaya: The Malayan Civil Service and its Predecessors, 1867-1942.* (Contributions in Comparative Colonial Studies, 6.) Westport, CT: Greenwood Press, 1981.

———. *Completing a Stewardship: The Malayan Civil Service, 1942-1957.* (Contributions in Comparative Colonial Studies, 15.) Westport, CT: Greenwood, 1983.

Hill, Ronald David. *Rice in Malaya: A Study in Historical Geography.* Kuala Lumpur: Oxford University Press, 1977.

———. *Agriculture in the Malaysian Region.* Budapest: Akademiai Kiado, 1982.

Hing Ai Yun. "Women and Work in West Malaysia." *Journal of Contemporary Asia* 14,2(1984a): 204-18.

———. "Capitalist Development, Class and Race." In *Ethnicity, Class and Development in Malaysia,* edited by Syed Husin Ali, pp. 296-328. Kuala Lumpur: Persatuan Sains Sosial Malaysia, 1984b.

———. "The Development and the Transformation of Wage Labour in West Malaysia." *Journal of Contemporary Asia* 15,2(1985a): 139-71.

———. "Work Orientation: A Case Study of Factory Workers in Peninsular Malaysia." *Journal of Contemporary Asia* 15,3(1985b): 267-87.

Hirschman, Charles. "Unemployment among Urban Youth in Peninsular Malaysia, 1970: A Multivariate Analysis of Individual and Structural Effects." *Economic Development and Cultural Change* 30(1982a): 391-412.

———. "Industrial and Occupational Change in Peninsular Malaysia, 1947-1970." *Journal of Southeast Asian Studies* 13,1(1982b): 9-32.

Hirschman, Charles, and Akbar Aghajanian. "Women's Labour Force Participation and Socioeconomic Development: The Case of Peninsular Malaysia, 1957-1970." *Journal of Southeast Asian Studies* 11(1980): 30-49.

Ho, Robert. "Rubber Production by Peasants of the Terachi Valley, Malacca." *Transactions and Papers, Institute of British Geographers,* Reprint 41, 1967a, pp. 187-202.

———. *Farmers of Central Malaya.* (Dept. of Geography, Australian National University Publications, G/4.) Canberra: Research School of Pacific Studies, Australian National University, 1967b.

———. "The Evolution of Agriculture and Land Ownership in Saiong Mukim." *Malayan Economic Review* 13,2(1968): 81-102.

————. "Land Ownership and Economic Prospects of Malayan Peasants." *Modern Asian Studies* 4,1(1970): 83-92.

Hopkins, Terence. "The Study of the Capitalist World-Economy: Some Introductory Considerations." In *The World-System of Capitalism,* edited by Walter L. Goldfrank, pp. 21-52. Beverly Hills: Sage Publications, 1979.

Horii, Kenzo. "The Land Tenure System of Malay Padi Farmers — A Case Study of Kampung Sungei Bujor in the State of Kedah." *Developing Economies* 10,1(1972): 45-73.

————. *Rice Economy and Land Tenure in West Malaysia: A Comparative Study of Eight Villages.* (Institute of Developing Economies Occasional Paper Series, 18.) Tokyo: Institute of Developing Economies, 1980.

Hua Wu Yin. *Class and Communalism in Malaysia: Politics in a Dependent Capitalist State.* London: Zed Press, 1983.

Huang, Yukon. "Tenancy Patterns, Productivity, and Rentals in Malaysia." *Economic Development and Cultural Change* 23(1974-75): 703-18.

Husin Ali, Syed. *Social Stratification in Kampong Bagan: A Study of Class, Status, Conflict and Mobility in a Rural Malayan Community.* (Royal Asiatic Society, Malayan Branch, Monographs, 1). Singapore: Royal Asiatic Society, Malaya Branch, 1964.

————. *Malay Peasant Society and Leadership.* Kuala Lumpur: Oxford University Press, 1975.

Hussein Alatas, Syed. *The Myth of the Lazy Native: A Study of the Image of the Malays, Filipinos and Javanese From the 16th to the 20th Century and Its Function in the Ideology of Colonial Capitalism.* London: Frank Cass, 1977.

Ibrahim Nik Mahmood. "The To' Janggut Rebellion of 1915." In *Kelantan: Religion, Society and Politics in a Malay State,* edited by William R. Roff, pp. 62-86. Kuala Lumpur: Oxford University Press, 1974.

Jaafar bin Hamzah. "The Malays in Tasek Glugor During the Japanese Occupation." *Malaysia in History* 21,2(1978): 56-64.

Jackson, James C. *Planters and Speculators: Chinese and European Agricultural Enterprise in Malaya, 1896-1921.* Kuala Lumpur: University of Malaya Press, 1968.

————. "Rice Cultivation in West Malaysia: Relationships Between Culture History, Customary Practices and Recent Developments." *Journal of the Malaysian Branch, Royal Asiatic Society* 45,2(1972): 76-96.

Jackson, R.N. *Immigrant Labour and the Development of Malaya 1786-1920.* Kuala Lumpur: The Government Press, 1961.

Jomo Kwame Sundaram. "Class Formation in Malaya: Capital, State and Uneven Development." Ph.D. diss., Harvard University, 1977.

———. "The Ascendance of Bureaucratic Capitalists in Malaysia." *Alternatives* 7,4(1981): 467-90.

———. *A Question of Class: Capital, the State, and Uneven Development in Malaya.* Singapore: Oxford University Press, 1986.

———. *Beyond 1990: Considerations for a New National Development Strategy,* Kuala Lumpur: Institut Pengajian Tinggi/Institute of Advanced Studies, Universiti Malaya, 1989.

———. *Growth and Structural Change in the Malaysian Economy.* London: McMillan, 1990.

Jomo Kwame Sundaram and Ishak Shari. "Income Inequalities in Post-colonial Peninsular Malaysia." *Pacific Viewpoint* 23,1(1982): 66-76.

Jones, Greta. *Social Darwinism and English Thought: The Interaction between Biological and Social Theory.* Sussex: The Harvester Press, 1980.

Kahn, Joel. "Social Context of Technological Change in Four Malaysian Villages: A Problem for Economic Anthropology." *Man* 16(1981): 542-62.

———. "From Peasants to Petty Commodity Production in Southeast Asia." *Bulletin of Concerned Asian Scholars* 14,1 (Jan.-Mar. 1982): 3-15.

Kaur, Amarjit. "Road or Rail? Competition in Colonial Malaya, 1909-1940." *Journal of the Malaysian Branch, Royal Asiatic Society* 53,2(1980): 45-65.

———. "Railroad in Malaya 1941-1957: The Japanese Interregnum, The Return of the British and Railroad Reconstruction." *Malaysia in History* 25(1982): 88-104.

Kaur, Amarjit, and Sharil Talib Robert. "The Extractive Colonial Economy and the Peasantry: Ulu Kelantan 1900-1940." *Review of Indonesian and Malayan Affairs* 15,2(1981): 32-91.

Keesing, Roger M. *Kin Groups and Social Structure.* New York: Holt, Rinehart and Winston, 1975.

Kessler, Clive. "Islam, Society and Political Behaviour: Some Comparative Implications of the Malay Case." *British Journal of Sociology* 23(1972): 33-50.

———. *Islam and Politics in a Malay State: Kelantan 1838-1969.* Ithaca: Cornell University Press, 1978.

Khasnor Johan. *The Emergence of the Modern Malay Administrative Elite.* Singapore: Oxford University Press, 1984.

Khoo Kay Kim. *The Western Malay States 1850-1873: The Effects of Commercial Development on Malay Politics.* Kuala Lumpur: Oxford University Press, 1972.

———. "Recent Malaysian Historiography." *Journal of Southeast Asian Studies* 10,2(1979): 247-61.

————. "Islam and Politics in Kelantan: A Review of *Islam and Politics in a Malay State: Kelantan, 1838-1969,* by Clive Kessler." *Journal of Southeast Asian Studies* 11(1980): 187-94.

————. "Sino-Malaya Relations in Peninsular Malaysia Before 1942." *Journal of Southeast Asian Studies* 12,1(1981): 93-107.

Kratoska, Paul H. "The Chettiar and the Yeoman: British Cultural Categories and Rural Indebtedness in Malaya." (Occasional Paper, 32). Singapore: Institute of Southeast Asian Studies, 1975.

————. "Rice Cultivation and the Ethnic Division of Labor in British Malaya." *Comparative Studies in Society and History* 24(1982): 280-314.

————. "'Ends that We Cannot Foresee': Malay Reservations in British Malaya." *Journal of Southeast Asian Studies* 14(1983): 149-68.

————. "Penghulus in Perak and Selangor: The Rationalization and Decline of a Traditional Malay Office." *Journal of the Malaysian Branch, Royal Asiatic Society* 57,2(1984a): 31-59.

————. "Review of *Issues in Malaysian Development,* edited by James C. Jackson and Martin Rudner." *Journal of Southeast Asian Studies* 15,2(1984b):401-03.

————. "The Peripatetic Peasant and Land Tenure in British Malaya." *Journal of Southeast Asian Studies* 16,1(1985): 16-45.

Kuchiba, Masuo, Yoshihiro Tsubouchi, and Narifumi Maeda, eds. *Three Malay Villages: A Sociology of Padi Growers in West Malaysia,* translated by Peter Hawkes and Stephanie Hawkes. (Center for Southeast Asian Studies, Kyoto University Monographs, 14.) Honolulu: University Press of Hawaii, (1976), 1979.

Kuchiba, Masuo, and Yoshihiro Tsubouchi. "Paddy Farming and Social Structure in a Malay Village: A Social Anthropological Study of a Community in Kedah." *Developing Economies* 5,3(1967): 463-85.

Lee Say Lee. "A Study of the Rice Trade in Kedah Before and During the Japanese Occupation." *Malaysia in History* 24(1981): 109-16.

Lee Suat Beng. "The Effects of Rubber Price Fluctuations on Rubber Smallholders: Gurun, Kedah, 1920-1950." In *Penghijrah dan Penghirahan (Kumpulan Esei Sejarah Malaysia oleh Pelajar-pelajar U.S.M.),* edited by Paul H. Kratoska, pp. 178-92. Pulau Pinang, Malaysia: Universiti Sains Malaysia, 1982.

Lent, J.A. "Human Rights in Malaysia." *Journal of Contemporary Asia* 14,4(1984): 442-58.

Leong, Stephen M.Y. "Sources, Agencies and Manifestations of Overseas Chinese Nationalism in Malaya, 1937-1941." Ph.D. diss., University of California at Los Angeles. Ann Arbor: University Microfilms, 1976.

Li, Dun J. *British Malaya: An Economic Analysis.* New York: The American

Press, 1955.

Lim Chong-Yah. *Economic Development of Modern Malaya.* Kuala Lumpur: Oxford University Press, 1967.

Lim Heng Kow. *The Evolution of the Urban System in Malaya.* Kuala Lumpur: Penerbit Universiti, 1978.

Lim Mah Hui. *Ownership and Control of the One Hundred Largest Corporations in Malaysia.* London: Oxford University Press, 1979.

————. "Ethnic and Class Relations in Malaysia." *Journal of Contemporary Asia* 10,1-2(1980): 130-54.

————. "The Ownership and Control of Large Corporations in Malaysia: The Role of Chinese Businessmen." In *The Chinese in Southeast Asia: Volume 1, Ethnicity and Economic Activity,* edited by Linda Y.C. Lim and L.A. Peter Gosling, pp. 275-315. Singapore: Maruzen Asia, 1983.

————. "Contradictions in the Development of Malay Capital: State, Accumulation and Legitimation." *Journal of Contemporary Asia* 15,1(1985a): 37-63.

————. "Affirmative Action, Ethnicity and Integration: The Case of Malaysia." *Ethnic and Racial Studies* 8(1985b): 250-76.

Lim Mah Hui, and William Canek. "The Political Economy of State Policies in Malaysia." *Journal of Contemporary Asia* 11,2(1981): 208-24.

Lim Teck Ghee. "Malayan Peasant Smallholders and the Stevenson Restriction Scheme 1922-28." *Journal, Malayan Branch of the Royal Asiatic Society* 47(1974): 105-22.

————. *Peasants and Their Agricultural Economy in Colonial Malaya, 1874-1941.* Kuala Lumpur: Oxford University Press, 1977.

Loh, Philip Fook-Seng. "Malay Precedence and the Federal Formula in the Federated Malay States, 1909-1939." *Journal of the Malaysian Branch, Royal Asiatic Society* 45,2(1972): 29-50.

Loh, Francis Kok-Wah. "Beyond the Tin Mines: The Political Economy of Chinese Squatter Farms in the Kinta New Villages, Malaysia." Ph.D diss., Cornell University. Ann Arbor: University Microfilms, 1980.

Malayan Law Journal Editors. Excerpts from Government *Gazette. Malayan Law Journal* 1981: xliii-xlv.

Malaysia, Government of. *Fourth Malaysia Plan 1981-1985.* Kuala Lumpur: National Printing Department, 1981.

Marx, Karl. *The Eighteenth Brumaire of Louis Bonaparte.* New York: International Publishers, 1963.

————. *Capital: Vol. 1, A Critical Analysis of Capitalist Production.* New York: International Publishers, 1967.

Marx, Karl, and Frederick Engels. *Marx and Engels on the Population Bomb: Selections from the Writings of Marx and Engels Dealing with the*

Theories of Thomas Robert Malthus, edited by Ronald L. Meek and translated by Dorothea L. Meek and Ronald L. Meek. Berkeley: The Ramparts Press, 1971.

Mason, Philip. *Prospero's Magic: Some Thoughts on Class and Race.* London: Oxford University Press, 1962.

Maxwell, W.E. "The Law and Customs of the Malays with Reference to the Tenure of Land." *Journal of the Straits Branch, Royal Asiatic Society* 13(1884): 75-200 (June).

McAllister, Carol Lynn. "Women and Feasting: The Impact of Capitalism and Islamic Revival on Ritual Exchange in Negeri Sembilan, Malaysia." Paper presented at Annual Meeting, American Anthropological Association, Chicago, IL, November 22, 1987.

McIntyre, W.D. *The Imperial Frontier in the Tropics, 1865-75.* London and New York: Macmillan and Co., 1967.

Meek, Charles Kingsley. *Land, Law and Custom in the Colonies.* 2nd ed. London: Oxford University Press, 1949.

Mehmet, Ozay. "Malaysian Employment Restructuring Policies: Effectiveness and Prospects under the Fourth Malaysian Plan, 1980-85." *Asian Survey* 22(1982): 978-87.

———. *Development in Malaysia: Poverty, Wealth and Trusteeship.* London: Croom Helm, 1986.

Meillasoux, Claude. *Maidens, Meal and Money: Capitalism and the Domestic Community.* Cambridge: Cambridge University Press, 1975 [trans. 1981].

Miliband, Ralph. "State Power and Class Interests." In *Class Power and State Power: Political Essays,* pp. 63-78. London: Verso, 1983.

Mills, Lennox. *British Rule in Eastern Asia: A Study of Contemporary Government and Economic Development in British Malaya and Hong Kong.* London: Oxford University Press, 1942.

Milne, R.S., and Diane K. Mauzy. *Politics and Government in Malaysia.* Singapore: Federal Publications, 1978.

Milner, A.C. *Kerajaan: Malay Political Culture on the Eve of Colonial Rule.* (Association for Asian Studies Monographs, 40.) Tucson, AZ: University of Arizona Press, 1982.

———. "Colonial Records History: British Malaya." *Modern Asian Studies* 21,4(1986): 773-92.

Mohamad Abu Bakar. "Islamic Revivalism and the Political Process in Malaysia." *Asian Survey* 21(1981): 1040-59.

Mohamed Amin. "Appendix: British 'Intervention' and Malay Resistance." In *Malaya: The Making of a Neocolony,* edited by Mohamed Amin and Malcolm Caldwell, pp. 64-72. Nottingham, England: Spokesman Books,

1977.

Mohamed Noordin Sopiee. *From Malayan Union to Singapore Separation: Political Unification in the Malaysian Region*. Kuala Lumpur, 1974.

Mokhtar Tamin. "Comments in the Colloquium, 'The Dynamics of Social Change and Economic Development in the Rural Sector of Malaysia'." In *Selected Papers Delivered at the Great Economics Debate*, edited by Fong Chek Kwai and Teh Swee Kiat, pp. 55-60. Kuala Lumpur: University of Malaya Economics Society, 1971.

Mokhzani Abdul Rahim. "Comments in the Colloquium, 'The Dynamics of Social Change and Economic Development in the Rural Sector of Malaysia'." In *Selected Papers Delivered at the Great Economics Debate*, edited by Fong Chek Kwai and Teh Swee Kiat, pp. 36-45. Kuala Lumpur: University of Malaya Economics Society, 1971.

Morgan, Michael. "The Rise and Fall of Malayan Trade Unionism, 1945-50." In *Malaya: The Making of a Neo-Colony*, edited by Mohamed Amin and Malcolm Caldwell, pp. 150-98. Nottingham, England: Spokesman Press, 1977.

Nagata, Judith. "Religious Ideology and Social Change: The Islamic Revival in Malaysia." *Pacific Affairs* 53,3(1980): 405-39.

————. "Islamic Revival and the Problem of Legitimacy Among Rural Religious Elites in Malaysia." *Man* (n.s.) 17(1982): 42-57.

Nash, Manning. *Peasant Citizens: Politics, Religion and Modernization in Kelantan, Malaysia*. Athens, OH: Ohio University Center for International Studies, 1974.

Ness, Gayl D. *Bureaucracy and Rural Development in Malaysia: A Study of Complex Organizations in Stimulating Economic Development in New States*. Berkeley: University of California Pres, 1967.

Newbold, T.J. *Political and Statistical Account of the British Settlements in the Straits of Malacca, With a History of the Malayan States*. (2 Vols.), 1839. Reprint. Kuala Lumpur: Oxford University Press, 1971.

New Straits Times. July 3, 1978.

————. July 1, 1979.

————. January 27, 1980.

————. "Consolidating Future of the Smallholders," July 16, 1985.

Nonini, Donald M. "Comment on 'Quantum Adjustment, Macroevolution and the Social Field: Some comments on Evolution and Culture' by Paul Diener." *Current Anthropology* 21,4(1980): 433-35.

————. "The Chinese Community of a West Malaysian Market Town: A Study in Political Economy." Stanford: Ph.D. diss., Stanford University, 1983.

————. "Varieties of Materialism." *Dialectical Anthropology* 9(1985): 7-63.

————. "Popular Sources of Chinese Labor Militance in Colonial Malaya." In
    The Politics of Immigrant Workers, edited by Carl Strikwerda and
    Camille Guerin-Gonzales. New York: Holmes and Meier. In press.
Ong, Aihwa. "Political Mobilization of Malay Women in Rural Selangor."
    Paper presented at the panel, "The Changing Role of Women in
    Malaysian Politics," Annual Meeting of the Association for Asian
    Studies, Philadelphia, Penn., March 22-24, 1985.
————. *Spirits of Resistance and Capitalist Discipline: Factory Women in
    Malaysia.* Albany: State University of New York Press, 1987.
Ooi Jin-Bee. "Rural Development in Tropical Areas, with Special Reference to
    Malaya." *Malayan Journal of Tropical Geography* 12(1959): i-x, 1-222.
————. *Peninsular Malaysia.* London: Longman, 1976.
Ormsby-Gore, W.G.A. *Report of The Right Honourable W.G.A. Ormsby-Gore,
    M.P. (Parliamentary Under-Secretary of State for the Colonies) on His
    Visit to Malaya, Ceylon, and Java During the Year 1928.* (Parliamentary
    Papers Cmd. 3235 of 1928), London: H.M.S.O., 1928.
Parkinson, Brien K. "Non-economic Factors in the Economic Retardation of the
    Rural Malays." *Modern Asian Studies* 1,1(1967): 31-46.
————. "The Economic Retardation of the Malays: A Rejoinder." *Modern
    Asian Studies* 2,3(1968): 267-72.
Parmer, J. Norman. *Colonial Labor Policy and Administration: A History of
    Labor in the Rubber Plantation Industry, c. 1910-1941.* (Association for
    Asian Studies Monographs, 9). Locust Valley, NY: J. J. Augustin Inc.,
    1960.
Patterson, Thomas C., and Christine W. Gailey, Eds. *Power Relations and State
    Formation: Essays From a Marxist Perspective.* (Archaeology Unit
    Special Publications, 1.) Washington, D.C.: American Anthropological
    Association, 1987.
Peacock, Frank. "The Failure of Rural Development in Peninsular Malaysia." In
    Issues in Malaysian Development, edited by James C. Jackson and
    Martin Rudner, pp. 375-96. (Asian Studies Association of Australia,
    Southeast Asia Publication Series, 3.) Kuala Lumpur: Heinemann
    Educational Books, 1979.
————. "Rural Poverty and Development in West Malaysia (1957-70)."
    Journal of Developing Areas 15,4(1981): 639-54.
Purcal, John T. *Rice Economy: Employment and Income in Malaysia.* Kuala
    Lumpur: University of Malaya Press, 1971.
Purcell, Victor. *The Chinese in Southeast Asia.* (2nd ed.) London: Oxford
    University Press, 1965.
————. *The Chinese in Malaya.* Kuala Lumpur: Oxford University Press, 1967.
Puthucheary, James. *Ownership and Control in the Malayan Economy.*

Singapore: Donald Moore for Eastern Universities Press, 1960.
Puthucheary, Mavis. *The Politics of Administration: The Malaysian Experience.*
   Kuala Lumpur: Oxford University Press, 1978.
Radin Soenarno. "Malay Nationalism 1900-1945." *Journal of Southeast Asian
   History* 1,1(1960): 1-33.
Ramli Mohamed. "The Role of the State in Economic Development: The
   Malaysian Case." Manoa: Unpublished MS, Dept. of Political Science,
   University of Hawaii, 1983.
Reid, Anthony, and Lance Castles, eds. *Precolonial State Systems in Southeast
   Asia.* (Malayan Branch of the Royal Asiatic Society Monographs, 6.)
   Kuala Lumpur: Malayan Branch of the Royal Asiatic Society, 1975.
Rice Production Committee. *Report of the Rice Production Committee.* Kuala
   Lumpur: Charles Grenier, 1953.
Richards, W. "The Underdevelopment of West Malaysia: A Survey." *Review of
   Indonesian and Malayan Affairs* 1(1973): 19-37.
Rimmer, Peter J., and George C.H. Cho. "Urbanization of the Malays Since
   Independence: Evidence from West Malaysia, 1957 and 1970." *Journal
   of Southeast Asian Studies* 12(1981): 349-63.
Rimmer, Peter J., and Lisa M. Allen. *The Underside of Malaysian History:
   Pullers, Prostitutes, Plantation Workers.* Singapore: Singapore
   University Press, 1990.
Roberts, Chester. *The Area Handbook on Malaya.* Chicago: The University of
   Chicago, 1955.
Robertson, A.F. *People and the State: An Anthropology of Planned
   Development.* Cambridge: Cambridge University Press, 1984.
Roff, William R. *The Origins of Malay Nationalism.* New Haven: Yale
   University Press, 1967.
———. "Translator's Introduction." In *Carving the Path to the Summit,* by
   Ahmad Boestamam, pp. xi-xxxii. Athens, Ohio: Ohio University Press,
   1979.
———. *Kelantan: Religion, Society and Politics in a Malay State.* Kuala
   Lumpur: Oxford University Press, 1974.
Rogers, Marvin L. "Patterns of Change in a Rural Malay Community: Sungai
   Raya Revisited." *Asian Survey* 22,8(1982): 757-78.
———. "Electoral Organization and Political Mobilization in Rural Malaysia."
   Manusia dan Masyarakat (n.s.) 4(1983): 13-24.
———. "Political Involvement and Political Stability in Rural Malaysia."
   Journal of Commonwealth and Comparative Politics 23,3(1985): 226-
   50.
———. "Changing Patterns of Political Involvement among Malay Village
   Women." *Asian Survey* 26,3(1986): 322-44.

Rubber Industry Smallholders Development Authority (RISDA). *Census of Rubber Smallholders in Peninsular Malaysia, 1977: Interim Report. (Laporan Sementara Banci Pekebun Kechil Getah Semenanjung Malaysia 1977: Analisa Profail Sosio-ekonomi Kemiskinan Dan Penyertaan Dalam Rancangan.)* Kuala Lumpur: RISDA, 1982.
————. *Census of Rubber Smallholders in Peninsular Malaysia, 1977: Final Report. (Laporan Akhir Banci Pekebun Kechil Getah Semenanjung Malaysia 1977: Analisa Profail Sosio-ekonomi Kemiskinan Dan Penyertaan Dalam Rancangan.)* Kuala Lumpur: RISDA, with Centre for Policy Research, Universiti Sains Malaysia, 1983.
Rubber Situation in British Colonies and Protectorates, Committee. (Stevenson Committee).
Report and Supplementary Report of the Committee. (Parliamentary Papers Cmds. 1678 and 1756 of 1922), London: H.M.S.O., 1922.
Rudner, Martin. "Malayan Rubber Policy: Development and Anti-Development during the 1950s." *Journal of Southeast Asian Studies* 7(1976): 235-59.
————. "Agricultural Policy and Peasant Social Transformation in Late Colonial Malaya." In *Issues in Malaysian Development,* edited by James C. Jackson and Martin Rudner, pp. 7-68. Singapore: Heinemann Educational Books (Asia) Ltd., 1979.
————. "Development Policies and Patterns of Agrarian Dominance in the Malaysian Rubber Export Economy." *Modern Asian Studies* 15,1(1981): 83-105.
————. "Changing Planning Perspectives of Agricultural Development in Malaysia." *Modern Asian Studies* 17,3(1983): 413-35.
Sadka, Emily. *The Protected Malay States 1874-1895.* Singapore: University of Singapore Press, 1968.
Sardesai, D.R. "Trade and Empire in Malaya and Singapore, 1869-1874." (Papers in International Studies Southeast Asia Series, 16.) Athens, OH: Center for International Studies, Ohio University, 1970.
Schlegel, Charles C. "Development, Equity and Level of Living in Peninsular Malaysia." *Journal of Developing Areas* 15, 2: 297-316.
Scott, James C., and Ben Kerkvliet. "The Politics of Survival: Peasant Responses to Progress in Southeast Asia." *Journal of Southeast Asian Studies* 4,2(1973): 241-68.
————, eds. "Special Issue: Everyday Forms of Peasant Resistance in South-East Asia." *Journal of Peasant Studies* 13,2 (January 1986).
Scott, James C. "Patron-Client Politics and Political Change in Southeast Asia." *American Political Science Review* 65,1(1972): 91-114.
————. *The Moral Economy of the Peasant: Rebellion and Subsistence in Southeast Asia.* New Haven: Yale University Press, 1976.

————. *Weapons of the Weak: Everyday Forms of Peasant Resistance.* New Haven: Yale University Press, 1985.

Shaharil Talib. "A Revolt in Malaysian Historiography." *Akademika* 20-21(1982): 445-67.

————. "Voices from the Kelantan Desa, 1900-1940." *Modern Asian Studies* 17,2(1983): 177-95.

————. *After Its Own Image: The Trengganu Experience 1881-1941.* Singapore: Oxford University Press, 1984.

Shahoran bin Johan Ariffin, and Walter E.J. Tips. "Income Levels and Basic Needs of Rubber Small-holders in Traditional Villages in Malaysia." *Southeast Asian Studies (Kyoto)* 19,1(1981): 63-76.

Shamsul Amri Baharuddin. "The Development of the Underdevelopment of the Malaysian Peasantry." *Journal of Contemporary Asia* 9,4(1979): 434-54.

————. "A Revival in the Study of Islam in Malaysia." *Man* 17(1982):399-404.

————. "The Politics of Poverty Eradication: The Implementation of Development Projects in a Malaysian District." *Pacific Affairs* 56(1983): 455-76.

————. *From British to Bumiputera Rule: Local Politics and Rural Development in Peninsular Malaysia.* Singapore: Institute of Southeast Asian Studies, 1986.

Shamsul Bahrin, Tunku. "The Pattern of Indonesian Migration and Settlement in Malaya." *Asian Studies* 5,2(1967): 233-57.

Sharifah Zaleha Hassan. "Institution vs. Technology in the Fishing Industry: A Case Study." *Kajian Ekonomi Malaysia* 13, 1-2(1976): 26-39.

Sharom Ahmat. "The Structure of the Economy of Kedah, 1879-1905." *Journal of the Malaysian Branch, Royal Asiatic Society* 43,2(1970a): 1-25.

————. "The Political Structure of the State of Kedah 1879-1905." *Journal of Southeast Asian Studies* 1,2(1970b): 115-28.

Short, Anthony. *The Communist Insurrection in Malaya, 1948-1960.* London: F. Muller, 1975.

Shukor Kassim, David Gibbons, and Halinah Todd. *Poor Malays Speak Out: Paddy Farmers in Muda.* Kuala Lumpur: Maricans, 1984.

Sidhu, Jagjit Singh. *Administration in the Federated Malay States 1896-1920.* Kuala Lumpur: Oxford University Press, 1980.

Silcock, T.H., and Ungku Abdul Aziz. "Nationalism in Malaya." In *Asian Nationalism and the West,* edited by W.L. Holland, pp. 269-346. New York: Institute of Pacific Relations, 1953.

Sinclair, Keith. "Hobson and Lenin in Johore: Colonial Office Policy Towards British Concessionaires and Investors, 1878-1907." *Modern Asian Studies* 1,4(1967): 335-52.

Skinner, G. William. "Overseas Chinese Leadership: Paradigm for a Paradox." In *Leadership and Authority,* edited by Gehan Wijeyewardene, pp. 191-207. Singapore: University of Malaya Press, 1968.

———. "Regional Urbanization in Nineteenth Century China." In *The City in Late Imperial China,* edited by G.W. Skinner, pp. 211-52. Stanford: Stanford University Press, 1977a.

———. "Cities and the Hierarchy of Local Systems." In *The City in Late Imperial China,* edited by G.W. Skinner, pp. 275-351. Stanford: Stanford University Press, 1977b.

———. "Marketing Systems and Regional Economies: Their Structure and Development." Paper presented for the Symposium on Social and Economic History in China from the Song Dynasty to 1900, Beijing, China, October 26 - November 1, 1980.

Smith, Carol A."Labor and International Capital in the Making of a Peripheral Social Formation." In *Labor Systems and Labor Movements in the World Capitalist Economy,* edited by C. Bergquist. Beverly Hills: Sage Publications, 1984a.

———. "Forms of Production in Practice: Fresh Approaches to Simple Commodity Production." *Journal of Peasant Studies* 11,4 (July 1984b): 201-21.

Snodgrass, Donald R. *Inequality and Economic Development in Malaysia.* Kuala Lumpur: Oxford University Press, 1980.

Spinanger, Dean. *Industrialization Policies and Regional Economic Development in Malaysia.* Singapore: Oxford University Press, 1986.

The Star. Penang, Malaysia. January 27, 1980.

———. "The Kedah Farmers' Demo: Looking into the Root of the Problem." Penang, Malaysia. January 28, 1980.

Stein, Burton. "The Malays in Malaya." In *Area Handbook on Malaya,* edited by Chester F. Roberts, pp. 394-499. New Haven: Human Relations Area Files, 1955.

Stenson, Michael. *Industrial Conflict in Malaya: Prelude to the Communist Revolt of 1948.* Kuala Lumpur: Oxford University Press, 1971.

———. "The Ethnic and Urban Bases of Communist Revolt in Malaya." In *Peasant Rebellion and Communist Revolution in Asia,* edited by John Wilson Lewis, pp. 125-50. Stanford: Stanford University Press, 1974.

———. "Class and Race in West Malaysia." *Bulletin of Concerned Asian Scholars* 8,2(1976): 45-54.

———. *Class, Race and Colonialism in West Malaysia.* Vancouver, Canada: University of British Columbia Press, 1980.

Stivens, Maila. "The Political Economy of Kinship in Rembau, Negeri Sembilan, Malaysia." London: Unpublished MS, Dept. of Anthropology,

University College, 1983.

———. *Women and Development in South-East Asia II: Sexual Politics in Rembau: Female Autonomy, Matriliny and Agrarian Change in Negeri Sembilan, Malaysia.* (Center of South-East Asian Studies Occasional Papers, 5.) Canterbury: Center of South-East Asian Studies, University of Canterbury, 1985a.

———. "The Fate of Women's Land Rights: Gender, Matriliny, and Capitalism in Rembau, Negeri Sembilan, Malaysia." In *Women, Work and Ideology in the Third World,* edited by H. Afshar, pp. 3-36. London: Tavistock, 1985b.

———. "Family and State in Malaysian Industrialization: The Case of Rembau, Negeri Sembilan, Malaysia." In *Women and the State,* edited by H. Afshar, pp. 89-110. London: Macmillan, 1986.

———. "Becoming Workers: The Social Context of Female Labour Migration in Rembau, Negri Sembilan." In *Women Workers in Malaysia,* edited by W. Smith and J. Ariffin. Singapore: Institute of Southeast Asian Studies. In press.

———. Workshop Paper: "Women and Their Land: Changing Property Relations among Rural Malays in Negeri Sembilan." London: Unpublished MS, Dept. of Anthropology, University College, n.d.

Stockwell, A.J. *British Policy and Malay Politics During the Malayan Union Experiment, 1942-1948.* (MBRAS Monographs, 8). Kuala Lumpur: Malayan Branch of the Royal Asiatic Society, 1979.

———. "British Imperial Policy and Decolonization in Malaya, 1942-52." *Journal of Imperial and Commonwealth History* 13,1(1984): 68-87.

Strange, Heather. "Education and Employment Patterns of Rural Malay Women 1965-1975." *Journal of Asian and African Studies* 13,1-2(1978): 50-64.

———. *Rural Malay Women in Tradition and Transition.* New York: Praeger, 1981.

Stubbs, Richard. "The United Malays National Organization, The Malayan Chinese Association, and the Early Years of the Malayan Emergency, 1948-1955." *Journal of Southeast Asian Studies* 10,1(1979): 77-88.

———. "Malaysia's Rubber Smallholding Industry: Crisis and the Search for Stability." *Pacific Affairs* 56(1983): 84-105.

Sullivan, Patrick. *Social Relations of Dependence in a Malay State: Nineteenth Century Perak.* (MBRAS Monographs, 10). Kuala Lumpur: Malaysian Branch of the Royal Asiatic Society, 1982.

Swettenham, Frank. *British Malaya: An Account of the Origin and Progress of British Influence in Malaya.* (2nd ed.), London: John Lane, 1929.

———. *British Malaya: An Account of the Origin and Progress of British Influence in Malaya.* (3rd. ed.), London: Allen and Unwin, 1948.

Swift, M.G. "The Accumulation of Capital in a Peasant Economy." In *Readings in Malayan Economics,* edited by T.H. Silcock, pp. 21-37. Singapore: Eastern Universities Press, 1961.

———. *Malay Peasant Society in Jelebu.* New York: Humanities Press, 1965.

———. "Economic Concentration and Malay Peasant Society." In *Social Organization: Essays Presented to Raymond Firth,* edited by Maurice Freedman, pp. 241-69. Chicago: Aldine, 1967.

Tan Loong-Hoe. "The State and the Distribution of Wealth Within the Malay Society in Peninsular Malaysia." *Southeast Asian Affairs 1981 (Singapore),* 1981, pp. 217-32.

Thio, Eunice. *British Policy in the Malay Peninsula, 1886-1901: Vol. 1, The Southern and Central States.* Singapore: University of Malaya Press, 1969.

Thompson, E.P. "The Moral Economy of the English Crowd in the Eighteenth Century." *Past and Present* 50(1971): 76-136.

Thompson, Virginia. "Notes on Labor Problems in Malaya." *Secretariat Paper.* New York: International Secretariat, Institute of Pacific Relations, 1945.

———. *Labor Problems in Southeast Asia.* New Haven: Yale University Press, 1947.

Tilman, Robert. *Bureaucratic Transition in Malaya.* Durham: Duke University Press, 1964.

Trocki, Carl. *Prince of Pirates: The Temenggongs and The Development of Johore and Singapore 1784-1885.* Singapore: University of Singapore Press, 1979.

Trouillot, Michel-Rolph. "Caribbean Peasantries and World Capitalism: An Approach to Micro-level Studies." *Nieuwe West-Indische Gid/New West Indian Guide* 58,1 (1984).

Vasil, R.K. *Politics in a Plural Society: A Study of Non-Communal Political Parties in West Malaysia.* Kuala Lumpur: Oxford University Press, 1971.

Visaria, Pravin. *Incidence of Poverty and the Characteristics of the Poor in Peninsular Malaysia, 1973.* (I.B.R.D. Staff Working Papers, 460.) Washington, D.C.: World Bank, 1981.

Vlieland, C.A. *A Report on the 1931 Census.* London: Crown Agents for the Colonies, 1932.

Voon, P.K. "Malay Reservations and Malay Land Ownership in Semenyih and Ulu Semenyih Mukims Selangor." *Modern Asian Studies* 10,4(1976): 509-23.

Wan Hashim. *A Malay Peasant Community in Upper Perak: Integration and Transformations.* Bangi, Malaysia: Penerbit Universiti Kebangsaan Malaysia, 1978.

Ward, Barbara. "Cash or Credit Crops? An Examination of Some Implications
    of Peasant Commercial Production with Special Reference to the
    Multiplicity of Traders and Middlemen." *Economic Development and
    Cultural Change* 8(1960): 148-63.
Wharton, C.R. "Marketing, Merchandizing, and Money-lending: A Note on
    Middleman Monopsony in Malaya." *Malayan Economic Review*
    7(1962): 24-44.
Wheelwright, E.L. "The Political Economy of Industrialization in Malaysia." In
    Radical Political Economy: Collected Essays. Sydney: Australian and
    New Zealand Press, 1974.
Wilder, William D. "Islam, Other Factors and Malay Backwardness: Comments
    on An Argument." *Modern Asian Studies* 2,2(1968): 155-64.
————. *Communication, Social Structure and Development in Rural Malaysia.
    A Study of Kampung Kuala Bera*. London: Athlone Press, 1982.
Wilkinson, Richard J., Ed. *Papers on Malay Subjects*. Selected and Introduced
    by P.L. Burns. Kuala Lumpur: Oxford University Press, 1971.
Wilson, H.E. "The Klang Strikes of 1941: Labour and Capital in Colonial
    Malaya." (Research Notes and Discussion Papers, 25.) Singapore:
    Institute of Southeast Asian Studies, 1981.
Wilson, Peter. *A Malay Village and Malaysia*. New Haven: Yale University
    Press, 1967.
Winstedt, Richard. "Kedah Laws." *Journal of the Malayan Branch, Royal
    Asiatic Society* 6,2(1928): 1-44.
Wolcott, H.F. "A Malay Village That Progress Chose: Sungai Lui and the
    Institute of Cultural Affairs. *Human Organization* 42,1(1983): 72-81.
Wong, David S.Y. *Tenure and Land Dealings in the Malay States*. Singapore:
    Singapore University Press, 1975.
Wong Lin Ken. *The Malayan Tin Industry to 1914*. (Association for Asian
    Studies Monographs and Papers, 14.) Tucson, AZ: University of
    Arizona Press, 1965.
————. "Review of *Peasants and Their Agricultural Economy in Colonial
    Malaya, 1874-1941* by Lim Teck Ghee." *Journal of Southeast Asian
    Studies* 10,1(1979): 194-203.
Worsley, Peter. "One World or Three: A Critique of the World System of
    Immanuel Wallerstein." In *The Socialist Register, 1980*, edited by R.
    Miliband and J. Saville, pp. 298-338. London: Merlin Press, 1980.
Yap Chan Ling. "Fishery Policies and Development with Special Reference to
    the West Coast of Peninsular Malaysia from the Early 1900's." *Kajian
    Ekonomi Malaysia* 13, 1-2(1976): 7-16.
Yegar, Moshe. *Islam and Islamic Institutions in British Malaya: Policies and
    Implementation*. Jerusalem: The Magnes Press, 1979.

Yeo Kim Wah. "Grooming of an Elite: Malay Administrators in the Federated Malay States, 1903-1941." *Journal of Southeast Asian Studies* 11(1980): 287-319.

————. "The Guillemard-Maxwell Power Struggle 1921-1925." *Journal of the Malaysian Branch, Royal Asiatic Society* 54,1(1981): 48-64.

————. *The Politics of Decentralization: Colonial Controversy in Malaya 1920-1929.* Kuala Lumpur: Oxford University Press, 1982.

Yeung Yue-man. "Economic Inequality and Social Injustice: Development Issues in Malaysia: Review Article." *Pacific Affairs* 55(1982): 94-101.

Zaharah binti Haji Mahmud. "The Period and Nature of 'Traditional' Settlement in the Malay Peninsula." *Journal of the Malayan Branch, Royal Asiatic Society* 43,2(1970): 81-113.

Zawawi Ibrahim. "Perspectives Towards Investigating Malay Peasant Ideology and the Bases of its Production in Contemporary Malaysia." *Journal of Contemporary Asia* 13,2(1983a): 198-209.

————. "Malay Peasants and Proletarian Consciousness." *Bulletin of Concern Asian Scholars* 15,4(1983b): 39-55.

————. "Investigating Peasant Consciousness in Contemporary Malaysia." In *History and Peasant Consciousness in South East Asia,* edited by Andrew Turton and Shigeharu Tanabe, pp. 135-60. (Senri Ethnological Series, 13.) Osaka: National Museum of Ethnology, 1984.

Index

"Standard Production" (rubber production quota), 86, 87
State formation: comparative literature on, 169n35; and kin-ordered village communities, 23-28; in precolonial period, 17-19; theories of, 8
State lands, 52, 63; rice production in, 100
State power, in "world-systems" theory, 4, 93
Stenson, Michael, 1, 3, 110
Stevenson Committee scheme (of restrictions on rubber), 85-88, 89, 91, 186n26
Straits Settlements: British influence in, 45; commerce in, 17, 30; revenue of, 50; rubber cultivation in, 68
Strikes, 109, 114, 200n48; in postwar period, 107
Suara Rakyat (newspaper), 114
Subaltern groups: in postwar period, 109-10; resistance to expansion, 4
Sullivan, Patrick, xiii
Sultan Idris Training College (Tanjong Malim), 106, 114, 191n37
Sumatra, 63; immigrants from, 24, 54
Sungei Manik, cultivation of, 81
Surat kuasa (empowering documents for *penghulu*), 49
Sustained yield strategy (of peasant labor), 40
Swettenham, Sir Frank, 32, 177n28
Swidden cultivation *(ladang)*, 24, 34, 79, 84
Swift, Michael G., 11; on slaughter-tapping, 141; on village economy, 130-31, 133, 135, 136
Tamil Immigration Fund Ordinance, 69
Tamil laborers, 55, 69
Tampin (district), 100
Tanah kampong (orchard land), 34
Tanjong Karang, cultivation of, 81
Taukeh ikan (fish trader-capitalists), 13
Taxes: in colonial period, 47, 65; evasion of by *ra'ayat*, 39; in precolonial period, 18, 29; on tin, 37
Temenggong of Johore, 29-30
Third World: capitalism in, 149, 158, 165; indeterminacy in, 4
Tin mining, 62, 67, 161; Chinese, 44, 52, 177n29; in colonial period, 43, 47; revenue from, 36, 41, 142
Tithes: in precolonial period, 18, 31-32, 36; as redistributive mechanism, 138

Tolong menolong (mutual help), 134-36, 141, 147
Topography: and precolonial trade, 19-20, 172n3
Torrens land registration system, 52, 58
Trade unions, 108; regulation of, 145. *See also* Labor unions
Trading systems, in precolonial period, 30, 41
Transfer of allegiance, peasant, 38, 40
Transport, in precolonial period, 19-20
Treaty of Pangkor (1874), 17, 19
Trengganu (state), 7, 14; British influence in, 45; commoditization of land in, 33; living conditions in, 198n8; uprising in (1928), 77
Tribe, Keith, 166n1
Tribute, precolonial, 29
Trocki, Carl, 30
Trouillet, Michel-Rolph, 167n1
Ulu Kelantan, 68
Ulu Langat (district): sharetapping in, 134-35
Ulu Langat valley, immigration into, 54
UMNO. *See* United Malays National Organization
Unfederated Malay States, 10, 61; British influence in, 46, 175n3; and McMichael Mission, 113. *See also* Johore; Kedah; Perlis
United Malays National Organization (UMNO), 103-5; accommodation with British officials, 105, 112-13, 114, 118-19, 123; after Independence, 144; challenges to authority of, 150; divisions within, 191n38; in Federation of Malaya, 116; founding of, 115; leadership of, 113; patronage system of, 119, 159
Wallerstein, Immanuel, 4, 5
Wan Hashim, 134
Wan Mat Saman canal, 37
Wet-rice cultivation, 70-71; after Independence, 144; British policy governing, 83, 98-102, 119-22, 141, 162; in colonial period, 81, 83-84; coordination of, 26-27; effect of business cycles on, 102; expansion of, 119-22; flight from, 164; impact of immigrants on, 54; laws governing, 74, 157, 181n39, 193n72-73; in postwar period, 110-11; in precolonial period, 23-24; and rubber cultivation, 91; sharecropping in, 135. *See also* Padi farmers; Rice
Wet-rice land *(sawah)*: in indigenous Malay law, 34